ETHICS, PSYCHE AND SOCIAL RESPONSIBILITY

Corporate Social Responsibility Series

Series Editor:
Professor David Crowther, De Montfort University, UK

This series aims to provide high quality research books on all aspects of corporate social responsibility including: business ethics, corporate governance and accountability, globalization, civil protests, regulation, responsible marketing and social reporting.

The series is interdisciplinary in scope and global in application and is an essential forum for everyone with an interest in this area.

Also in the series

Higher Education and Civic Engagement: International Perspectives
Lorraine McIlrath and Iain Mac Labhrainn
ISBN 978-0-7546-4889-5

Managing Corporate Social Responsibility in Action: Talking, Doing and Measuring
Frank den Hond, Frank G.A. de Bakker and Peter Neergaard
ISBN 978-0-7546-4721-8

The Employment Contract and the Changed World of Work
Stella Vettori
ISBN 978-0-7546-4754-6

The Cooperative Movement: Globalization from Below
Richard C. Williams
ISBN 978-0-7546-7038-4

Capitalist Networks and Social Power in Australia and New Zealand
Georgina Murray
ISBN 978-0-7546-4708-9

Stories, Visions and Values in Voluntary Organisations
Christina Schwabenland
ISBN 978-0-7546-4462-0

Whistleblowing and Organizational Social Responsibility: A Global Assessment
Wim Vandekerckhove
ISBN 978-0-7546-4750-8

Ethics, Psyche and Social Responsibility

Edited by

ANA MARIA DÁVILA GÓMEZ
University of Quebec, Canada

and

DAVID CROWTHER
De Montfort University, UK

ASHGATE

Published by
Ashgate Publishing Limited
Gower House
Croft Road
Aldershot
Hampshire GU11 3HR
England

Ashgate Publishing Company
Suite 420
101 Cherry Street
Burlington, VT 05401-4405
USA

Ashgate website: http://www.ashgate.com

British Library Cataloguing in Publication Data
Ethics, psyche and social responsiblility. - (Corporate
   social responsibility series)
   1. Social responsibility of business 2. Social pyschology
   I. Dávila Gómez, Ana Maria II. Crowther, David
   658.4'08

Library of Congress Cataloging-in-Publication Data
Ethics, psyche, and social responsibility / edited by Ana Maria Dávila Gómez and David Crowther.
      p. cm. -- (Corporate social responsibility series)
   Includes index.
   ISBN 978-0-7546-7089-6
   1. Social responsibility of business. 2. Corporations--Sociological aspects. 3. Industrial relations. 4. Job stress. I. Dávila Gómez, Ana Maria. II. Crowther, David.

   HD60.E845 2007
   658.3'12--dc22

                                                                      2007003832
ISBN 13: 978 0 7546 7089 6

Printed and bound in Great Britain by Antony Rowe Ltd, Chippenham, Wiltshire.

Contents

List of Figures and Tables

Notes on Contributors

Emmanuelle Avon Ph.D. is a professor at the Université du Québec en Outaouais (UQO) in Administrative Sciences. She holds a Ph.D. from École des Hautes Études Commerciales (HEC) in Montréal, Canada. She is also a member of the Research Centre Humanism, Management and Globalization at École des Hautes Études Commerciales (HEC) in Montréal, Canada. Her area of research is organizational change, leadership and human aspects. She has been a Director in Organizational Change and Corporate Strategy for Bell Canada and a Sociologist-Economist at Statistics Canada. She has published in the Association of Administrative Sciences of Canada (ASAC), at the Institut de socio-economie des enterprises et des organisations (ISEOR) and at the International Journal of Management Concept and Philosophy (IJMCP).

David Crowther is Professor of Corporate Social Responsibility, De Montfort University, UK. His career also includes service as general manager, consultant and accountant in a wide range of organisational settings. The author or editor of 18 books and more than 200 papers, on various aspects of organisational behaviour, knowledge management, environmentalism, corporate reporting and social accounting, he is also founding member of Association for Integrity in Accounting. His research interests cover a wide area but are primarily concerned with issues surrounding the accountability of organisations to their wider stakeholder community. He is founding editor of *Social Responsibility Journal* and also on the Editorial Boards of several journals and has organised a number of conferences and symposia in a variety of areas.

Ana Maria Dávila Gómez is a professor in the Department of Administrative Sciences at the *Université du Québec en Outaouais (UQO)*, Canada, where she teaches Management and Organizational Change, conducts researches on the managerial challenges towards more social responsible organizations. She holds a Ph.D. from the *École des hautes etudes commerciales de Montréal*, and an MBA and an Industrial Engineer degrees from the *Universidad del Valle*, Colombia. For seven years, she worked at various private and public organizations in Colombia (e.g. *Emcali* – governmental service; *Unitel* – telecommunications; *Lloreda* – processed food manufacturing) supporting and implementing Information Technology (IT) and Business Process Reengineering projects. Her recent doctoral research treated the human implications of IT in management education.

Jelena Debeljak is a teaching assistant in Business Ethics and Corporate Social Responsibility, and Introduction to Philosophy Courses at Zagreb School of Economics and Management, Croatia. Having graduated from the university in year 2006 in philosophy and religion sciences, she is preparing for a masters degree in business. Since 2003 she has been working actively in the Business Ethics Centre of the Faculty of Philosophy of the Society of Jesus in Zagreb. Her interests relate to broad area of (human) relations phenomenon, manifested in public and private life, specifically, business in encounter with multiculturalism and managing process' of positive change.

Jacques-Bernard Gauthier, Ph.D., is a professor in the Department of Administrative Sciences at the Université du Québec en Outaouais (UQO), Canada, as well as associate professor in the Faculty of Social Sciences at the Université Laval, Québec, Canada. While studying his doctorate in Management, he discovered a truly passion for theoretical and methodological concerns regarding Organizational Studies, passion that he continues to develop nowadays throughout his teachings and actual researches. As the holder of the courses of Epistemology of Management, Organization Theory and Research Methodology, his research works, academic papers and actual projects are concerned for the application, many times upon a critical and reflective view, of the Structuralism Theory towards organizations.

Mirna Koričan is Assistant Professor on courses in Management, Human Resources Management, Strategic Management and Social Psychology at Zagreb School of Economics and Management in Zagreb, Croatia. She holds a BA in Psychology and is in the last stage of her MA program in Management and Organization. She is a project manager and a researcher in the field of Corporate Governance and Corporate Social Responsibility and author of several articles in the field of management and psychology.

Kristijan Krkač is Professor of Business Ethics and CSR, Zagreb School of Economics and Management, and of Analytical Philosophy, Jesuit College in Zagreb, Croatia. He is author of 3 books and more then 50 papers on topic of Wittgenstein and European pragmatism in fields of religion, epistemology, ontology, and ethics. In CSR he is co-editor of "Business Ethics and Corporate Social Responsibility" (2006), and editor of textbook on BE and CSR (in Croatian). His interests cover topics from Wittgenstein, pragmatism, normative ethics, business ethics, and CSR. In last few years his interest covers influence of local European cultures on business vice versa, especially vis-à-vis principal relation of these phenomena, and also regarding particular cultural and business activities as it were particular business practices. He has co-organized philosophical symposia and symposia and scientific colloquia on CSR, and he is administrator of the journal "Disputatio Philosophica".

Pierre-Paul Morin is a Civil Engineer and holds an MBA from the University of Miami as well as a Doctoral Degree in Project Management from the Université d'Aix-Marseille. A full-time teacher at the Université du Québec en Outaouais for the last five years, his research focuses on the management of technical processes and projects. He had a 25 year career as a CEO of consulting firms and Hi-Tech companies. His recent doctoral thesis was on human resource and change management in projects.

Yaromir Munoz Molina is Associate Professor in the Department of Marketing at EAFIT University in Medellin, Colombia, where he teaches Analysis of consumer behaviour and Issues in social marketing, conducts researches on the consumer behaviour and the social marketing in the private business organizations as well as in the public sector. He is actually a Ph.D. candidate from the École des hautes etudes commerciales de Montréal (HEC Montréal), and holds an MBA from *Instituto de Empresa* in Madrid, Spain. He has published one book entitled *"El mercadeo social en Colombia"* (Social marketing in Colombia) and more than ten articles related with consumer behavior topic.

Andrijana Mušura is Assistant Professor at Zagreb School of Economics and Management in Zagreb, Croatia, assisting in courses in Social Psychology, Organizational Behaviour and Consumer Behaviour. She is a psychology PhD student at University of Zagreb, Croatia. Her research interests include corporate social responsibility and she is author of several articles in the field of CSR.

Jair Nascimento Santos is a professor in the University of Salvador (Unifacs) and State University of Feira de Santana (UEFS), Brazil, where he teaches Organizational Theory, Management, Human Resources Strategic Management and Organizational Change, conducts researches on the human resources, networks, leadership, managerial changes and local development towards more social responsible organizations. He holds a Ph.D. from the Federal University of Minas Gerais (UFMG) and *École des hautes etudes commerciales de Montréal* (HEC Montreal), an Administration Master Science degree from Federal University of Bahia (UFBA), Brazil. He worked at various private and public organizations in Brazil (e.g. supermarket, department store, and engineering enterprise – governmental service of transit) supporting and implementing Gestion Technology and Business Process Reengineering projects. His recent doctoral research treated the leadership in the networks contexts

Introduction

Ana Maria Dávila Gómez and David Crowther

The last couple of decades have seen considerable change in the structure of business organisations, caused largely by their desire to gain competitive advantage and by their desire to make use of the technological infrastructure available. Often this has been legitimated as a reaction to the increasingly deregulated free market environment brought into being as a consequence of globalisation. Equally often it has been legitimated as a reaction to the need to create value for shareholders. This has been manifest in the explicit aims of organisations, in three main areas:

- The desire to cut costs primarily through reductions in employee costs; this has led to a reduction in the number of direct employees as organisations have sought to downsize;
- The desire to return to core competencies through the divestment of non-core businesses and functions; access to essential but non-core functions is now achieved mainly through outsourcing the functions from specialists in these areas;
- The desire to flatten the hierarchical structures of organisations through a reversion to flatter structures; this has led to the shedding of large numbers of middle managers whose jobs are no longer essential in the changed business environment.

As a consequence of these drivers of business management, organisations are now leaner and fitter but inherent in these changes are certain dangers as organisations seek to capitalise on their restructuring and achieve continued competitive advantage and growth in this new environment. These dangers can be summarised as follows:

- The socio-demographic structures of organisations have changed through the loss of mainly older employees, with consequent implications for career structures and succession management;
- Essential skills have been lost from within the organisation and now have to be bought in as required;
- Spare capacity (slack resources) have disappeared thus affecting the ability to cope with crises and future expansion;
- There is an implicit assumption that the technological changes which have facilitated such restructuring will adequately compensate for staff changes
- Employees remaining with the company have been affected by the uncertainty regarding job security and future prospects, and this has affected motivation;

- Recruitment and training problems have become more significant in this new environment, particularly when societal demographic changes are considered.

More recently it has started to be discussed and recognised that this focus of organisations in cutting costs through labour force reductions, while providing short term benefit, is not without its problems and that problems have potentially been stored up for the future. Thus managers are starting to recognise that there is a need for them to manage their way out of the current short term focus on business activity and build for the future. What is less certain however is that managers understand the implications of the actions of the last decades upon their existing, and potential, workforce, and the importance of the psychological contract between employer and employee and the way this has been changed by this new environment. Equally there is considerable uncertainty concerning what can be done to bring about changes to this contract and invest in the future of organisations.

The Sins of Accounting

Much of the change has been expressed in terms of the creation of value for shareholders. And this has been used as a legitimation for change which has ignored many of the consequences which we wish to focus on in this book. This change has of course been firmly located and justifed within the discourse of accounting.[1] The discourse of accounting can be interpreted as being concerned solely with the operational performance of the organisation. Contrasting views of the role of accounting in the production process might therefore be epitomised as either providing a system of measurement to enable a reasonable market mediation in the resource allocation problem or as providing a mechanism for the expropriation of surplus value from the labour component of the transformational process. Both strands of the discourse however tend to view that labour as a homogeneous entity and consider the effect of organisational activity upon that entity. Labour is of course composed of individual people; moreover these individual people have a lifetime of availability for employment and different needs at different points during their life cycle. The depersonalisation of people through the use of the term labour however provides a mechanism for the treatment of labour as an entity without any recognition of these personal needs – merely another raw material in the manufacturing process. Thus it is possible to restrict the discourse to that of the organisation and its components – labour capital etc. – and to theorise accordingly.

This therefore illustrates the sins which are legitimated through the use of accounting:

---

1   One of the authors of this introduction is qualified as an accountant.

Labour as a Variable Cost

The use of the term labour is a convenient euphemism which disguises the fact that labour consists of people, while the treatment of people as a variable cost effectively commodifies these people in the production process. In order to create value in the transformational process of an organisation then commodities need to be used efficiently, and this efficient use of such commodities is measured through the accounting of the organisation. When this commodity consists of people then this implies using them in such a way that the maximum surplus value can be extracted from them. The way in which this can be achieved is through the employment of young fit people who can work hard and then be replaced by more young fit people. In this way surplus value can be transferred from the future of the person and extracted in the present. Thus in a competitive environment the worker blames his fellow workers rather than the accounting which has legitimated his sacking. This blame is caused by the competitive environment which has caused this striving for jobs to be important and was recognised by Marx (1866: 91) in stating:

> The discussion of the workmen is created and perpetuated by their unavoidable competition amongst themselves.

Labour and Machinery are Interchangeable

As people have been constituted as a commodified variable cost then they become merely a factor of production which can be exchanged for another factor of production, as the costs determined through the use of accounting legitimate. Thus it is reasonable, through an accounting analysis, to replace people with machinery if more value (profit) can be extracted in doing so, and this has provided the imperative for the industrial revolution which has continued up until the present. Accounting is only concerned with the effect of the actions of an organisation upon itself and so the effect of mechanisation upon people need not be taken into account. Thus if mechanisation results in people becoming unemployed (or possibly unemployable) then this is of no concern – except to the people themselves. Equally if jobs are relocated and stress levels changed dramatically this is of no concern. The use of accounting however still legitimates the ignoring of these effects by the organisation and the replacement of people with equipment. The only change in the present is that people tend to be replaced by technology rather than machinery but the effects upon those individuals is still equally devastating.

Wealth Equates to Welfare

The quantitative nature of accounting tends to focus upon the economic foundations of the discipline and thereby to reinforce the preconception that it is only those things which can be measured in financial terms, and thereby expressed as accounting information, which have value. Thus economic wealth is all that matters. Economic rationality presupposes that organisations, and the people within those organisations, behave in a rational manner in terms of maximising utility, and the underlying assumption of such rationality is that the organisation is attempting to maximise utility for its owners, or shareholders. Under economic rationality this utility is presumed to be synonymous with wealth,[2] perhaps because such wealth can be quantified in accounting terms and thereby become subject to mathematical analysis. It is also assumed unquestioningly in the discourse of economic rationality that what benefits the shareholders of a business will also benefit the other stakeholders to the organisation as well as society at large. Thus the monistic viewpoint of economic rationality is based upon a stance within the discourse of modernity and accepts the philosophy of classical liberal economics. Indeed this view also accepts the tenets of classical liberalism in general.

In the present some things are different. Thus part of the discourse of accounting at the present is concerned with how and to what extent environmental accounting should be adopted by organisations. There is great concern, at least in Western countries, about the effects of pollution – certainly in the context of global warming. It is one of the dominant issues of the present and the effects on the future in terms of effects upon lifestyle is the subject of much consideration. The unquantifiable aspects of welfare however are still not considered to be a legitimate concern of accounting and are removed from the discourse, although emotional and spiritual welfare are considered to be important – and a subject of many of the contributions to this volume – and subject to degradation at the present time. Equally other types of pollution, such as noise pollution are of increasing concern at the present time.

Enacting Performance and its Consequences

Delivery of an organisation's strategic objectives can be achieved through the use of a system of performance indicators (Meekings, Dransfield and Goddard 1994) but such a system needs appropriate linkages between top level strategy and lower level operationalisation. More significantly the culture of the organisation must be transformed to meet the strategic objectives of the organisation. Indeed strategies at different levels within the organisation need to be coherent (Nath and Sudharshan 1994) and need to be reflected in the culture of the organisation. Appropriate indicators used appropriately can build this coherence and facilitate the necessary cultural transformation while inappriopriate indicators can have a dysfunctional consequence for operational performance.

These dynamics reflect the dominant managerial approach that answers to the neoliberal (positivist) conception of organizations, in which, everything that includes thinking, proposition, and conception, belongs to the higher levels of the hierarchy, where employees with no authority are conceived only as executors. In this way, labour workers, whose definition is presented in previous points, have no right to think, or to feel discomfort or fatigue, given that they risk losing their jobs or they fear being replaced by someone cheaper in salary that can perform at least

---

2   See Crowther (2002) for a more detailed critique of these assumptions and the underlying philosophy of liberalism.

as much as them. Thus the introduction of processes conceived in other parts of the world and performed by other cultures – a feature of globalisation – produces not only misunderstanding but also stress in employees. For instance, regarding back office services, a common operation which is realocated in the drive to create shareholder value, we know that many times people operating in other countries follow predetermined orders, procedures, and ways of acting. These are the excess of rationalisation seeking performance growth, which is enhanced with the help of many strategic and managerial models such as process reengineering. The effects of this kind of managerial decision making is one the things discussed in this volume.

This introduction of ways of doing, often strange for local people, requires then an accommodation and an organizational change, which most of the time is conducted by some senior manager that belongs to the foreign country, in order to preserve the mission and culture of the organization's headquarters.[3] Simultaneously, in the few cases where the manager is someone from the country where the back office operates, the way of managing is also something ruled by the foreign country perception; it is a situation that is also accepted by managers because they want to perform, and the western way of operating business is the dominant thought paradigm worldwide.

In this process, the natural stress of employees is most of the times neglected by the theory of organizational change, as discussed by Bareil and Savoie (1999) who explain how a process of change inflects affective and cognitive anguish in people; however those realities are not yet widely accepted nor considered. Hence, change resistance, or stress, are seen as an impediment for the new way of operating, as a source of conflict, moreover, as something that has to be anticipated in order to elude its occurrence. However, employees at any level, as human beings, will always have interests, interpretations and expectancies, that are not necessarily the same for everyone (see Enriquez 1997). Therefore, conflicts or differences in points of view are a natural state of our integrity. Thus, when dominant organizational theory neglects the reality of our individual and social beings, a false and an incomplete set of managerial tools for strategic success is developed.

For instance, the mere fact of imposing a foreign procedure as an "adoption activity" that must be performed with no questioning by those who will execute it later, implies the neglecting of an "adaptation process" to a different cultural context. Here, managers operate organizational change with no consultation to foreign values, culture or beliefs. They only drive their performance seeking actions answering corporate rules, procedures, and therefore, pre-established indicators (either quantitative or qualitative). Hereby, in organizational change theory, a supposition is made about the participation of personnel, upon which, in order to eliminate change resistance, there is a need to inform the personnel about what is going to be introduced, and to allow a communication channel while the process is conducted in case problems arise. Our practical experiences tell us that even though the latter includes personnel, it does not integrate the complete interaction between persons, because, the fact of giving information does not necessarily allow the receptor of

---

3   In fact, in international organizations, the manager level in the foreign country is filled with people belonging to the owners' country in order to assure control, loyalty and a sense of organizational identification.

the information the right to answer nor to give opinions. In communication, there is a difference between information, consultation, and dialogue. Furthermore, the information activity (wrongly called communication process) is operated by managers without consultation of propositions, because changes are already conceived. Here, the change or activities to be modified are never consulted with the final executors. Our research (see for example Crowther and Dávila Gómez 2006) also suggests that in this sense, stress is reinforced when an employee dares to give an opinion that is contrary to the imposed rules, because it represents the possibility of being fired or psychologically mistreated. Hence, punishment for misbehaving become examples to reinforce the silent role that employees are called to play.

Thus, upon the positivist philosophy of organizational theory, strategic and managerial methods of transformation and change, treat the cultural component as something that can be predicated upon few rules, therefore anticipated, and well managed. Following these precepts, the works of Hoftstede (1980) and Hampden-Turner and Trompenaars (2004) count among the most used approaches to deal with cultural differences. Summarizing, these approaches presuppose four cultural variables (individualism/collectivism; gender; hierarchical distance recognition and control of the uncertain) that will allow any manager to perform well. However, our practical experiences tell us that even though the definition of these variables may identify some global characteristics of some societies, they do not identify the particular cultural environment of any organization, nor the different and mixed cultural values among personnel in various hierarchical levels; they are more likely tied with anthropological community trails rather than with entire countries' precognized stereotypes. As expressed by Berne (1996: 1036):

> From diversity to humanism. Diversity programs can have significant inherent problems. They can encourage resentment in majority employees. They can also give rise to feelings of mistrust and agitation in minority employees who then question the motives and sincerity of management's push to diversify. [...] What values are reflected in the objectives of managing diversity? [...] Typical managing diversity programs have arisen from an attempt to "right the wrongs", in an obligation to rectify injustices (races, gender). [...] When diversity management programs are administrated without a moral dimension, there may be the appearance of success as judged by raw numbers, but underneath will be anger, hostility and frustration [...] Diversity consciousness cannot simply be mandate into a system, be trained into a corporate culture, or motivated by economic and promotional incentives. It is reflective of an attitude which will appear when organizations, and the people who comprise them, change their basic, fundamental concepts about who we are as workers and why we work as we do [...] The success of managing diversity will come from a collective perceptual shift which by its nature converts notions of them into the notion of us.

The previous shows us that in the current globalized economic world, more than talking about national cultures, there is a mix of values, a transcultural composition of groups, of individuals, where quantifiable precodification of variables will not solve the problems of adoption or adaptation. There is the sharing and it enriches values for all of us. Therefore, when managers try to apply the previous cited cultural approaches to deal with cultural issues, they encounter many obstacles and realities that have no explanation, in consequence, no way to deal with, no possible exit, no solution. At this point, the weak trial for cultural consideration is no longuer possible and imposition of foreign values and change procedures regain their status.

On the contrary, a few managers, and in parallel, few organizational theory and change procedures, follow a complementary approach of interpretative and culture co-construction. Hereby, we talk about, for example, the works of d'Iribarne (1989),[4] who insists on taking a deterministic framework of cultural classification, and insists on the need to interpret the organizational culture as a result of society's representations and symbolism, as well as the pluralistic mix of values of different people within the organization. At the same time, we identify then that (as considered by Zghal 2003), the organizational culture is the result of many complex subcultures operating simultaneously. Our demand is then the need for those who own power (shareholders and managers), who hold the imposed cultural values, to open a communication dialogue process where other real and factual cultures may speak out. As presented by Swanson (1975: 441–443 in Sills, ed.)

> [...] symbolic interaction refers to the process by which individuals relate to their own minds or the minds of others; the process, that is, in which individuals take account of their own or their fellows' motives, needs, desires, means and ends, knowledge, and the like [...] among sociologists it is often called social interaction [...] When individuals take account of the one another's minds, they observe, and adapt to, the existence of these instrumental process as such.

This dialogue will then allow the unveiling of others' values, anguishes, expectancies, and stress. Only in that way, the recognition of reality is possible in order to jointly (by the different groups of stakeholders) propose solutions and procedural changes. In doing so, we do not only allow cultural expressions as the voice of groups, but also individuals' meanings and symbolic representations of reality (ontological senses). That means then the possibility to "adapt" and to "rearrange" with concerning for those who will execute, and for those who will be served (customers).This is an open process of interaction; where managers should develop attitudes of listening, coherence and concern. Hereby, an interpersonal approach is therefore needed in order to comprehend other ways of conceiving activities, meanings of action, and as a result, mutual understanding and solution propositions. A path to start thinking about 'us', not only 'otherness' but mostly about 'wholeness'.

The Current Contribution

We have been researching and writing in this area for some time and the focus of our attention has been on the effects of these changes upon individual people – not just in their working lives but also in their social and family lives – and the effects upon the people, particularly family, that they interact with. We have found ourselves making extensive use of psychological theory in developing our understanding, and particularly psychoanalytic theory as a helpful mechanism for explanation –

---

4   See also approaches of this kind in Alvesson (2002), who follows a more hermeneutical and deconstructive methodology.

although we are fully aware that many people would dispute any claim to it being a theory at all. Nevertheless we have found it helpful and it has been a major part of the initial conceptualisation of this book. Our work has brought us into contact with like minded people and this book is the outcome.

The contributions in this book are diverse in their topics, and this selection is deliberate. So too is the selection of contributions from authors with a wide range of backgrounds – both geographical and disciplinary. While these chapters may initially appear to be diverse and unconnected, they are in fact linked by a common theme in that they are all concerned with the usually neglected margins of corporate activity and the various approaches to social responsibility. In other words the focus of the various contributions is firmly upon the effects on people – employees and their relatives – of the various aspects of corporate activity. We aregue that this is a rich field for research which has been ignored to a large extent. This book is an attempt to redress this absence.

In the first chapter Ana Maria Dávila Gómez and David Crowther start from the position that the drive for shareholder value which has been a feature of business over the past two decades has had many effects on business organisation and many consequences not just for organisational behaviour but also for the people who work within those organisations. So while much of the shareholder value which has been created has been a cynical exploitation of power in adjusting the distributional benefits of organisational activity and appropriating an increased share at the expense of other stakeholders, there have been many other effects as the psychological contract between employer and employee has been redrawn. Thus alongside a reduced share of the value created in the transformational process employees have lost any expectation of permanence of employment. Concurrently people have become units of production rather than individuals as the newly created human resources function has replaced the personnel department and techniques such as knowledge management have been introduced to deskill people and make them perfectly replaceable, one by another.

So while it is generally accepted that organisations have always been normalising machines in which the individual is subjugated to the requirements of organisation the uncertainties caused by the changes in business organisation have exacerbated this effect. Certainty has been to a large extent replaced by uncertainty and this has introduced an element of fear into the workplace. Fear of course is viewed as a motivational factor because of its effect in shaping and controlling behaviour towards the desired organisational goals; which means of course that more surplus value can be extracted. At the same time however the soul of the organisation is jeopardised as people's behaviour changes in response to the organisational pressures. Consequently risk minimisation governs people's behaviour not just as far as organisational behaviour is concerned but also at a personal level. In other words, as human beings we are afraid to express our most profound feelings (those ontological) because that could represent risk for our work assurance. It is argued that this is not just detrimental for the goals of the organisation but also for the psychological and emotional welfare of the people concerned. The purpose of this chapter is to explore and analyse the effects of this facet of organisational life, from the perspective of individuals within organisations and to speculate upon a prognosis.

In the second chapter Emmanuelle Avon argues that a new phenomenon emerged in Canada and has affected every sphere of the Canadian economic sectors and human aspects of society. Strategic organizational transformations have been undertaken to unprecedented levels, scope, scale and depths. The only way this paradigm shift has been possible is by breaking the tacit moral contract that underlined this economic and social effort. Leadership practices have been standardized in respect with the teleological management practices. The social interaction contracts and the determinist community social bonding determine this tendency to create a disruption in the basic trust toward the leadership practices. The consequences are already alarming for the human and economic costs. This chapter presents a structured argumentation based on the most up to date empirical data to present organizational change as a new capitalist phenomenon, the human conditions it has created and the break of tacit moral contract.

In the third chapter Yaromir Munoz Molina returns to one of the themes addressed by Dávila Gómez and Crowther, namely the effect upon family members arising from the stresses of corporate life. In this chapter the focus is upon the use of alcohol and its deleterious effects. Drinking during pregnancy remains as a great health public problem, which is explored in detail in this chapter by Molina. Each year, only in United States, more than 40,000 babies are born with some degree of alcohol related problems and the life health care for each one in 2000 reached at $588.000. Although the beverage-warning label is on the containers since 1989, at least 3.3% of pregnant women interviewed in 1999 reported frequent drinking (Hankin, 2002). However, the data gathered does not reflect the true reality because, according to Hankin et al (2000), there were at least three limitations; first, data were self-reported and might be subject to reporting biases. Second, homeless women or in homes without telephones were not surveyed. Third, there were statistical limitations of the sample because the proportion of the women who were drinking during pregnancy was limited. These arguments allow suspect that the proportion of women who are drinking during pregnancy is higher than is currently reported. The situation in low development countries might be strongest because of alcohol consumption is high, people are less educated, and data are not well known yet.

The main problem of drinking during pregnancy is the consequences on the fetus. The most severe is Fetal Alcoholic Syndrome (FAS), which produces growth retardation and developmental abnormalities in the central nervous system; the most severe impact is mental retardation (Hankin, 2002). It is important to note that those birth defects are preventable, and one way to prevent it named universal prevention is putting beverage warning labels on the containers (Warren and Foudin, 2001; Hankin, 2002). Since the law for warning started in 1989, many researches have tried to establish effectiveness on prevention because it offers information about risks related alcohol consumption (DeCarlo, 1997; Andrews, Netemeyer, Durvasula, 1990, 1993; Hilton, 1993; Hankin et al, 1993; Laughery, Young, and Vaubel, 1993; Hankin, Sloan, and Sokol, 1998). This represents a critical social responsibility issue for alcohol industries. It is imperative to address the question of conscious and humanistic actions from inside marketing activities, moreover, while we know that most organizations only take into account these issues when a governmental prerogative is mandatory. It is also important to recognise the causes of such alcohol use and the strains of corporate life are one important, and often neglected, reason for this.

In Chapter 4 Jacques-Bernard Gauthier takes as his starting point the assertion that organization theories are in continuous questioning. The bases of its questioning are various. Among them, we find the debate between structure and action. Inside social sciences, Giddens (1984) is one of the authors who studied the subject. Essentially, he proposes an important reflection concerning the idea that structures do not exist in an independent way form actions. Equally, for him, while individuals are acting they are producing and reproducing the structures of the social systems. He calls that principle the duality of the structure. Those interactions presented by Giddens as one of the dimensions of the duality of the structure, unfold themselves mainly as a co-presence. Giddens utilizes the notion of co-presence in the same sense that Goffman (1959) does: "co-presence is anchored in the perceptual and communicative modalities of the body" (Giddens, 1984, p. 67).

As Gauthier shows, the theory of structuralism does not deal directly with the organization. However, it is seen by several authors as a conceptual architecture that is very interesting as it studies daily interactions between individuals inside organizations (Hatch, 1997). With the support of this point of view about the structure of social systems, Giddens (1984) calls for a conscious awareness concerning the relevance of the co-presence in organizations. In fact, the majority of interactions with other individuals in organizations (whereas employees, clients, shareholders, citizens, etc.) is developed in a context of co-presence. On the other hand, the theory of structuration invites us to reflect about the absence as a modality of interactions with other individuals (the alter-ego). Interactions with the alter-ego are more particularly examined from the point of view of the capacity of responsibility, a capacity of ethical nature of the human agents. These are the points that Gauthier have been developed in this chapter.

Pierre-Paul Morin is concerned with suffering in the next chapter. As he asserts, the word suffering is rarely found in business literature. It refers to a strong emotion that also deals with personal and collective values. Suffering can be useful when it is properly diagnosed and taken into account. It can be seen as a symptom of something needing attention. It can be an opportunity to learn about oneself or about group behaviours. It may be the catalyst to collective change. It can even be essential to taking *rational* decisions. All suffering is not positive. Some is pathological, either individually or even in a group. If it can sometimes be an occasion to redefine and adjust values and beliefs, it can also come from the expression of power and create a spiral of greater suffering. Suffering is part of being human. When recognized, it is an opportunity for people to share their humaneness. It opens the door to tolerance, courage, loyalty and friendship. It sometimes creates freedom, justice and love.

As David Crowther and Ana Maria Dávila Gómez state, there are many theories concerning the formation of personality and the way this formation affects behaviour in organisations, one large body of thought is concerned with psychoanalysis. Psychoanalysis is well known and it arouses strong feelings for most people: some reject it absolutely while others think that it provides insights which are not apparent elsewhere. Among academics some hold that it is coherent body of theory while others claim that it is not theory at all as the explanations it gives are untestable. Here they do not enter this debate but rather look at the perspective it offers upon behaviour in organisation, through a focus upon corporate communications and the associated myths surrounding behaviour in organisations. In this chapter they do this through the lens of semiology, focusing upon an examination of corporate communication while considering this in the context of some key psychoanalytic theorists, with particular emphasis being placed upon the work of Jung and Lacan.

In Chapter 7 Jelena Debeljak, Mirna Koričan, Kristijan Krkač and Andrijana Mušura are concerned with the ethics of care and with the role of women in society in general and business in particular. They distinguish between female characteristics and male characteristics and introduce the Ethics of Care as a different approach to moral behaviour. They take a philosophical stance in their analysis of care which is complemented by a righteous indignation that women are generally worse paid than men and less likely to be promoted into the topmost echelons of the corporate hierarchy. They also make a clear link between care, as an attribute, and corporate social responsibility.

Dávila Gómez and Santos are concerned with the role of education in the development of managers. As they state, as professional managers, we search to contribute for change in society. On the other hand, we realize that there is a gap in management training, because the trainees are stimulated to get success at any cost. Beyond all traditional concepts that support unrealistic approaches, they try to discuss the need to develop individuals with their minds open to plurality within organizations. According to this, we try to figure out how to stimulate changes in the attitudes of managers in order to get a real change in social reality. To find an answer to that question, this article takes into account the philosophical support that guides the education and the cycle of processes of education: planning, direction, evaluation and controlling. Additionally, they have chosen a critical pedagogy approach as strategy for management development, which emphasizes the process of direction. In order to take into account the other three processes of the cycle, and to make more practical this pedagogical approach, they introduce the concept of intersubjectivity as a complementary tool that generates examples of reflections and tasks for the students. They also show how that pedagogy is articulated and applied, and they we make some comments concerning its implementation. Finally, they put in question the limitation or possibility of applying the critical pedagogy, trying to search for a hopeful and positive answer to that question.

As already stated, the diversity of contributions to this volume shows the broad range of issues which need to be addressed in considering the effects of corporate activity upon people – both employees and extending out from the working environment to their families also. At the same time this diversity has a danger of obscuring the commonality of the themes being addressed. This is a danger which we accept in our desire to show the range of issues involved in, and range of people concerned with this field. We hope that this book succeeds in opening up the discourse in this neglected area.

References

Alvesson M. (2002), *Understanding Organizational Culture*; Sage: London.

Andrews, J. Craig, Richard G. Netemeyer, and Srinivas Durvasula (1990) "The Role of Cognitive Responses as Mediators of Alcohol Warning Label Effect", *Journal of Public Policy and Marketing*, Vol. 12 (1), pp. 57–68.

Andrews, J. Craig, Richard G. Netemeyer, and Srinivas Durvasula, (1993), "Effects of Consumption Frequency on Believability and Attitudes Toward Alcohol Warning Labels", *The Journal of Consumer Affairs*, Vol. 25 (2), pp. 323–37.

Bareil et Savoie (1999), Comprendre et mieux gérer le sindividus en situation de changement organisationnel; *Gestion* Vol. 24 No. 3 automne pp. 86–94 HEC: Montréal.

Berne R. (1996), Diversity; in Warner M. (eds) 1996 *International Encyclopedia of Business and Management.* P Routledge: USA, Canada.

Crowther D. (2002), *A Social Critique of Corporate Reporting*; Ashgate: Aldershot.

Crowther D. and Dávila Gómez A-M. (2006), Stress in the back office; Proceedings of India – The processing Office to the World; Kochi, January 2006; pp. 27–38.

DeCarlo, Tomas E. (1997), "Alcohol Warnings and Warning Labels: An Examination of Alternative Alcohol Warning Message and Perceived Effectiveness", *The Journal of Consumer Marketing*, Vol. 14 (6), p. 448.

Enriquez E. 1997; Imaginaire social, refoulement et répression dans les organisations; in Enriquez E. (1997), *Les jeux du poivoir et du désir dans l'entreprise*, pp. 75–112; (ed.), Desclée de Brouwer: Paris.

Giddens , A. (1984), *The Constitution of Society*. Polity Press: Cambridge.

Goffman, E. (1963), *Behavior in Public Places. Notes on the social organization of gatherings*. The Free Press: Cambridge.

Hampden-Turner and Trompenaars (2004), *Au-délà du choc des cultures: dépasser les opositions pour mieux travailler ensemble*; trans. Larry Cohen, (ed.), d'Organisation: Paris.

Hankin, Janet R., James J. Sloan, and Robert J. Sokol, (1998), "The Modest Impact of the Alcohol Beverage Warning Label on Drinking During Pregnancy Among a Sample of African and American Women," *Journal of Public Policy and Marketing*, Vol. 17 (1), pp. 61–70.

Hankin, Janet, Mary E. McCaul, and Janet Heussner, (2000), "Pregnant, Alchol-Abusing Women", *Alcoholism: Clinical and Experimental Research*, Vol. 24 (8), pp. 1276–86.

Hankin, Janet R. (2002), "Fetal Alcohol Syndrome Prevention Research", *Alcohol Research and Health World*, Vol. 26 (1), pp. 58–65.

Hankin, J.R., I.J. Firestone, J.J. Sloan, J.W. Ager, A.C Goodman, R.J. Sokol, and S.S. Martier, (1993), "The Impact of the Alcohol Warning Label on Drinking During Pregnancy", *Journal of Public Policy and Marketing*, Vol. 12 (1), pp. 10–18.

Hatch, M. J. (1997), *Organization Theory. Modern, symbolic and postmodern perspectives*. Oxford University Press: Oxford.

Hilton, Michael (1993), "An Overview of Recent Findings on Alcoholic Beverage Warning Label", *Journal of Public Policy and Marketing*, Vol. 12 (1), pp. 1–9.

Hofstede G. (1980), *Culture's consequences: international differences in work-related values*; Sage: Berverly Hills, California.

d'Iribarne P. (1989), *La logique de l'honneur: gestion des enterprises et traditions nationales*; (ed.), De Seuil, Paris.

Laughery, K.R., S.L.Young, K.P. Vaubel, and J.W. Brelsford, (1993) "The Noticeability of Warnings on Alcoholic Beverage Containers", *Journal of Public Policy and Marketing*, Vol. 12 (1), pp. 38–56.

Marx K (1866), Instructions to delegates to the General Congress in *Political Writings*, Vol. 3; Penguin: Harmondsworth.

Meekings A., Dransfield J. and Goddard J. 1994; "Implementing strategic intent: The power of an effective business management process" in *Business Strategy Review*, Vol. 5, No. 4, pp. 17–31.

Swanson 1972, in Sills L. (ed.) (1972), *International Encyclopedia of the Social Sciences*; Collier-Macmillan Publishers: USA.

Warren, Kenneth, R., and Laurie L. Foudin (2001) "Alcohol-Related Birth Defects-the Past, Present, and Future", *Alcohol Research and Health*, Vol. 25 (3), pp. 153–60.

Zghal 2003, Culture et gestion: gestion de l'harmonie ou gestion des paradoxes?; *Gestion* Vol. 28, No. 2, pp. 26–32, HEC: Montréal.

Chapter 1

Psychological Violence at Work: Where does the Human Dignity Lie?

Ana Maria Dávila Gómez and David Crowther

Global Competitiveness, Organizations and Human Distress

In the academic discipline of business, and more specifically in management, the main concern has been mostly concentrated on providing new methods and tools in order to enable managers to operate their firm in a way which will increase the shareholder value of the firm; and of course these shares are owned by a small percentage of the world population.[1] Meanwhile the majority of the population works to gain an adequate wage that allows them to survive, and in many cases, to enter into the consumption cultural behaviour that surrounds us all worldwide. In this sense, Ritzer (1996) criticizes the actual MacDonalization of the economy, as being not only an organizational phenomenon, but also as being a cultural phenomenon: in almost every community around the world it has become a way of living. There is an urge to accomplish competitiveness, to follow in time operational procedures, to answer to powerful agents' pressures immediately. Consequently, these practices lead to detachment towards the human being,[2] given that inside these practices, the human being is conceived mostly as a link of a chain inside an unquestionable macro-social set of rules.

This dynamism of the macro-economic world concerns the individuals living a daily experience in organizations, both local and multinational. The way in which the economy is driven nowadays is reflected directly in the way of living of individuals inside and outside organizations. Our research and observations indicate to us that

---

1   See the latest United Nations' report "World Economic and Social Survey 2006" (United Nations, 2006) which criticizes the increasing inequities between countries' GDP, and also reveals how over the past 50 years, the richest have become richer (what they call the developed world) and the poorest still remain poor (what they call the developing world); even though an improvement has been made, however, this is not significant in absolute values of improving the population's quality of life.

2   Of course the whole language of business relegates the human being to a mere part of the production process, rather then recognizing people as entities in their own right. Thus personnel management has become renamed and we talk about human resources management as a way of utilizing people as a resource in the production process alongside other resources such as finance or raw materials. Thus the whole language of business dehumanizes the worker and encourages (or at best condones) the problems with which we are concerned in this chapter.

these pressures and their consequences contain psychological violence as one of the means by which some obtain utility from the actions from others and vice-versa; and in this way, a social reproduction continuum of violence takes place. Economics and a concern for shareholder value added techniques do not distinguish between economic wealth and welfare, assuming that maximising wealth also maximises welfare (Crowther et al 1998). Thus the automobile industry, for example, assumes that increasing wealth increases demand for cars which thereby increases welfare. In fact, evidence exists to suggest that welfare is reducing as wealth is increasing (Mishan 1993) and that this situation is therefore untenable.

A highly concentrated interest in excessive competitiveness is not without its consequences for human dignity. Even though it is possible to demonstrate in a mathematical and rational way that the economic contributions that corporations make to a country's development, throughout taxation or donations, support the economical growth of the country concerned as a whole (e.g. through indicators such as GNP, GDP, etc.), it has been impossible to demonstrate that the majority of the population involved has reached a better quality of life while regarding the very individual separately.[3] As discussed by Shaw (2006a), with globalization, misery and inequities increase constantly. A neo-liberalist market opens the door for the disregarding of others because there are not sufficient international protective laws, and therefore, and as explained by Crowther and Ortiz-Martinez (2006), a free market represents for multinational corporations an opportunity to legally avoid social responsibility when there are no statutory duties regulated by local laws in some of the countries where corporations operate – which unfortunately are normally developing countries. It is sad but true that justice and ethics do not belong to legislation but to the consciousness of managers and owners when they are acting.

Poverty and inequities are not exclusive to developing countries of course, but also to strong economies. For instance, the United States has the higher GDP in the world,[4] but at the same time, it has a high rate of domestic and urban violence – indicators of poverty. By the same token, socially developed countries suffer also from problems regarding human integrity. For instance, in Canada (and specifically the province of Quebec), as well as in some Scandinavian countries, regardless of different economic models – some call it social capitalism which enforces rules and norms for collecting taxes and avoiding evasion, in order to making a better redistribution of the national wealth – they show the highest indexes of suicide in the world,[5] a fact that could be linked in some way with a sentiment of dissatisfaction and human emptiness. Furthermore, a country's economic wealth does not assure a

---

3   The foundations of economic activity in the free market are of course based on the philosophy of Utilitarianism and under this philosophy it is sufficient to determine the growth in welfare through summation of individuals welfare. In other words many can lose as long as the gain for the few outweighs the losses of the many and welfare has increased.

4   Ibid 1. See also GNP and GDP indicators at World Bank (2006) latest statistics for 2004.

5   See some statistics and reports at the *Institut national de santé publique – Québec* (2003), and *Crise – Center for Research and Intervention on Suicide and Euthanasia* (2006).

fair and equitable distribution of income[6] for all the social and collective sectors. As another example, we comment on the case of the Quebec province in Canada, whose economy is stable and normally operates with a balanced budget or even in surplus; nonetheless, the health sector[7] has critical problems to be solved, among which is the difficulty to answer in time the average patients' needs (e.g. critical disease diagnosis, emergencies, etc.). It is a problem of failing to cover the population's health needs and not a problem of competitiveness inside a global market.

The previous examples show us that the social and economic development of the conglomerate may satisfy primary biological needs but not necessarily emotional or psychological health issues. At the same time, the magical strategic formulas of competitiveness do not solve crucial human and social problems. Following Karaset and Theorell (1990), it is a fact that nowadays the typical work climate induces so much pressure and stress on employees (workers or managers) that heart disease has become an occupational disease. Furthermore, burn-out has increasingly become a disease that many people have suffered in work environments (Maslach, 1998), which for us is a result of the excessive demands of the increasing levels of productivity and performance asked by directors in order to achieve the organisation's competitiveness goals. Furthermore, even in the richest and socially most developed countries,[8] human dissatisfaction is experienced even though a lack of a competitive wage may be compensated by a governmental program of financial assistance to help families in distress.[9]

This occurrence is not only a responsibility of governments or social movements, but also of individuals because in every single decision, in every single choice made, there is power in action that concerns others. As the integral beings that we are, we suffer in our familiar, ontological and emotional life the positive or negative consequences of the economy and organizations' activities. As stated by Sen (1998), an economy with ethics is needed. For us, the ethical decisions to change the aforementioned situations are made by people – by human beings at any private firm or at the stage of any governmental or political institution. Decisions are made by human beings who act also as organizational managers given that they invest the organizational responsibility of their institution.

We talk here about the virtues of the being, as presented by Socrates (in Plato, 399–384 B.C.) in the *Alcibiades*, and *Second Alcibiades* dialogues; in order to rule, we need to question how to act morally when someone is in power. In the context

---

6   It is well known, for example, that the USA is the richest country in the world but that this income distribution is so unequal that 20% of the population have difficulty in even managing to get sufficient wealth to feed themselves, let alone engage in any capital accumulation.

7   Many public, professional or academic sources confirm it. See some examples explaining the situation in Radio-Canada (2006); Castonguay, C. (2004).

8   Ibid 1, 2.

9   For instance, in Canada, recently unemployed people may benefit from a monthly amount (about 2/3 of their salary) for up to 9 months (with some exceptions), when if they are not back in the labour force, they will be eligible for the welfare program as a last resource (see Human Resources and Social Development Canada, 2005). But in other developing countries this program or this consideration does not even exist.

of a manager, Dávila Gómez (2003) treated this to some extent upon the concept of human qualities. For organizations, as the social actors that they are (Giddens, 1987), it is critical, therefore, the way in which the individuals with more power treat those with less power, and also how they treat themselves because their own actions and behaviours represent an opportunity to feel empty or fulfilled: the moral consciousness (see Dewey, 1975).

The aforementioned situations call for a critical regard of managerial techniques and practices.[10] Among the great variety of authors in management, our research and bibliographical reviews show us that only a few pose a critical regard to the actual organizational responsibility towards the social and human needs, given that the majority of the attention is drawn towards new rational ways to increase productivity and competitiveness. Then, as we seek to elucidate some causes of this detachment towards the human aspect of the organization, we refer to what some of these few authors consider. For instance, Crowther and Dávila Gómez (2006a) explore the way in which strategy and management theories are driven mostly by new modes such us Business Process Reengineering, Knowledge Management, Supply Chain Management and Human Capital, among others, which, in the end, are a mere sophistication of the Taylorism movement that gave birth to our scientific administration (less cost, more products, more sales) and that was reinforced by the specialized in-line production practice or Fordism. Furthermore, the latest productivity approaches of outsourcing, offshoring and empowerment that corporations begin to implement as their salvation while having financial problems or wanting to increase profit, are again a rational sophistication of the utilitarian paradigm of conducting business. In fact, in outsourcing there are not only financial issues, but also human and cultural concerns (see Tripathy and Chavan, 2006; Crowther and Dávila Gómez, 2006b), as for example, massive layouts in the country of origin to the detriment of the families' quality of life, mistreatment of new employees on the new country, disregard of native cultures on the new country, among others.

Thus Crowther and Dávila Gómez (2006a) state that a transformation of the terms and an increased use of technology do not change either the principles or the philosophical underpinnings of actions. Indeed Crowther (2002a) has already demonstrated that Utilitarianism, as an organizational approach that follows a neo-liberalist orientation in which, blindly seeking financial growth for shareholders, disregards many of the responsibilities towards other stakeholders and the environment. It has also been stated by other authors (e.g. Chanlat, 1998; Alvesson and Wilmot, 1996) that the way in which business is conducted nowadays lacks a critical concern for the pursued purposes, given that no reflexivity is exercised by managers who seek mostly pragmatic behaviours that allow them to conduct strategically successful businesses. Equally, some others authors (e.g. Banerjee, 2004; Crowther and Green, 2004; Chanlat and Bédard, 1990) have been preoccupied by some aspects of the human integrity inside organizations: e.g. human respect, social interactions, and right of speech.

---

10   See for example Crowther, Carter and Cooper 1997 and Ortiz-Martinez and Crowther 2004).

Following the previous authors' critical precepts, we have observed that the aforementioned situations generate in employees, at any hierarchical level, a psychological pressure to perform in order to fit in the pre-arranged social order. This causes distress, discomfort and also other mental health consequences affecting the integrity of the human being, which we have previously documented in Crowther and Dávila Gómez (2006b). This happens not only to the specific person who is being mistreated, but also to the other human beings dependent on him or her: family members, friends, etc. In some cases, this also implies mistrust for a better future, which many times results in a person to abandoning his ideals. As such, dissatisfaction and emptiness arrive late in life, and the family that the being is a part of, will very likely suffer from this. A new generation inherits the disenchantment.

In order to generate some changes in the actual reality, a deep comprehension of the psychological violence being inflicted at work is needed. As follows, we explore and discuss some of its representations, its causes and, in some cases, some suggestions about what could be done. We will do this by exemplifying some of the psychological situations faced on a daily basis in the work environment, such as: ethnic discrimination, psychological intimidation, and physical violence, all acting to the detriment of the human and collective aspects. In parallel, we explore some behaviours that result in this violence as compensatory and balancing aids for the human being. We subject managers to questioning their ethical choices. For this, we make use of some extracts of Freud's theory of the psyche (Freud, 1856–1939a,b), and while exploring behaviours, we do it not only by examining external stimuli but also mostly by reflecting on the inner self and the possible past and actual experiences motivating him or her. We take an in depth look at 'behaviours' from a psychoanalytical perspective[11] and not a mere conditioned-conductive behaviourist perspective (see how Graham (2002) distinguishes them).

From Ethnical Discrimination to Forced Isolation

While discussing about social and cultural issues, we know that some developed countries are recognized worldwide for their openness to immigration and cultural diversity.[12] However, and as shown by some cultural research conducted by Chevrier (2000),[13] a multicultural environment or a protective legislation do not assure per se either acceptance or integration at the workplace. Equally, Bataille (1997) denounces various forms of cultural discrimination at work, such as isolation or impediment to

---

11   In doing so we recognise the alternative explanation provided by Crowther (2002b) which is predicated in managers seeking to restate to themselves that they are actually important people and that all action is inwardly directed in this manner rather than directed against others. The Lacanian view (Lacan 1977, 1988, 1991) expounded in that paper is particularly important for this explanation. We consider however that recognising this alternative interpretation does not detract from our argument here.

12   See for example the Canada's official source of immigration and citizenship information – CIC (2006).

13   Some in Canada and others in Europe.

obtain promotions, among others, which represent nothing else than a manifestation of racism at work.[14]

We align our observations with the statements of the former authors. For instance, there are many programs that purport to encourage immigrants to integrate into the labour market,[15] but in reality, as our observations show us, their implementation depends on the will of those in charge of engaging employees: shareholders and managers, either for private or public organizations. The person who makes these kind of decisions (approving or denying someone else's chance to integrate into the labour market), reminds us not only of the importance of the quality of the individual's free will, his ethical choices and his moral behaviour, but also of his personal fears of being socially condemned or socially isolated if rules are not followed.[16] Even in the worst case scenario, intelligence may be put into damaging others by means of installing new barriers against integration into organizational life. For example, this occurs throughout committees evaluating résumés – prospective employees – with the aid of requirements that are impossible to meet for many immigrants who, paradoxically, are considered by the law as experienced workers. Here, the promise of a better future is broken. In this case, a feeling of frustration is many times experienced by those who left their home and their country, in search of a better life for themselves and their families. Feelings of unworthiness and non-accomplishment begin to invade the ontological security of these people, and their children recognize instinctively that something is going wrong regarding their family's means of support. Consequently, emotions erupt at home through forms of, for example, parents' detachment among themselves or indifference towards their children's anguish, verbal abuse, or even physical violence, all of which may result in a situation that the children grow developing resentment not necessarily only against their parents, but also against the social order: a country, a government, a specific social group. As we discuss later, this implies a reproduction of violence for oncoming generations inside the collective.

Moreover, and as our observations confirm, even for those qualified immigrants who got a qualified job, there is a long path to walk in order to be accepted as an equal by some colleagues and managers. There is a need to demonstrate that the new employee is as worthy as the native employees are, and that becomes a daily struggle, a psychological pressure. This deteriorates relationships at work and degrades the human integrity of the person that is trying to fit into an environment where he or she is not necessarily welcome by the social consensus, even though the high direction has found a person worthy of working with them. Therefore, as we have observed, the intercultural dynamic expected at political levels is not achieved. From the above, acculturation produces in the being a sense of discomfort and emptiness, even if he is already working and earning a very competitive salary while occupying a professional job. Similar cases of racism and discrimination occur when

---

14   Indeed the academic environment is one such environment of discrimination – not just of racism but also of sexism – which the unions in the UK are constantly highlighting.

15   Ibid 7.

16   See for example in the province of Quebec, how this is a major concern, still addressed nowadays (*Secrétariat du Conseil du trésor – Québec*, 2006).

a multinational of a developed country operates an outsourcing and offshoring process in a developing country: most of the time, directors come from the more developed country, and the management style is elitist and socially discriminating against powerless personnel. There is a need for a true acceptance and an acknowledgment of equitable opportunities.

As we see, most of these well founded precepts of human equity and justice remain in the supranational law and in the normative social rules, which are followed only when governmental instances are deeply looking into the daily basis of the social life in specific cases, or only by those people who feel afraid of constraining the law, or in the best case scenario, by those individuals who are convinced about the philosophy of the rule.

Psychological Intimidation, Actions, Motives and Compensatory Behaviours

As we are concerned by human fulfilment, and within this, throughout behaviours representing ethical consideration towards others (Dávila Gómez, 2005), our research allows us to identify that there is a need for exploring to what extent the described human disregard in organizations affects the human's mental and physical health. As we discussed in previous paragraphs, the state of the individuals' mental and physical health conditions him or her to adjust (or misadjust) to a collective social life, and therefore, to feel free, repressed, or even, in the best case scenario, fulfilled. By this, we aim to elucidate hidden emotions at the workplace, as well as repressive and compensatory behaviours that on a daily basis inflict suffering and pain on a person during his other activities, and in many cases, demand on people conformism in order to avoid adding more conflicts or problems to their lives, given that at least, the fact of having a stable job gives them a salary to survive, in order to fit into the established social regime.

Inside the economic dynamics in which we live, it is understandable that a person wants to enter a competitive way of living, given that as human beings we have desires, we want more of what we already have,[17] regardless of whether this entails a material or an emotional aspect. Our brain's bio-chemical structure allows us to learn more and more, and in consequence, to develop cognitive processes that makes us conscious about our environment and ourselves. Bloom (1957) explains how the capability of the human mind allows it to pass from a cognitive level to another more complex: e.g. to pass from the comprehension and understanding of things, to analysis of causes and effects, to synthesis of the context of things, to evaluation of moral values, purposes and contents of things, to abstraction of concepts that change reality. Despite of this wide range of possibilities that the human mind offers, our research tells us that under the sign of competitiveness, the comprehension and analysis levels are the most privileged. The reflexivity we refer to (see also Reynolds, 1998) needs synthesis to contextualize situations, as well as evaluation and abstraction in order to unveil the motives of actions and to act with

---

17   This is of course exacerbated by the consumerist society of the present – arguably one of the main causes of economic migration.

consequent responsibility for the previous established context where stakeholders and their interests would be taken into account. For example, when employees and other stakeholders are suppressed from their right to participate in organizational decisions and planning, there is as well a restriction to exercise the evaluation and abstraction of human capabilities. In this sense, people feel empty; their integral possibility of shining is not taken into account. Their dignity is diminished.[18]

On the one hand, the process of the human cognitive development is not only biological but also intellectual and emotional. Piaget (1977a, b) shows how the individual, sustained by the cognitive development, starts his progression at birth (and biologically before birth), passing through the subject's detachment of the mother until he recognizes the existence of external objects as well as other beings. Nevertheless, this development is not always done (for each being) in a healthy way, and as a consequence, psychological traumatism might well emerge later in adulthood.

On the other hand, Freud (1856–1939a) explores the psyche and identifies that even though a being is conscious of an action, it is possible for him or her to be unaware of some of the motives that remain in the unconscious. By the same token, in some cases, the being is conscious of the motives but he or she does not do anything to change that behaviour. This happens, in some cases because the person is afraid to being socially reprimanded for not following the collective's accepted way of doing things; in other cases, because the being is simply not interested in doing so, he or she has chosen to follow other life priorities rather than the understanding of their inner selves. To the latter Freud (1856–1939a) gives the name of super-ego (what we relate to the subconscious) in which value judgements are made, based on what the subject has learned from his cultural or family background. Here, knowing about motives, even consequences of the actions, the external reality intimidates the security of the self and therefore the final action is not consistent with the inner self but with others' external expectations. In the superego may lie a fear to change, to act, to take more ethical decisions. This may also be accompanied by past experiences of not knowing why a fear of acting continues to be persistent in the unconscious. As pointed out by Chanlat (2002: 65):

> How many people have chosen one profession or another in order to satisfy a desire of which they are more or less conscious: to save humanity, to take revenge against destiny, to transform the world, to heal a narcissistic wound, to come out of mourning, or to please their parents? [...] how many workers, employees, directors and managers have also seen themselves represented, nourished by their professional activities, how many of these activities have been associated to a gender (thirty years before, the image of a managers was related to a man) and how many, at least for some, retirement is a difficult experience?[19]

---

18   In extreme circumstances this can result in a person resorting to madness by attempting to hold what Laing (1961) describes as an untenable position. They can also result in paranoid behaviour through the dominance of feelings of guilt (Klein 1932) or in psychosis (Lawrence 1995).

19   Free translation from the original text published in French.

The above is not exclusive to the choice of a profession, but as our previous research and organizational observations indicate to us, it is something that also drives the way in which individuals behave in the work place. Thus, and basing our analysis on Freud's precepts and in our reflections, formerly presented, and while exploring the possible motives of repression in organizations, we identify that when it comes the time to look at managerial action, the manager feels pressure on a daily basis.

The manager has to demonstrate to the shareholders his or her ability to compete, to excel in a world of economic competition. Unfortunately, in doing so without a critical human perspective, managers representing shareholders' interests defend the emblem of free market per se with no restrictions or laws for the protection of the weakest, or at least for those who have less chance to fight for their rights in political and social arenas.[20] In the cases where there is not enough protective legislation, the latter emblem is a favourable environment for unethical actions,[21] and therefore irresponsible behaviours. However, as we have highlighted, a free market practice or a competitive environment does not rule out responsibility for action by the actor, because the consequences for others may always be evaluated; the decision to act is more of an ethical and moral concern (see Rousseau, 1712–1778a; Socrates – in Plato, 399–384 B.C. – among others, as well as Dávila Gómez, 2005 in a managerial context), a free will choice, a decision, even if there is no legislation; it is then an individual responsibility.

On the other hand, unconscious motives may trigger new unsatisfactory experiences for the acting being. It is here, then, when Freud (1856–1939a, b) proposes the need to reflect upon oneself in order to identify these motives, and as found not only by Freud, but also by Winnicott (1965) and Khan (1983), among others, these motives are anchored either during infancy, where the capability to reason was developing, or later during childhood, where incoherence in the behaviour of power figures was observed by the child with no logical explanation given to him or her that would have clarified any doubt. As explained by Klein and Riviere (1964:115):

> We hate in ourselves the harsh and stern figures that are also part of our inner world, and are to a large extent the result of our own aggression towards our parent. At the bottom our strongest hatred, however, is directed against the hatred within ourselves. We so much dead the hatred in ourselves that we are driven to employ one of our strongest measure of defence by putting it on to other people – to project it. But we also displace love into the outer world; and we can do so genuinely only if we have established good relations with the friendly figures within our minds. Here is a benign circle, for in the first place we gain trust and love in relation to our parents, next we take them, with all this love and trust, as it were, into ourselves; and then we can give from this wealth of loving feeling to the outer world again. There is an analogous circle in regard to our hatred; for hatred,

---

20   Sadly the Utilitarianist norms of society seem to require the imposition of regulation to mitigate against the tendency to exploit the relatively powerless by the powerful which is considered the norm. This is evidenced by the vast body of evidence concerning corporate abuse and excess which is readily observable throughout the world.

21   See only as a typical example what happened in the US with the recent Enron and Arthur Andersen scandals. See also what happens daily in places where both governmental and private corruption takes place.

as we have seen, leads to our establishing frightening figures in our minds, and then we are apt to endow other people with unpleasant and malevolent qualities. Incidentally, such an attitude of mind has an actual effect in making other people unpleasant and suspicious towards us, while a friendly and trusting attitude on our part is apt to call forth trust and benevolence from others.

As we grow up and interact with powerful figures – parents, teachers – or equals – brothers and colleagues – we experience various situations that produce in us joy, pain, satisfaction, hatred, or even disconcert. Our experiences imprint in our brain emotions of fear, security, or shame, which will reproduce later in life, when new similar situations may trigger inside of us, either the desire of reliving joyful sensations, or the need to unconsciously avoid new pain. As the integral beings that we are, these experiences reproduce themselves in our working environment. As organizational actors, we are also human beings that have experienced love and hatred on different levels, in early stages of our lives. Therefore, our present behaviour at work and our attitudes reflect our life, and also, our potential to change when surrounded by compassionate figures who inspire trust and benevolence in us (as explained by Klein and Riviere), which in an organizational environment are those with power (managers, directors, shareholders).

Seeking to generate change, it is necessary to continue to unveil the motives of the unconscious in order to act on them. As discussed previously, incoherent behaviours from adults, observed by children without receiving a logical explanation, leads to storing the unanswered issue in the unconscious. Thus, compensatory behaviours manifest in the being when he or she has to defend him/herself against those with more power, proposing a similar situation to one lived in the past, in which the being was confronted by and was unable to avoid the aggression. Our observations indicate that some of the compensatory behaviours with which the being seeks to obtain protection from others, inside organizations, are: aggressiveness (either having power or not), evasion of the responsibilities anchored in a duty or a mission, isolation from others, evasion of additional endeavours, overindulgence towards those with power, hypocrisy towards aggressors and therefore living a double life.

On the other hand, following Merleau-Ponty (1975), when a person has been raised by extremely authoritarian figures (a parent, a tutor, etc.), free speech as well as free mind are relegated to develop quietly in the mind of the subject because there is neither a place to freely express feelings nor for freely speaking out. According to Merleau-Ponty, when this authoritarianism is accompanied by physical or verbal violence, disastrous consequences for the person as a future adult arise, some of which we discuss in the following paragraphs as confirmed by our observations: vulnerability for allowing others' intimidation and integrity trespassing, hiding the true self, reproduction of violent behaviours towards others.

From the above, and aiming to diminish the effect of reality as detrimental to human integrity, we present a point of view where, following a philosophical orientation of the being's transcendence (see Schelling, 1775–1854), powerful figures should inspire confidence, freedom and credibility instead of fear, hatred or psychological damage on those who are under their development responsibility, as is the case of managers with their employees. As discussed, many of the aforementioned abuses are perpetuated because of a physical impossibility of the oppressed being to bring the power figure face to face with him or her, or because of the psychological intimidation that power figures exercise.

Inside the physical impossibilities we refer mostly to the cases when, for example, parental figure, much stronger than the child, beats or spanks him or her. This case is not only experienced during childhood but also during adulthood with domestic violence[22] where, for example, a lot of women are still beaten by their husbands, and many of those women go to work convinced of the male dominance of their working peers. Here, we identify the phantom figure of believing in a practice as the correct norm to follow – even if it is unfair – as explained by Freud (1856–1939a, b). Some managers or employees who may have experienced violence from their loved ones, see no conflict in inflicting pain to others who do not represent any emotional tie for them, basically, as a degenerative and pathological response. As such, a manager who was abused during childhood may have no problem in intimidating his employees. However, childhood mistreatment does not justify its reproduction during adulthood given that, as social and collective beings that we are, we have learned also the forgiveness and the compassion that others might have had for us. At the same time, we always claim the ethical consciousness that should accompany free will action, even not knowing the unconscious motives of past suffering. This is why a morbid motive like experiencing satisfaction while inflicting pain on others answers more to a pathology or to a mental trouble. As sustained by Khan and Freud, it is through the questioning of the inner self that there is always a possibility to unveil and heal the unconscious. It demands willpower and determination from the being.

On the other hand, regarding psychological intimidation we identify cases in which, for example, an adolescent is afraid of losing financial support if he goes against his parents rules, or in organizations when an employee risks losing his job when questioning the finalities of an order or a command – and here, we are not only referring to employees without power, but also to managers who also receive shareholders' directives which may not always seem to be an ethical course of action. As a consequence, in the few cases in which the powerless being confronts the powerful being, another psychological phenomenon arrives and it is the case of psychological violence in which not only the being with more power threatens the stability and security of the less powerful, but also inflicts the pain of verbal violence by adopting a dominant tone of voice, or even using abusive language. When this occurs, a physical confrontation may take place, and we can reproduce, in an organizational environment, the street violence that we find worldwide. In the worst case scenario, this violence ends up escalating to the broader scope of countries with ethnic military conflicts in which many consider that those who are different have fewer rights than themselves.[23]

---

22   See for example what the *Santé et services sociaux Québec* (2006) stipulate, asking parents to behave humanly, allowing at the same time legal denounces of mistreatment.

23   See Crowther and Green, 2002.

The Manager's Ethical Choices

In a sense, because of the intimidation the manager may have experienced previously as a child who had to excel and perform in order to make his or her parents proud, the need to please the director (or shareholder) arises and makes him or her proud of the strategic ability to carry on successfully with the business in a reality of competitiveness (see Crowther and Jatana, 2005). Thus, a reproduction of the phantom of identification has taken place. At the same time, the manager here may be abiding by his or her director's rules or else, he or she may be fired, becoming professionally unfulfilled. In some cases, having already suffered from psychological violence, this last episode is one that he or she does not want to recreate. The manager feels obliged to perform blindly, because he does not want to reproduce the painful event he or she suffered during his childhood, which was inflicted by his parents, who loved him or her very much. An unconscious protective barrier is then erected. However, as we are also conscious beings, even though we are unaware of some of our motives, we have the capacity of awareness for the consequences of our actions towards other people, and therefore, towards ourselves. We can therefore be ethical in our actions and accountable for their consequences.

Many times, managers in organizations know their workload will represent for them less time spent with their families, therefore, less opportunity to share quality time with their kids. In this case, the manager is devoted to his or her professional career, which, at that moment seems more important than his or her family's emotional satisfaction. However, if we ask any manager about this, he or she will probably say that family comes first and that everything that is humanly possible is being done in order to give them a better quality of life than he or she ever had.[24] In this, the unconscious manifests in the sense that the person is aware that in order to obtain something (some material improvement quality of life, represented many times in more income) sacrifices must be made resulting in less time spent with family and less direct attention to his or her role as a parent. However, the unconscious is present when even the person, understanding the aforementioned reality, does not know why he or she is actually doing this. Hereby, as we discussed previously, and as some of our empirical data and observations confirm, in the psychological childhood experience of the actual parent, he or she could have suffered some privations (e.g., his or her own parents might have lived on a low income), or he could have suffered from psychological or verbal violence (and sometimes physical abuse to "correct misbehaviours" in the eyes of his or her parent). This attitude of evasion is in many cases not recognized by the parent, the actual manager. As Freud (1856–1939a, b) explains, many painful experiences lie repressed in the unconscious, and consequently, a compensatory behaviour in the present or in the future that could attempt to relive them, is avoided and cut off from the individual's life.

In other cases, an actual manager that has been abused during childhood (either by his or her parents, or by a school teacher), may not remember the situation as

---

24   Of course the pressure of the culture at work exacerbate this tendency by requiring workers to be present in excess of their normal contracted hours in order to be seen to be enthusiastic.

something shameful but as something necessary, and therefore it is a natural and good way of proceeding towards his or her own children, or spouse (situations may aggravate if the manager saw his or her parents being violent towards each other). Hereby, we refer to a superego (which we relate to a subconscious) of accepted social rules, even if the concerned being knows that ethically it may be wrong. As highlighted by Socrates (in Plato, 399–384 B.C.) in the *Menon* dialogue, and by Rousseau (1712–1778b), the fact of following the law does not imply that the law is just. Not always regulations and norms are justice. Justice, as a virtue, is something that has to do more with the ethical integrity of the being when he is acting, and therefore it is a question of choices.

Consequences for the Collective Well-being

When a person has lived any of the previous experiences during childhood, there are some consequences that become apparent in his or her framework of conduct as an adult. Among these consequences we have observed in organizations, basically, the following three.

We identify that first of all, there is a consequence of *hiding* of the true self through the acceptance of impositions by others. As pointed out by Khan (1983), the life that others expect to be lived by the being remains in his or her superego (what we relate to a subconscious) and dominates his or her inner and truthful desires. Hereby, as life goes on and, in cases when, from a materialistic point of view, if the life of the individual has been rewarding, it is easy to hide the emotional desires to do other things, because change might cost so much, in time and money, and many times, in family tranquillity.

As a second consequence, we identify the *aggressive* attitude in which the individual explodes with fury in the workplace and takes revenge on account of his or her past, though not against the initial perpetrators of his or her problems (the people of his past), but against people who are now under his own power (the actual employees). Here, the new powerful being may desire to make some people pay for the faults of others in the past; even if it is an unconscious desire, it is, however, a conscious decision to act as such. Likewise, the being may want for others to experience what he or she has suffered in the past while they are being promoted to higher positions. As a norm of life, things are difficult, they were difficult for him or her in order to obtain his actual position, so, therefore, it has to be difficult for others as well. In this case, we identify a level of hatred that surpasses the angry resentment against a person of the past; as life goes on, it transforms itself into hatred for the system, or in many cases against life itself.

As a third consequence we identify that some individuals, in the desire for changing reality, decide to take action and develop a *fighting* behaviour against the system from inside, which could represent for the being, new occasions to suffer more psychological violence coming from those who are more powerful than him.

In the first consequence, the hiding, we find a silent being, whose acts are not without consequences for his family or his colleagues, as his example encourages others to follow him. Whether individuals are threatened or suffer from any kind of violence at work with no chance to protest, or whether they are the ones creating violence, any of these situations will generate other spaces for individuals exploding with anger (see Crowther and Dávila-Gómez, 2006c). As the individuals hide their true emotions in the workplace, it is the family environment, or community life that will be suffering. Suicide becomes an alternative, physical violence in families increases, isolation and family disruption occurs, and in other cases, urban and civil violence is affected.

Equally, in the second consequence, the aggressive being who has a legitimized power, may be seen by others who want to progress with a successful career, as exhibiting a conduct to follow. Hereby, a violent way of conduct is replicated by many, not only in the workplace, but also at home and in community life. Hence, generations to come will reproduce this conduct. However, there are also those who suffered violence from aggressive beings, but instead decided not to reproduce this behaviour, and seeking for emotional security, ended up acting as in the first consequence that we already described (the hiding).

Finally, in the third consequence, for the fighting being who aims to change reality to some extent, there is some hope. As presented by Courcy and Savoie (2003), the number of cases of psychological harassment that are denounced are increasing thanks to new governmental regulations in some countries such as United States, Canada and France, inter alia. Before then, the situation was utterly complicated as only a few cases were formally declared. However, and as our observations confirm, there are structural barriers to overcome in the organization such as norms, procedures, hierarchy, the right to free speech, etc.. There are also new occasions to suffering psychological intimidation because the authority's legitimacy is questioned by a fighting being that falls into this type of behaviour. The person with more power sees in the fighting being a threat, therefore, new intimidation opportunities appear.

Even though, increasingly, governments and organizations are implementing proceedings and policies to prevent and to resolve conflicts coming from psychological intimidation, the truth that we have observed is that in many cases, those in power arrange the situation in order to hide the truth or to perpetrate violence in spaces, places or times where there will be no witnesses to advocate later in favour of the case of the fighting being. In this manner, regardless of laws, intimidation and violence continues to occur. In some cases, especially with bigger organizations, norms and procedures are so bureaucratic, that it will take a long time to apply the law when the fighting being makes a complaint, even in the case in which the organizational direction admits he or she is right. Therefore, as we have observed, even if in some cases justice was done, times and procedures demand so much energy from the being, that his or her integrity is also in peril. In this situation, even if the being may be answering to his or her true self, it will be him or her, in the future, who will suffer the denigration of his or her integrity, as well as his or her family's. Sometimes, sentiments of anger or hatred may be developed, not by the fighting being, but by one of his colleagues or a member of his family. In this way, cases one and two (hiding or violent beings) will reproduce in the future.

In general, among the observed behaviours that come from the consequences of psychological violence, we see that the three that we have detailed are also repetitively reproduced, not only by those in a power relation (manager – employee), but also by those that share the same power: the colleagues. As such, we have various managers responsible for operations in different departments, whom, competing for promotions or for excelling in their duties in order to obtain the directors' or shareholders' preference, commit many times acts of sabotage against their colleagues, or even in other cases, steal from another manager a magnificent idea and present it as their own. This competitiveness is also reproduced by colleagues within the same department, in which employees will fight to be the manager's favourite in order to gain a promotion, or to be the next successor in power. In doing this, people are constantly repeating the three conducts we described, because, among others, as human beings, the idea to perform exists; it is important to obtain acknowledgment from the "actual father", or simply, to gain the power that was denied to him, in other stages of life. This dynamic is intrinsically linked with the necessity experienced in a world of competition as a request for gaining respect, acknowledgment, or in some cases, morbid motives of satisfaction while inflicting pain to others.

The three consequences for the collective well-being that we have explored in this point are not the only ones. In fact, we have also analysed others related with compensatory behaviours, some of which have already been presented in some extent in previous points as we discussed physical impossibility and psychological intimidation. Continuous exploration and more reflection about consequences of psychological violence in the workplace is a theme that needs continual exploration. As such, a deep analysis of this kind allows to undercover the very motives and roots of behaviours that a manager, or any person (e.g. an employee), should change in order to regain his or her human dignity.

Is there Some Hope?

Managers, as responsible as they are for the continual development of people working with them, are called to acknowledge and to act, consequently, according to what we have discussed. The need to develop solidarity, empathy and willingness in search for togetherness becomes a moral imperative for organizational life given that organizational actions are driving humanity's reality. The reflections we have presented allow us to identify that it is like if all the repression and violence experienced worldwide, since infancy and throughout childhood, finds its way out to reproduce in collective environments, either in organizations or in the constitution of new families. Projections of hatred, non-conformity and violence are perpetuated continuously, leaving deep psychological wounds that do not seem to heal.

There is a need to stop the reproduction of this human violence (either physical or psychological) from generation to generation. There is a need to regain the integrity, the dignity of the human being. In this way, organizations have a serious duty of responsibility towards the collective, and in this, the action, the consciousness and ethics of those in power are crucial. As stated by Shaw (2006b), there is a need to find again the love lost in organizations; the very meaning of their existence is increasingly forgotten. In the same sense, Haw (2004) expressed that managers must procure compassion, understanding and satisfactory jobs for their collaborators (e.g. employees). There is a need to re-educate a blessed adult through active social life.

There is a need for managers to become healers, or at least, generous providers of healing environments at the workplace through humanistic attitudes and treatment, coherent behaviours and ethical exemplarity. Helping to heal individuals while working (taking here the precepts of Klein and Riviere, as well as those of Merleau-Ponty we presented before), or at least, not deteriorating the actual situation to the detriment of humanity, contribute to inspire, on others, humanistic conducts and behaviours to reproduce in other social and collective environments (e.g. family, school), and as such, to improve the present and the future human and social life. This implies acting with forethought.

Many strategic authors and also the positivist organizational orientation may see the above as simply rhetorical or utopian good wishes. Nevertheless, inside a critical perspective, we believe that only a change of values in the human being may help change the results of the actions, and therefore, with more ethical and moral actions and decisions, organizational actions, as a result, will help to change social and collective environments for the best. Even in governmental institutions, the improvement of laws and structures are a result of individuals' social consciousness in action. As behaviours experienced inside the workplace are transferred and reproduced in families, therefore in society, a need for human change is imperative. For any firm, as well as for any governmental institution, regardless of the importance of seeking high productivity levels, the main aim of its organizational success should be the accomplishment of its mission regarding society.

References

Alvesson, H. and Willmott, H. (1996), *Making sense of management: a critical introduction*, London: Sage.

Banerjee, R.P. (2004), "Beyond Human Values: Divine Values for New Era Corporations", in Gupta, A.D. (ed.) *Human Values in Management*, UK: Ashgate, pp. 112–126.

Bataille, P. (1997), *Le racisme au travail*, Paris, Ed. La Découverte.

Bloom, B.S. (1957), *Taxonomy of education objectives: Handbook I, cognitive domain*, New York: Longmans, Green and Co.

Canada's official source of immigration and citizenship information – CIC (2006), http://www.cic.gc.ca/english/index.html, consulted in July 2006.

Castonguay, C. (2004), *The Future of the Health Care System: Are we condemned to never-ending crises?*, Montreal Economic Institute – IDEM, http://www.iedm.org/main/publications_en.php, consulted in July 2006.

Chanlat, A. and Bédard, R. (1990), "La gestion, une affaire de parole", in Chanlat, J.F. (ed.) *L'individu dans l'organisation: les dimensions oubliées*, Québec: Presses de l'Université Laval; Paris: Eska, pp.79–99.

Chanlat, J.F. (2002), "Le défi social du management: l'apport des sciences socials" in Kalila and Michel (eds.), *Les défis du management*, Ed. Liaisons, Paris, pp.59–82.

Chanlat, J.F. (1998), *Sciences sociales et management: plaidoyer pour une anthropologie générale*, Sainte-Foy, Québec: Presses de l'Université Laval; Paris: Eska.

Chevrier, S. (2000), *Le management des équipes interculturalles*, Paris: Presses universitaires de France.

Courcy, F. and Savoie, A. (2003), "L'agression au milieu de travail: qu'en est-il et que faire?", *Gestion*, HEC Montréal, summer 2003, vol. 28, no. 2, pp. 19–25.

Crise – Center for Research and Intervention on Suicide and Euthanasia (2006), *Topics and Orientations*, http://www.crise.ca/eng/cr_problematique.asp, consulted in July 2006.

Crowther, D. (2002a), *A Social Critique of Corporate Reporting*; 2002; Aldershot; Ashgate.

Crowther, D. (2002b), Psychoanalysis and auditing; in S Clegg (ed), *Paradoxical New Directions in Management and Organization Theory*; Amsterdam; J Benjamins; pp 227–246.

Crowther, D., Carter, C. and Cooper, S. (1998), A treatise on Business Process Engineering; *Proceedings of Business Process Track at BAM97* pp. 293–312.

Crowther, D., Davies M. L. and Cooper, S. (1998), Evaluating Corporate Performance: a Critique of Economic Value Added; *Journal of Applied Accounting Research* Vol 4 No 2 pp. 2–34.

Crowther, D. and Dávila Gómez, A.M. (2006a), "Is lying the best way of telling the truth", *Social Responsibility Journal*, vol. 1, no. 3 and 4, pp. 128–141.

Crowther, D. and Dávila Gómez, A.M. (2006b), "Stress in the Back Office", in *Proceedings of India – The Processing Office of the World*; Kochi, January 2006, pp.27–38.

Crowther, D. and Dávila Gómez, A.M. (2006c), "I will if you will: risk, feelings and emotion in the workplace", in Crowther, D. and Caliyurt, T.K., (eds.), *Globalization and Social Responsibility*, UK, Cambridge Scholars Press, pp. 163–184.

Crowther, D. and Green, M. (2002), Balancing the books: an amoral accounting of retribution; paper presented at the European Critical Accounting Studies Conference; Leicester; July 2002.

Crowther, D. and Green, M. (2004), "Re-placing People in Organizational Activity", in Gupta, A.D. (ed.), *Human Values in Management*, UK: Ashgate, pp. 264–282.

Crowther, D. and Jatana, R. (2005), "Modern epics and corporate well-being", in Crowther, D. and Jatana, R. (eds.), *Representations of Social Responsibility Vol 2*; Hyderabad; ICFAI University Press, pp. 125–166.

Crowther, D. and Ortiz-Martinez, E. (2006), "The Abdication of Responsibility: Corporate Social Responsibility, Public Administration and the Globalizing Agenda", in Crowther, D. and Caliyurt, T.K., (eds.), *Globalization and Social Responsibility*, UK, Cambridge Scholars Press, pp. 253–276.

Dávila Gómez, A.M. (2005), "Beyond Business Ethics: Managers' Ethical Challenges Concerning Community and Employees", in Crowther, D. and Jatana, R (eds.) *Representations of Social Responsibility Vol 1*, Hyderabad, India: ICFAI University Press, 2005, pp. 74–104.

Dávila Gómez, A.M. (2003), *Hacia un Management Humanista desde la educación a distancia: intersubjetividad y desarrollo de cualidades humanas,* Doctoral thesis, École des HEC de Montréal, Canada.

Dewey, J. (1975), *Moral Principles in Education*, copyright 1909, Southern Illinois University Press U.S.

Freud, S. (1856–1939a), *Nouvelles conferences sur la psychanalyse*, France: Gallimard, coll. Idées, 1984.

Freud, S. (1856–1939b), *Métapsychologie*, France: Gallimard, coll. Idées, 1968.

Giddens, A. (1987), *Social Theory and Modern Sociology*, Stanford, Calif. Stanford University Press.

Graham, G. (2002), "Behaviourism, and Psychoanalysis", in Erwin, E. (ed) *The Freud Encyclopedia – Theory, Therapy, and Culture*, New Youk, London, Routledge, , pp. 43–44.

Haw, R. (2004), "Management by Love and Kindness and the Consequent Implications", in Crowther, D. and Rayman-Bacchus (eds.), *Perspectives on Corporate Social Responsibility*, UK, Ashgate, pp. 205–228.

Human Resources and Social Development Canada (2005), *Employment Insurances (EI) – Acts and Regulations*, Government of Canada, http://www.hrsdc.gc.ca/en/ei/legislation/ei_act_entry_page.shtml, consulted in July 2006.

Institut national de santé publique – Québec (2003), *La mortalité au Québec – une comparaison internationale*, http://www.inspq.qc.ca/pdf/publications/, consulted in July 2006.

Karaset, R. and Theorell, T. (1990), "Psychosocial Job Characteristics and Heart Disease", in Karaset, R. and Theorell, T. (ed.) *Healthy Work, Stress, Productivity and the Reconstruction of Working Life*, New York, Basic Books.

Khan, M. (1983), *Hidden selves: between theory and practice in psychoanalysis*, London: Hogarth and the Institute of Psycho-Analysis.

Klein M (1932), *The Psychoanalysis of Children*; London; Hogarth.

Klein, M. and Riviere, J. (1964), *Love, Hate and Reparation*, New York, W.W. Norton and Company. Eds.

Lacan J (1977), *Ecrits: a selection*; trans A Sheridan; London; Tavistock.

Lacan J (1988), *The Seminars of Jacques Lacan Book II: The Ego in Freud's Theory and in the Technique of Psychoanalysis 1954–1955*; trans S Tomaselli; New York; Cambridge University Press.

Lacan J (1991), *The Seminars of Jacques Lacan Book I: Freud's papers on Techniqu 1953–1954*; trans J Forrester; New York; W W Norton and Co.

Laing R D (1961), *Self and Others*; London; Tavistock.

Lawrence W G (1995); The seductiveness of totalitarian states of mind; *Journal of Health Care Chaplaincy*; October, 11–22.

Maslach, C. (1998) "A Multidimensional theory of Burnout", in Cooper, C.L. (ed.) *Theories of Organisational Stress*, UK, Oxford University Press.

Merleau-Ponty M. (1975), *Les relations avec autruit chez l'enfant*, Centre de documentation Paris V, France.

Mishan E J 1993, The Costs of Economic Growth: London; Weidenfeld and Nicolson.

Ortiz-Martinez, E, and Crowther, D. (2004), ¿Son compatibles la responsabilidad económica y la responsabilidad social corporativa?; Documentos, IX Congreso del CLAD, Madrid, November 2004.

Piaget, J. (1977a), *Mes idées*, Denöel Gonthier, coll. Médiations.

Piaget, J. (1977b), *El nacimiento de la inteligencia en el niño*, Ed. grijalbo, 1994, Bogotá, trad. Delachaux et Niestlé, 1977.

Plato (399–384 B.C.), Socrates – *Alcibiades, Second Alcibiades,* and *Menon* dialogues, in Plato, *Complete Works,* Ed. By Cooper, J., M. and Hutchison, D.S., Indianapolis, Tacket publishing company, 1997, pp. 557–608.

Radio Canada (2006), "Le privé dans la santé : le patients seront-ils gaganates?", in Radio Canada, *Nouvelles science et santé,* http://www.radio-canada.ca/nouvelles/science-Sante/, consulted in July 2006.

Reynolds, M. (1998), "Reflection and Critical Reflection in Management Learning," *Management Learning,* vol 29 (2), Sage: London, pp.183–200.

Ritzer, G. (1996) "An Introduction to McDonalisation" in Ritzer, G. (ed.) *The McDonalisation of Society,* London, Pine Forge Press.

Rousseau, J.J. (1712–1778a), *Emile: or, On education,* trans. by Bloom, A., 1979, New York, Basic Books.

Rousseau, J.J. (1712–1778b), "Discourse on the Origin and Foundations of Inequality Among Men," in Rousseau, J.J, *The First and Second Discourses,* Ed. By Masters, R, D, Translated by Master, R and Masters, J, 1964, New York, St.Martin's Press.

Secrétariat du Conseil du trésor – Quebec (006), *Budget de dépanses 2006–2007 – Vol.II,* http://www.tresor.gouv.qc.ca/fr/publications/budget/06–07/06–07_vol2.pdf, consulted in July 2006.

Santé et services sociaux Québec (2006), *Domestic violence,* Gouvernment du Québec, http://www.msss.gouv.qc.ca/en/sujets/prob_sociaux/domestic_violence.html, consulted in July 2006.

Sen, A. (1998), *On Ethics and Economics,* UK, Blackwell.

Schelling, F.W.J.(1775–1854), *System of Transcendental Idealism (1800),* trans. by Heath, P., Charlottesville: University Press of Virginia.

Shaw, J. J. A. (2006a), "Globalization: A Tale of Corporate Dominance, Diminished Responsibility and a Disenchanted World", in Crowther, Crowther, D. and Tunca Caliyurt, K., (eds.), *Globalization and Social Responsibility,* UK, Cambridge Scholars Press, pp. 253–276.

Shaw, J. J. A. (2006b), "Where is the Love?", *Social Responsibility Journal,* vol.2, no. 1, pp.112–119.

Trypathy, K. and Chavan, S. (2006), "Managing Cross-Cultural issues in BPOS: the HR Imperative", in *Proceedings of India – the processing Office of the World*; Kochi, January 2006, pp. 39–45.

United Nations (2006), *World Economic and Social Survey 2006,* http://www.un.org/esa/policy/wess/index.html, consulted in July 2006.

World Bank (2006), *Data and Statistics – 2004,* http://www.worldbank.org/, consulted in July 2006.

Winnicott, D. (1965), *The maturational processes and the facilitating environment: studies in the theory of emotional developments,* NewYork, International University Press.

Chapter 2

Organizational Change, Human Condition and the Moral Contract

Emmanuelle Avon

Introduction

When I started to work on this chapter, I wanted to address some of the ethical decisions that executives debate on when they have to implement radical organizational transformation while they have to pursue the ever increasing operational performance objectives. My previous title for the chapter was therefore: "*Crossroad Leadership between Teleological and Deontological Ethical Practice: A Corporate Rule of Conduct or an Individual Choice*". My chapter was structured by the ethical leadership literature approach on the individual leadership behaviour facing a difficult crossroad between the ongoing performance process which normally requires teleological ethical practices and the organizational changes that induce a genuine deontological ethical practice. The current literature provides a logical framework to structure a sound analysis of this dilemma and my action-research allowed me to respond with empirical data.

Within my action-research in large Canadian corporations, I saw business executives facing a constant struggle between new market pressures on the one hand and major organizational transformations on the other. In other words, the pressure is constantly pushing for higher operating performance levels while these very same operating processes are being transformed. The individual leader has to make an ethical choice between a teleological focus on the shareholder value and a deontological conduct of ethics focussing on employee well being and work condition. The leadership ethics literature supports the idea that this decision will be directly influenced by the individual traits and moral maturity (Kanungo and Mendonca 2001, Aronson 2001, Kanungo 2001). Based on our research, I tend to believe that this decision is institutionalized in the legal framework, the corporate rules of conduct and the social norms carried in the business management practice. I will revisit these elements to see how it leads to a teleological perspective for shareholder value over any other form of considerations.

The challenge organizations and executives are increasingly facing since the 1990s is that they can not expect a stable, predictable and very effective operating process to achieve higher performance levels like it used to be. Now, they have to work within an unperfected and unpredictable operating process to make it more effective despite the ongoing changes. The challenge for those executives is therefore to mobilize and motivate the employees and middle managers to cope and work even more to compensate an imperfect workflow environment while continuously ensure commitment to the organizational transformation.

The result, in my view is devastating. The corporation's productivity and even profitability is still at stake, the people's work environment and social climate is deteriorating affecting the workplace climate. Ultimately the middle managers and executives are facing this "double contradiction" where they can't aim for higher competitiveness without implementing these major organizational transformations which in return are weakening their work force (Duxbury and Higgins 2003).

My empirical research leads me to a whole other level of analysis going from the individual leader facing this crossroad and the organizational structural rules of conduct to the organizational change as a phenomenon and a management practice. In other words, I believe that the ethical decision about how to treat employees within an organizational transformation embedded in the operating structure is not individually determined. It is organizationally, legally and socially determined to adopt a teleological ethics. This behaviour determinism is not a decision left on the individual's shoulder or the organization's culture. It is a well defined behaviour rule of conduct in the capitalist system. The issue we face today is that organizational changes have become so intensified in terms of human conditioning of the employees' work experience and at such a large scaled (corporate and economic infrastructure) that we are facing a breach of tacit moral contract. The ethical dilemma can no longer be on the individual's moral responsibility or on the corporation's human consciousness but is becoming a collective political debate.

I adopted the assumption that the organization is a social system that determines and structures all human decisions and actions including these ethical practices. The organization is not an entity as such, it is the result of individual relations and interactions with one another where individuals perceive themselves in relation with a legal corporate entity (Eraly 1988).

First of all, this chapter will look at the phenomenon of organizational transformation as a new form of "industrial revolution" embracing the basic capitalist principals of the organization operational engineered improvements. This will introduce the current context in which organizational transformation has changed in terms of strategic initiative.

On the second phase, I will pay a special attention to this new phenomenon on the executive function in terms of leadership and management practices. I will revisit the conceptual framework on organizational change facing empirical data. We will see how this new management practice is becoming a routine and path dependent. It will lead us to revisit the day-to-day new ethical practices executives are facing. I will therefore address the very contradictions executives have to deal with.

The third step of my analysis will focus on the human and economic consequences of this change phenomenon and new management practices have on the Canadian society over the last 15 years. It will allow us to look more closely at the new human conditions it has created within the Canadian corporations.

Finally, I will discuss the consequences of this new economic, managerial and social context on the tacit moral contract. I will revisit Adam Smith, Jean-Jacques Rousseau, John Stuart Mill and Karl Marx as utopian philosophers of our modern world. I will pay special attention to their definition of our tacit moral contract to see if we are still meeting it or not. Our preliminary conclusions lead us to believe that our current context has engaged a breach of moral contract. The current management practices are going deeper in dehumanizing people and reducing people's humanity to a production factor. I believe, based on the empirical data that the current ethical practices have changed the human condition and consciousness to a new form of technical instrument. These new management practices have, by all means, broken the tacit moral contract of our capitalist system.

This analytical research is based on two sets of data. My empirical analysis focuses on data related to the Canadian economy and society from 1990s to 2006 because the current outstanding transformation of our society is known to have begun in the 1990s. The empirical data on change management leadership behaviours is based on corporate annual reports and on my action-research in large Canadian private owned corporations. The empirical data on the Canadian economy and social fabric comes from the national bureau of Statistics Canada and a longitudinal research published in 2003 entitled "The 2001 National Work-Life Conflict Study" by Dr. Linda Duxbury and Dr. Chris Higgins (2002). I also look at large Canadian based Corporations since 2000. Finally, I completed my analysis by reviewing the literature on leadership, management, ethical practices and social responsibility. I revisited classical literature of political philosophy to understand our tacit capitalist moral contract and put it in perspective with the current managerial ethical practices on change.

Organizational Change

Organizational change is not new to the capitalist system. In fact, it is part of the fundamentals of what capitalism system really is. We can go back as far as the classics like Adam Smith in the 18th century in his perspective on creating the nations wealth to see that the division of labour, the task specialization and free labour market was the innovative approach to our modern economic system. For the first time it was understood that a division of labour allowed to create added value which would sum up to become great wealth for the nation and its people.

By the mid-ninetieth Century, Karl Marx revealed the increasing industrial phenomenon where the manufacturers perfected even further the division of labour redefining the meaning of work in terms of dehumanized labour tasks. A new form of human exploitation under the private production ownership allowed to go so far that it transformed society. He foresaw a destructive process affecting not only the meaning of work, but also the work environment that affected the human conditions and consequently the human consciousness. In fact, these changes were expending to an intensity and rhythm that generated what we call today, the Industrial Revolution. Joseph Schumpeter, in the early 20th century recognized this creative destruction process as the only possible economic evolution. In fact entrepreneurs were the only type of individuals that could invent, innovate and take the business risks to generate these necessary ongoing changes to continue to create wealth through these technological innovations as well as creating new markets, building new business partnership and redesigning the operation processes.

On the organizational perspective, change has always been fundamental to maintain business competitiveness and profitability. Frederic Taylor, in the early Twentieth Century, designed and perfected an engineered way of creating more efficient, productive and effective methods through "scientific division of labour in the organization" to increase each task's performance. Taylor introduced a new way of understanding the organization of labour as a whole mechanic where scientific rational engineer knowledge could rethink the operations to find the best way to operate effectively and improve its productivity.

In the early Twentieth Century, private corporations were also able to legally get the corporate legal entity recognized as a legal person that could be responsible for its actions (Crawford 2003). This new legal approach limited the shareholders legal responsibility. The Corporation could therefore expend its economic activities in multiple industrial sectors, in diverse geographic regions.

We also know that the industrial economic system increased its operations a mass production capacity. By the 1950s we saw a mass consumption develop creating local captive markets. By the 1970s and 1980s, the economic system was facing some cycles which slowed down the mass production and mass consumption. The Corporations had to find new ways of building on this creation of wealth. By the early 1990s, this is when we saw the beginning of a new knowledge economy infrastructure emerge while the consumer and labour market had to face new challenges. This particular moment in our recent history is the one I want to focus on because it has all the creative destruction's signature our capitalist system has. I will look at the organizational change as a new capitalist phenomenon. I will see how it transformed leadership into a management practice. I will review this whole transformation to understand the ethical practice dilemmas executive have to face.

A Capitalist Phenomenon

The capitalist industrial revolution has always been profoundly marked by its ability to reinvent itself. At the early stages it was to improve productivity, later on, in the 20th century it was to create new products and new improved processes. In the 1980s, corporations had to be strategic and adapt to a changing environment (Porter 1985). There was also, in the late 1980s, the need to develop organizational culture to reach excellence (T. Peters and R. Waterman 1983).

In every capitalist transformation phase, the Corporation embraced a specific change to maintain its competitiveness and performance. It was not any different in the 1990s. However, the specificity of the 1990s is that the Canadian economy and society has experienced an extraordinary level of change. In fact, corporations have made what used to be exceptional organisational transformations an ongoing operating driver as a general accepted competitive advantage.

During most of the 20th century, it was common to improve the operations for cost controls and adopt very effective problem solving approaches to innovate. By the 80s, the need to improve on the corporate culture toward excellence brought the attention on the employees' ability to impact performance through their own behaviours. Organizational development was an art because it required competencies to read the social and human aspects of the organization from a psychological, political, sociological and cultural perspective to align employee behaviours through a corporate wide belief and value system coherent with the corporate strategy.

Over the last decade, change management has perfected itself to such a degree that these managerial methods are so effective that very large corporations can count on 2 to 4 years to undergo major organizational transformation and make it financially affordable and timely effective. At a corporate level, change management methods have been improved and perfected to a level never encountered in the capitalist history. It is now common to see CEO presenting the next level of organizational major changes. Just to look at some of the major labour intensive large Corporations operating in Canada that are also highly vertically integrated in the economy with other sectors, lets look at three major firms.

In 2006, Ford Motor Company announced their need to restructure their manufacturing operating infrastructure across the globe to improve their efficiency. It was also very clear that a new innovative, organic, entrepreneurial corporate culture had to be embraced. In January 2006, William Clay Ford, Jr., Chairman and CEO has announced Ford strategic plan. Here are the key elements that affected their employees directly:

> Ford Motor Company was solidly profitable and growing around the world in 2005. (…) When I took over as CEO at the end of 2001, Ford Motor Company was unprofitable, losing more than $5 billion that year. In 2002, we launched a major effort to revitalize our company. (…) but the conditions we confronted represented a turning point in our industry unlike anything we've experienced in the last 50 years. The automotive business had shifted, completely and permanently, to full-scale global competition. The days of unlimited, inexpensive gasoline are gone forever. It is time for a bold new approach that goes beyond anything we have done in the past. So, in January 2006, we launched the most fundamental restructuring in our history, which we call "Way Forward" plan. (…) Way Forward is a comprehensive plan for restructuring and reinvigorating our automotive business in North America. It touches every piece of our North American business to make it more customer-focussed, product-driven and efficient, including: (….)

> • North American capacity will be realigned to match demand – with 14 manufacturing facilities to be idled – resulting in significant cost savings and reduced employment of 25, 000–30,000, Capacity will be reduced by 1.2 million units, or 26 percent, by 2008, which represents the majority of actions within the plan's 2006–2012 period.
> • Salary-related costs cut 10 percent in North America, with the reduction of the equivalent of 4, 000 salaried positions by the end of the first quarter 2006. In addition, the company's officer ranks are being reduced 12 percent by the end of the first quarter.

> (…) This plan will restore our North American automotive operations to profitability by 2006. (…) Along with our substantial cost restructuring, we are changing the business model that's existed for many decades at Ford. (…) First, we are taking a more far-sighted approach to creating shareholder value. (…) We also will be managing to allow our employees more freedom, to take smart risks and to demonstrate their creativity. (…) We are unleashing our spirit of American innovation. (…) Addressing the challenges we face, particularly in North America, is going to be difficult and at times painful. Winning will

require sacrifices by the people of Ford, and there will be fewer of us in the future than there are today." (2006, Annual report, pp.2–5)

In North America, including Canada, Ford Motor Company had 140 000 employees in 2005 which represent 47% of the company's work force (2006:102). It is important to realize that this company being in the manufacturing industry is highly integrated in the Canadian economy (natural resources, professional services, other manufacturing companies, retail, wholesale etc.). Any major changes in its operating structure will have a major impact in the Canadian economy.

Bell Canada Enterprises also goes toward the same strategic challenge in terms of major transformation. In the 2002 Annual Report, Michael J. Sabia, Chairman and CEO of Bell Canada recognized, when he took over the leadership that the company needed to focus on its core business and its productivity level. He encouraged viewing this performance objective as a discipline and initiative behaviour and ultimately a cost structure. He wanted every employee to adopt the attitude of working hard to earn their job (2003:15).

> We are emphasizing productivity improvements, focussing on the right metrics, including return on equity and free cash flow. We have set aggressive targets, but it's important to be clear: We are not pursuing productivity strategies to hit a given target. We're pursuing productivity as a discipline, not an initiative. (2003:16)

In the 2003 Annual Report, Michael J. Sabia was able to confirm that the organizational changes to improve productivity were successful. It reduced the cost structure by \$636 million (2004:20). He also continued to encourage reinventing the company constantly as to overcome the new competition. This statement not only reflects the new operating structure but also a new organizational culture and behaviour.

In the 2004 Annual Report, Michael J. Sabia announced the formal launched Galileo initiative. That initiative is an effort to revisit all aspects of the business to radically simplify all activities, products as well as internal and external business processes to reduce even more the cost structure. He reduced this organizational transformation to a simple equation: "simplicity = Service = economies (cost savings) = growth" (2005:5). The objective is to reduce costs by \$1 to 1.5 billion by the end of 2006. The ultimate objective is to increase shareholder value while investing in new sectors.

Finally, in the 2005 Annual Report, Michael J. Sabia announced in June 2006 to the shareholder meeting that Galileo allowed the company to reduce \$524 million in costs which is according to the annual cost reduction objectives of \$500 to \$600 million a year.

These costs savings were mainly from:

- The 2004 employee departure program
- Lower procurement costs
- Call center efficiencies and optimization initiatives
- Eliminating network elements and standardizing core operating processes.

In 2006, we will continue to transform our cost structure to support our operations. (…) Our process transformation initiative will include:

- Continuing to actively encourage customers to adopt new IP-based services
- Developing end-to-end process improvements for sales and ordering, installation, billing, collection, and maintenance and repair, which will allow us to deliver our products and services more efficiently
- Optimizing management support to reduce costs in our corporate and support functions. (2006:11)

BCE is still focussing on even more cost structure reduction of $8.5 billions by the end of 2006. It means even more pressure for productivity and cost reduction initiatives. The social workplace climate has been relatively stable over the years 63% (2003–2004) to 65% (2005) but still bellow the best in class performance of 84% (2005), 83% (2004), 81% (2003). The improvement has been on the job challenge, autonomy to do the work and leadership from the supervisors. The absenteeism has slightly been reduced (0,69 in 2004 to 0,63 in 2005) while the employee program has increased in usage (11% in 2004 to 13% in 2005).

Based on this information, we can see that the company has implemented very important changes through restructuring, reduction of employees, reorganization of the processes, cost savings structure, improved productivity while maintaining employee satisfaction level. I believe that this implies that the executives and the middle managers have internalized the change strategy at all level of the organization to optimize the shareholder value as the primary objective without compromising on the employee satisfaction.

To support this leadership capability, BCE has launched the PRIDE initiative to identify leaders who have the ability to motivate their employees and share their stories. This level of balanced change leadership requires a very high level of leadership integrity both on the teleological and deontological ethical perspective. It is particularly challenging to manage since a teleological ethic is characterized by its aims to pursue a particular end such as self interests while a deontological ethics focuses on the moral aspects of the means. The leadership ethical literature considers both mutually exclusive and therefore incompatible in management practices (Aronson 2001, Kanungo 2001, Kanungo and Mendonca 2001). In this respect, we believe that the day to day management practice remains to be seen through an in-depth research of the firm to see how this level of leadership integrity is accomplished. However, we can propose our preliminary conclusions that change management practices at BCE have been so well developed that by the years 2000 it is more easily adapted by leaders of every levels of command because the strategic change is reaching every level of the organization.

The third business case is Air Canada. The firm was restructured into ACE Aviation Holdings, starting as of April 1st 2003 after 18 months under CCAA creditor protection of strict supervision. As Robert A. Milton, Chairman and CEO of ACE Aviation Holdings Inc. explains:

By grouping all Air Canada operations into subsidiaries of ACE, we are remaking each as a separate business with financial and operational benchmark, sensitive to both internal and external customers and with a mandate to contribute more to the overall profitability of the Corporation."(2005:2)

ACE Aviation Holdings has engaged important cost structure such as labour cost reduction of $0.9 billion through outsourcing, automated services, more part time jobs, flexible working hours and optimized work management (2004, Annual Report, 2005).

> Based on our current business plan, Management is targeting $2 billion in annual cost savings by 2006 (as compared to 2002) derived mainly from new labor and supplier arrangements. The labor component is worth about $0,9 billion of the annual cost savings. Much of that is in the form of more flexible scheduling, more efficient work processes and rules as well as flexibility to use more automation, contract out some functions, cross-utilize more staff and use more part timers and vacation relievers. That will drive further productivity improvements for years to come, creating an environment for relatively low-cost, low-risk growth. (2005:3)

By the end of 2005, ACE Aviation Holdings has rationalized and simplified its processes along with other strategic restructuring.

> Our objective is to foster a culture of perpetual cost reduction that focuses on productivity enhancement and process reform, especially simplification. (2006:3)

Through the overall cost structure reduction ACE Aviation Holdings also reduced the number of employees, the salary base and increased productivity. Again, despite the overall instability in this aviation sector, the company is able through major organizational and cultural transformation to rebuild its profitability.

As these corporations can show, since the year 2000, the large labour intensive private firms established in traditional industrial sectors are able to embrace this new organizational behaviour toward change. In other words, since the 1990s, the change phenomenon changed itself. It was not the "what do we need to change" but rather, "let's change the change process, behaviour and experience, and let's make it permanent". It focussed not only on improving the operating processes, but restructuring the operations as a whole. The incremental result is changing the very foundations of Canadian economic infrastructure of all private industries.

At a nation level, these changes are transforming the economic infrastructure. I will focus on three types of significant indicators of this change phenomenon and its impact on the overall economy. These indicators are the level of outsourcing, the level of offshoring and the level of GNP in comparison with other OCDE countries.

Statistics Canada reveals a steep trend to outsourcing, which increases economic wealth for Canada, but also offshoring which exports wealth creation to other countries. The overall economy transformation occurs in the manufacturing labour intensive sector and in the science and technology human capital labour market (Beckstead and Brown 2006). In other words, it appears that at a structural perspective, we are moving towards a knowledge based economy while our natural resources sector gain in market value.

One of the Canadian firms' ability to intensify this new "change paradigm" shift is through outsourcing within the national economy and through offshoring by sending their operations outside the country, which increased imports of unfinished goods.

> A related factor is imports. Not only can manufacturers carve up their production process by purchasing from other firms in Canada, they can also import parts from abroad. (...) firms significantly increased this form of vertical dis-integration during the 1990s. (Cross and Ghanem, 2006:3.16)

From 1986 to 2002, the Canadian economic infrastructure has been influenced by a both an industry vertical integration through outsourcing and a dis-integration by offshoring (Cross and Ghanem 2006). It has influenced the Gross National Product industry contribution.

> The pervasive trend to higher multipliers suggests most private sector industries are specialising in their core area of expertise and purchasing other inputs. This is hardly a new phenomenon-it was Adam Smith's major insight into the division of labour back in the 18th century." (Cross and Ghanem 2006:3.9–3.10) (...)"The GDP multipliers have fallen for 20 of the 22 industries over the last 15 years (education edged up while non-profit was unchanged). Most goods-producing industries posted slightly larger declines than services, perhaps because they can more easily use imports in their production. But the uniformity of declines is in striking contrast with the across-the-board increase for revenue multipliers. This adds weight to the idea that the increase in revenue multipliers was driven by a trend to outsourcing the provision of inputs to other firms in Canada. (Cross and Ghanem 2006:3.16)

This change in the Canadian economic infrastructure is therefore unnoticed in terms of industrial revenues but in terms of GDP contributions. Manufacturers raised their imports of 37% while the other goods-producing industries increased of 20% in the 1990s. It means that the industries that used to contribute the most in the GDP have reduced their contributions. We should keep in mind that this is the result of individual corporations to reduce operating costs and increase efficiency to maintain a competitive edge. It is the consequences of this capitalist phenomenon of change.

> Whether outsourcing to other firms in Canada or offshoring to firms around the globe, the motivation is the same-to boost efficiency and lower the costs. (Cross and Ghanem 2006:3.10) (The preferred outsourced services are business-process operations such as payroll administration and computer services). (...) "The increase in outsourcing also has implications for the analysis of industry shares in GDP. Industries such as manufacturing that have rapidly increased outsourcing (both here and abroad) will see their share of GDP decline as other industries, especially services. (Cross and Ghanem 2006:3.11)

As a consequence of the dis-integration of the economy, is on the labour market. The offshoring and outsourcing change strategy has created a new labour market. The first change is noticed on the decline quality of jobs created. In 2002, the number of non-full time permanent jobs has reached 47.2% of the labour market (Tabi and Langlois 2003). 19% are part time jobs, 13% are temporary jobs, 15.2% are self employed. It is well known that these part time, temporary and self employed jobs have a lower wage, have less paid hours of work, have less stability and have less medical collective insurance. It is important to notice that these full time permanent jobs are generally occupied in the public sector like health and education where employees are generally older (median age in 1999 is 40 years old and older in 1999 in health and education).

The only labour market sector where Canadians has improved is in the science and engineering based occupations. We have compared the actual science and engineering employment shares almost doubled for both Canadian (2.3% in 1980–1981 to 4.5% in 2000–2001) and American economies (2.6% 1980–1981 to 4.5% in 2000–2001) since 1980 (Canadian Economic Observer 2006). In fact this category of occupation is the human capital indicator of economic growth because these organizational investments are associated with higher productivity growth and long term economic growth. In the highly integrated North American labour market for skilled professionals, Canadian cities have raised their competitive advantage (Table 2.1).

Table 2.1   Science and engineer labour force

Percentage of science and engineer labour force	Canadian Cities	American Cities
1980–1981	2,9%	3,0%
2000–2001	5,6%	5,1%

Source: Canadian Economic Observer 2006, p.7

However, this category of occupation is sensitive to the concentration of large cities creating a disruption of well qualified job creations between large and small cities (Table 2.2). On the other hand, given the American large scale cities, it is impressive enough to see how Canadian cities have been able to create a competitive advantage.

Table 2.2   Science and engineer labour force disparities between large and small cities

	Canada		United States	
	Large cities	Small cities	Large cities	Small cities
1980–1981	2.9%	1.3%	3.0%	1.6%
2000–2001	5.6%	2.0%	5.1%	2.3%

Source: Canadian Economic Observer 2006, p.7

We can only wonder about the overall quality of work condition and income Canadian workers have over American workers. According to the purchasing power studies, Canadian workers have lost not only on their purchasing power compared to the American workers, but the quality of products has decreased (Kemp 2002). I will review these studies later on the Canadian human condition.

A New Management Practice

In 2002, J. Kotter and D. Cohen and in 2002 J.M. Kouzes and B.Z. Posner, all well known gurus in change literature, restated their observations made respectively in 1947 and 1945 that leading change demanded extraordinary people leadership abilities. They sustain that the leadership is a social and relational ability that every executives in charge of leading change has to have. Kotter and Cohen recognize the large-scale change programs large corporations have to engage and review the leadership practice in order to manage this intensified process. In Table 2.3, are the principal change leadership practices still vastly encouraged.

Table 2.3   Change leadership practices

Kotter and Cohen (2002)	Kouzes and Posner (2002)
Building a social movement toward change by preventing resistance to change	True leadership is based on credibility, authenticity, true commitment for the stakeholders
Increase Urgency Step 1: Raising the feeling of urgency and inevitability of change	**Model the Way** Step 1: The executive must clarify your personal values
Step 2: Prevent resistance by reducing fear, anger, complacency	Step 2: Lead by example by aligning actions with values
Build the Guiding Team Step 3: Build the team with change advocates	**Inspire a Shared Vision** Step 3: Envision the future of the corporation
Step 4: Enabling the team creating a climate of trust and emotional commitment to one another	Step 4: Mobilize the stakeholders to share that vision
Get the Vision Right Step 5: Create a shared vision for the guiding team	**Challenge the Process** Step 5: Challenge the status quo and seek opportunities, innovative ways to change, improve
Step 6: Support the guiding team to develop strategies to make the vision a reality	Step 6: Experiment by taking risks and initiating small wins

Continued on page 46.

Kotter and Cohen (2002)	Kouzes and Posner (2002)
Communicate for Buy-In Step 7: Communicate with charisma credible messages that will clarify the direction and overcome confusion and distrust	**Enable Others to Act** Step 7: Build climate of trust and collaboration with face-to-face interaction with employees
Empower Action Step 8: Remove organizational and cognitive barriers for the change advocates to create new behaviours	Step 8: Share power and accountability, develop sense of self confidence and competency – "strengthen others"
Create Short Terms Wins Step 9: Building momentum through visible, fast, easy, simple and significant results to diffuse cynicism, pessimism and scepticism.	**Encourage the Heart** Step 9: Reward and recognize through social recognition of excellence
Don't Let Up Step 10: Sustain the effort especially to overcome bigger emotional barriers while avoiding personal exhaustion as the leader	Step 10: Create a sense of community by celebrating victories, behaviours and values
Make Change Stick Step 11: Institutionalize new behaviours in the promotional, performance evaluation, rewards and recognition programs and emotions to create new social norms and shared values to sustain the new behaviours.	

Kouzes and Posner (2002) point out John Gardner's four moral goals in leadership:

- Releasing human potential
- Balancing the needs of the individual and the community
- Defending the fundamental values of the community
- Instilling in individuals a sense of initiative and responsibility

Attending to these goals will always direct your eyes to higher purpose. As you work to become all you can be, you can start to let go of your petty self-interests. As you give back some of what you've been given, you can reconstruct your community." (Kouzes & Posner 2002:393)

In our new context of complex organizational transformations, I believe these best practices of leadership have changed. The pressure is on the corporations to engage strategic change more intensively then ever before. It has transformed change management practices.

However, as Kotter and Cohen point out, most of the leadership strength will be the ability to organizationally "manage" people's perception, emotional experience, and the social bonds in terms of social norms and shared values that determine human behaviour. It means that the changed management practice will change the way we experience humanity.

> In highly successful change efforts, people find ways to help others see the problems or solutions in ways that influence emotions, not just thought. Feelings then alter behaviour sufficiently to overcome all the many barriers to sensible large-scale change. (Kotter and Cohen 2002:x)

This particular way of addressing emotional, social and spiritual human experience of change stakeholders are troubling because this managerial practice embraces the idea of including the human dimensions beyond the work force capability to ensure mass production of strategic change initiative programs across the corporations. It is even more important since Kouzes and Posner recognize the moral risks of abusing these managerial practices to manipulate people's experience. Aubert and Gaulejac (1991) were already raising concerns about this trend to move from an external concern toward an internal control where people are pressured to internalize conditioned self-control and corporate defined behaviour norms. It means that the managerial practices are not only defining actions, decisions, tasks and the actual work effort, but it also aims at controlling human desires, emotion, spiritual and subjective experience to reduce it to the level of an instrument of production (1991:61). We need to step back and review how extensive the change phenomenon is and see if, where and how it may have invaded our Canadian society and economic infrastructure.

Since the 1990s, organizations engaged into reorganization, restructuring, massive regular layoffs, outsourcing, wage freeze and cut backs, pressure for more productive unpaid working hours and ongoing process reengineering culture implementation. This trend of transformation of the very nature of organizational change has increased in its intensity, complexity, and organizational scope to a level never met before. In fact, it is so well managed that corporations include it in a permanent strategic change program where it monitors and drives ongoing multiple strategic change initiatives.

Kouzes and Posner (2002) present this careful advice:

> Any leadership practice can become destructive. Virtues can become vices. There's a point at which each of the five practices, taken to extremes, can lead you astray. (2002:395)

The contemporary Canadian economic infrastructure and competitive edge have indeed pushed managerial practices to the extremes because organizational transformation is massively implemented and market pressures expect it to be done more efficiently and effectively. Leaders have no choice but to focus on the process rather then the people.

Through my action-research, I was able to understand how leaders were caught between their individual morality and the transformed organizational behaviour framework. Not only the organizational change has become a phenomenon, but the managerial practice it enforces generates ethical practices contradictions. The ethical contradictions have a consequence on the overall human condition and therefore the organization capability to perform. I believe, this contradiction is breaking the tacit moral contract of the capitalist system.

Ethical Practice Dilemmas

Friedman (1970) is clear on the executive ethics by recognizing that the only ethical accountability is to the shareholder. Anything else is politically and socially against good capitalism. It implies that any executive decision has to be teleological in terms of the shareholder value as the only viable economic and social interest.

> In a free-enterprise, private-property system, a corporate executive is an employee of the owners of the business. He had direct responsibility to his employers. That responsibility is to conduct the business in accordance with their desires, which generally will be to make as much money as possible while conforming to the basic rules of the society, both those embodied in law and those embodied in ethical custom. (1977:573)

However, the leadership literature recognizes that teleological ethics in change management initiative is devastating. It is encouraged to perform charismatic transformational leadership styles (Kanungo and Mendonca 2001, Kanungo 2001, Aronson 2001). In an organizational change initiative, leadership effectiveness improves when it moves from a transactional to a transformational leadership. But the charismatic transformational leadership is an exceptional transcendent behaviour (Aronson 2001). Conceptually, it is judged to be unethical to approach an organizational strategic transformation with a teleological transactional leadership.

The leadership literature brings together a logical management ethical practice by attributing a teleological ethics to the transactional leadership located in the operating management styles. The strategic change initiative is believed to be driven by high level executives capable of transcending the operations to lead the transformation and embracing the human aspects of change through a moral altruism. In that leadership style, the top executive is invited to forget personal interests and focus on the followers' well being and self-actualization. The tacit collective moral contract would therefore lead his actions toward a collective shared vision of the firm.

Table 2.4   Situational leadership ethical behaviour

Transactional leadership	Transformation leadership
Objectives: 1) Achieve performance objectives 2) Mutual motives and actions will generate mutual benefits	Objectives: 1) Achieve strategic change initiatives through people and behaviour change. 2) Change the followers core attitudes and values according to the leader's vision of the organization.

Effectiveness: is based on the improved processes	**Effectiveness**: is based on the people relationships. The leaders represent a shared perspective in terms of behaviour, moral values and authenticity

Ethical leadership

Teleological ethics	Deontological ethics
Motive: 1) Egotistic intent: mutual altruism and utilitarianism to serve personal interests (gain power, status, material benefits) 2) Idiocentric self-concept: individualistic rules of conduct	**Motive:** 1) Moral altruistic genuine motives. 2) Allocentric self-concept: collectivist moral norms of actions
Behaviour: Using power and authority of the position Using rewards and sanctions to control behaviours Using coercion to get compliance, commitment and loyalty from the followers	**Behaviour:** Empowering others Increase followers self-efficiency and their capacity for self determination Generate a sense of self-growth, self worth and autonomy
Social context: Reciprocity principal: doing good to those who do good to us	**Social context:** Leader self sacrifice through a sense of duty and obligation toward the followers Social responsibility: belief of moral obligation to help others without personal considerations.
Organizational context: Applied to ongoing operations	**Organizational context:** Applied to extraordinary strategic organizational change

Source: (Kanungo 2001)

In principal, I fundamentally agree with the literature by differentiating the transactional and transformational leadership and the ethical practices. But empirical data contradict the assumptions. First of all, the strategic change initiative are no longer the sol top executive accountability, it has been decentralized in terms of implementation and design. Most corporations have demanded that all stakeholders participate in their ongoing organizational transformation (BCE 2006, Ford 2006, ACE 2006). Change initiative overlap operations. They are not addressed as separated activities from the operations. Ultimately, there is a need to embed major transformations within the ongoing operations through internalized the new social norm of a "changing behaviours". Stakeholders have to embrace the "change" experience as a new way of experiencing their working conditions.

On the official corporate ethical business conducts, Corporations kept their traditional perspective. For example, Ford (2006) and BCE (2006), focus on the conflict of interest. They leave out any formal considerations on the way executives manage people with respect and dignity. In fact, annual reports minimize or ignore any environmental and social externalities (Crowther 2005, Crowther and Rayman-Bacchus 2004 a, b, c).

An ethical leadership will therefore adopt a teleological perspective despite individual preferences because it is the executive legal obligation to comply with the shareholder's economic interests. In the day to day management practice, the individual leader will face two factors facilitating this ethical decision: 1) their own performance evaluation is based on the operation performance and the shareholder value; 2) employees are laid-off on an annual basis, they are outsourced, and they are evaluated on the operation performance and the shareholder value. Ultimately, when the change management practice focuses on shared value to lead changes, the first and most important corporate shared value is and will always be the shareholder value. This shareholder value is the ultimate guide to change management practice.

Human Condition

Hertzberg and Maslow (1972, 1976) have studied the human motivation and have influenced the management literature. We can see that the hygienic factors identified by Herzberg (1966) also refer to the lower levels of human needs identified by Maslow. The interesting observation is that these working conditions only neutralize the employee dis-satisfaction. In other words, optimizing the hygienic factors, which correspond to the basic human needs doesn't motivate employees as such. It only meets their human basic functional needs. Managing the motor factors of the motivation, however, will stimulate the motivation and respond to the higher levels of the human hierarchy of needs. These are the principals of Hertzberg and Maslow findings on motivation. I believe, based on the traditional view of charismatic transformational leadership that change management practices used to work on these higher level of human needs fundamental to the motivation.

Based on the new massive change phenomenon across North America (especially in Canada) the current change management practices have shifted from deontological transformational leadership to a teleological transactional leadership. As a consequence, Canadian workers are facing more pressure for productivity under extremely difficult working condition. It appears, based on Maslow's work that the basic motivation driving the Canadian workers is at the physiological needs and some level of security level of needs. Based on the Hertzberg's motivation factor, it appears that the corporations have redefined the hygienic factors. It can only lead us to wonder what would be the social compromise accepted to continue to motivate the workers to contribute to the productivity level expected.

Table 2.5   Motivation factors

Herzberg (1966)	Maslow (1972, 1976)
Motor factor of motivation	Human needs of motivation
· Meaning of the work and tasks	· Transcendence, spirituality
· Autonomy	· Self actualization
· Sense of responsibility	· Self Esteem and esteem from others
· Sense of decision ownership	
Hygienic factor of motivation	Human needs of motivation
· Salary	· Love and friendship
· Work relations	· Security
· Work environment	· Physiological needs
· Work schedules	

A Canadian research has revealed that by 2001 more than 3/4 Canadian workers have giving priority to work over their family life (Duxbury and Higgins 2003). This proportion has doubled in a decade. In 1991, one Canadian out of ten worked more than 50 hours a week while in 2001, that proportion increased by one Canadian out of four. In fact, 88% of Canadians have a surcharge of roles. As a result, one out of three respondents has a high level of depressive moods and exhaustion. Stress levels have increased from 44% Canadians in 1991 to 55% Canadians in 2001. Only 41% of the Canadian workers are satisfied of their lives making this Canadian working environment a health risk hazard. Again the higher level of motivation needs and factors of motivation are not met. The conclusions are devastating for the management practices. Duxbury and Higgins (2003) identify the ways Canadian employees are treated and their relations with their colleagues and their supervisors as the main reasons for their overall social consequences.

Duxbury and Higgins (2003) have estimated that the economic costs affecting productivity are between $1 billions to $6 billions a year only on absenteeism costs. In 2003, Marshall (2006) reported that 720 000 Canadians have taken sick leaves of absence of roughly $8 800 (an average of two weeks) which represents $6.3 billion. Marshall is careful to point out that only 200 000 workers have taken work related sick leaves which represents approximately $1.8 billion. Furthermore, it is important that these work-related sick leaves have to meet specific official guidelines to be considered as such. It is therefore legitimate for Duxbury and Higgins to consider the whole range of absenteeism to measure the overall productivity loss in Canada. This economic cost is not considering the other hidden social costs such as fewer children, an unsatisfying family and parental life, a decrease on the overall quality of life, health and general well being.

The poor quality of jobs has also influenced the purchasing power of Canadian families. Canadian families have decreased their capacity to consume in volume and in expenditures. In 1981, Americans consumed 12% more than Canadians while at the end of the 1990s it was 50%. When we consider the public services provided by Canadian government, this consumption gap is brought back to 27% lower than the

American individual. It is still considerably a high difference. In the OECD country ranking, Canada was in the 8th place while the United States are in the second place after Luxembourg. As a comparison, Japan moved from the fifth place in 1996 and dropped on the 13th place in 2001. Ireland moved from the 19th place in 1996 to the 7th place in 2001.

Canadians have lost a significant purchasing power but have continued to consume through increased debt. Since 1990, the ability for Canadians to pay their debts with the available net income has increased from 60% to 110% in 2003 (Archambault and Laverdière 2003). It means that a Canadian who wants to payback their debts other then their mortgage has to take more than a full year of their total net income. The level of individual bankruptcy has increased of 11.3%. The general profile of the individual bankruptcy is a married person, age 42 of a net monthly revenue of $1 479 and has $57 199 average debt. These debts are composed of credit cards, student loans, other personal bank loans (except mortgage) and government unpaid bills. The Canadians have less income but want to maximize their ability to consume to the point of taking personal debts on credit cards to pay for their mortgage and day to day expenditures. In other words, the GNP may increase but the available personal income has proportionally decreased.

This consumption profile raises the question of the ability to save for retirement. Based on the Canadian study, 44% of Canadians have not saved enough for their retirement (Maser and Dufour 2001). Generally, 32% of the retirement capital is on the principal residence and 29% is personal savings. Unfortunately, in 1999, 60% of the Canadian families have only $50 000 which is not enough to cover 80% of their net income before retirement. This leads us to believe that elderly people will suffer of a very poor quality of life with increasing health issues while the younger generations will have less available income to support their children and elderly parents.

In overall, the quality of life for Canadians has significantly decreased and will continue to aggravate since a great majority of workers will retire with insufficient retirement private funds, that the quality of jobs has all the sign of deterioration given the economic infrastructure transformations, and that the health, well being and overall quality of life will also deteriorate because of the increased levels of stress and working conditions.

The Moral Contract

In the 18th century, Adam Smith and Jean-Jacques Rousseau have imagined an utopian society based on a tacit moral social contract. Rationality allows humanity to determine our individual and collective destiny, but the moral and emotional dimensions of humanity will always dominate mankind actions. Morality will translate economic cooperation into mutual benefits for humanity.

Adam Smith's perspective stipulates that the economy defines society (Heilbroner and Milberg 1995, Coase 1994). The creation of wealth is possible through individual actions. Freedom of enterprise and egoism of mankind is the motor of this wealth. However, altruism and sympathy to others will ensure the moral standards for the well being of the species. Beyond individual self interests, man is connected to its humanity from within his moral sentiments while his utilitarian reason will connect him to his society. The individual is fundamentally a social being because he has passion, sentiments, emotions, imagination, and sympathy, as well as a need for love and for recognition from others. Each individual is born free in terms of this moral contract. Ethic and justice will be the basis for society. Ethics is emotion, virtue, the morally good for all. This moral rule of conduct should be fund in the laws and jurisprudence. Smith was careful about the vices. He saw how merchants and manufacturers of the capitalist system could generate egoistic vices. The only way to counterbalance these vices is through moral education of the masses, or the human consciousness of the majority, and government wisdom. The government role is to redistribute wealth between the wealthiest and the poorest.

Jean-Jacques Rousseau also believed that the individual is born free but that he consents to the social contract (1994 a, b). Law is therefore the incarnation of this social contract. Rationality is created by mankind, it does not pre-exist humanity. It is only logical that mankind is fundamentally influenced by its passion and emotion. Again, the goal of society is to educate on morality. In fact, Rousseau believed that the economic system, its progress and commerce will erase morality and virtue. The individuals have to create a social contract to maintain this morality to self-preserve society as a whole. The government has the mission to compensate for economic inequalities by dominating the individual actions and will. Again, love for ourselves and love for others is the only way to maintain this tacit moral contract and ensure the well being for all.

John Stuart Mill and Karl Marx, in the 19th century when the capitalist system was expending, were concerned respectively with happiness and the human condition (Heilbroner and Milberg 1995, Dupuis 1990). For Mill, progress for humanity is possible only through science. In that sense, rational and utilitarian actions are good for humanity. For Mill, the individual is always seeking pleasure and avoiding sufferings. His motivation is therefore driven by his hierarchy of pleasure. It is close to Maslow hierarchy of needs. For Mill, the ultimate pleasure is the intellectual one. He encourages a moral education to reach that intellectual pleasure for the majority of the people. Ultimately, for Mill, the utilitarian action is morally turned toward progress. Progress is defined by the individual emancipation and happiness. Logically, the only way to achieve this is by allowing the individual to pursue self interest for as long as they are morally educated and guided.

Karl Marx was not as optimistic as Mill. Based on empirical observation of the workforce he believes that the human condition determine the human consciousness. The mode of production and consumption will therefore structure social conduct. He starts with the inequalities between the poorest and the wealthiest to explain that the capitalist system is performing so well that it destroys the workforce. The consciousness is the essence of humanity. The capitalist mode of production and consumption is breaking its consciousness and the morality. Mankind is reduced as a means of production losing its humanity.

These four political philosophers present some of the fundamental debate we need to re-establish to understand our preliminary conclusion about the tacit moral contract. Mill is the philosopher who inspired the utilitarian teleological ethics in management. It was therefore believed that by pursuing self-interests, human kind is logically reinforcing both collective wealth and morality. According to the ethical leadership literature, this utopian philosophy is destructive when the leaders pursue only their self interest and manipulate others to earn more power, more material benefits and a better social status.

On the other hand, Karl Marx allows us to understand the consequences of poor human condition on humanity. It is obvious in this paradigm that the capitalist system does not aim at a moral and social justice as such but only at its own profitability in the shareholders' interests. It leaves us to understand that the current human condition deterioration is a destruction of our consciousness and therefore our humanity.

Rousseau and Smith saw our humanity as the emotional, spiritual, love and friendship, our overall ability to care for one another. Our ability to cooperate is translating our spirit of freedom and individual emancipation, self actualisation. Breaking down our human condition would consequently destroy our consciousness, our ability to care for one another, to self actualize, to innovate and ultimately to pursue our progress as society.

Based on this accelerating phenomenon of change at the macroeconomic, corporate and management practice levels, it appears that we have to be sensitive to the human consequences. In fact these human consequences are intimately related to the economic performance of this change phenomenon. At a first glance of the economic indicators, it appears that Canadians have collectively lost on the quality of jobs, income, purchasing powers and household wealth. On the human consequences we can observe fewer children, more health risks, more stress and pressure to overwork, less satisfying family life and overall well being and pleasure of living. Based on the three business case, the largest corporation strategic plans are showing no signs of slowing down the change phenomenon and the Canadian economic infrastructure is increasingly integrated globally. Canada has increased values in our natural resources and invested in the knowledge economy which appears to be positive except that it does not translate in the individual and family reality in terms of wealth. All these significant factors indicate that the change management practices have not improved its deontological ethics. It has, on the contrary, increased its teleological transactional management practices to the point of intensifying the pressure for productivity at a dehumanizing cost.

Previous research on the social logics of organizational change and innovation has shown that it is the social bonding; the way people experience the organization and the cooperation at the workplace that will influence the firm's ability to change and innovate (Avon 2003, 2005). The social contracts are setting the context for social interaction and relations as well as individual behaviour and decisions. There are two trends of social contracts, the individualist, from John Locke tradition, and collectivist, from Thomas Hobbes tradition, contracts based on which, the individual or the community, is the priority for any social conduct over the other. It is fund that large firms may embed both forms of these social contracts. The individualist social contract will favour teleological ethics in behaviours while the collectivist social contract will favour deontological ethics.

Contrary to the ethical literature, both ethical rules of conduct can be fund in the same organization within a logical consensus. The actual determinant of the moral system is the social bonding. There is the determinist community social bond that will condition the individual to a social, organizational conformity and there is the individuality bonding based on freedom of the individual. That form of bonding is favouring the self actualization of the individual as the ideal form of organizational experience. This form of bonding will encourage, for instance, any form of entrepreneurial initiatives and innovations. It is the later form of bonding that will generate the most organizational agility. But it will require a transcending form of leadership where accountability and recognition is truly decentralized. It is the most difficult form of bonding that organization can achieve. On the other hand the determinist community bonding will limit the individual creativity and initiative. This form of bonding tends to exhaust individual and collective human vitality. It is however the most common form of bonding because it ensures the executive a better sense of control.

Based on the current information across the Canadian economy, it appears that the large corporations have kept collectivist social contract and community determinist social bonding. It is the most difficult form of organizational social predisposition toward change. Pushing for major organizational transformation under such a social logic will create devastating effects we currently observe. It would only be logical that managers that have to deal with these changes and high operating performance levels tend to manipulate their employees and their basic needs for security and physiological needs to push them to adopt and internalize these new social norms of risk taking, uncertainty and accept this constant pressure in the workplace.

Our analysis leads us to conclude that by the 1990, Canadian corporation and society has breach a tacit social and moral contract. The contract used to be that the employees work hard, contribute to the productivity level, reduce costs to maintain and improve shareholder value. This effort would lead to a more stable growth and eventually to a better workplace where innovation, individual initiatives, entrepreneurial behaviours, self actualization initiatives would be encouraged through this transformation leadership. Risk takers, smarter initiatives, creativity would be socially recognized and rewarded because it ensured growth. The workforce, the unions and the government accepted to support this paradigm shift and these massive change initiatives. In fact business and industrial transformation were possible because Canadians have prioritized this collective effort. However, the social and human counter part has yet to be shown 15 years later. Not only the productivity level of the Canadian economy is not showing the increase level expected, but the workers show signs of fatigue, consumption denial, stress, dis-satisfaction, lower loyalty, lower empowerment. These are the reasons for supporting the idea that we have beached our collective tacit moral contract.

Conclusion

I may appear to criticize change management and organizational transformation but I am a strong believer in the need to pursue evolution. My concern is the direction it takes, the manner by which we make it happen and the reasons we make it. The current leadership practices have broken a trust level between the stakeholders and the top executives. It is even becoming a shareholder concern for social stability, social justice and wealth distribution. The change phenomenon has grown, but management practices have broken the tacit moral contract. We did not need to forget about humanity on the workplace. We do not need to destroy our social fabric. We should consult our political philosophers to understand how government or other institutional representations of social justice can induce a deontological ethical leadership practices and an overall moral system because the issue is the dehumanization of the people. We can already see the early consequences of these capitalist strong forces of destruction on our society and the way caring for one another has little meaning in the workplace.

References

ACE Aviation Inc., (2006), *2005 Annual Report*; website: http://www.aceaviation.com/en/investors/annual.html; consulted in June 2006.

ACE Aviation Inc., (2005), *2004 Annual Report*; website: http://www.aceaviation.com/en/investors/annual.html; consulted in June 2006.

Archambault, R., Laverdière, D. (2005), *Un modèle macroéconomique d'analyse et de prevision de l'insolvabilité commerciale et des consommateurs au Canada*, Canada, Congrès de la Société Canadienne des Sciences Économique.

Aronson, E.. (December 2001) « Integrating Leadership Styles and Ethical Perspectives » *Canadian Journal of Administrative Sciences*, Canada ASAC, vol. 18, no.244–256.

Avon, E., (2005); "Organisational Predisposition Toward Change and Innovation", International Journal of Management Concepts and Philosophy, vol.1, no.2, Great Britain, Inderscience Enterprises Ltd.

Avon, E., (2003); *La gestion stratégique des logiques socials du changement*, Thèse de doctorat, Montréal, HEC.

Beckstead, D. Brown, M.W. (2006) "Innovation Capabilities : Comparing Science and Engineering Employment in Canadian and U.S. Cities", in *The Canadian Economy in Transition Series*, Ottawa, Statistics Canada, cat. 11-622-MIE, no.12.

Bell Canada Enterprises, (2006) *2005 Annual Report*; website: http://www.bce.ca/en/investors/financialperformance/corporatefinancial/bec/; consulted in June 2006.

Bell Canada Enterprises, (2006) *Vision and Strategy,* website: http://www.bce.ca/en/; consulted in June 2006.

Bell Canada Enterprises, (2006) *Code of Business Conduct,* website: http://www.bce.ca/ ; consulted in June 2006.

Bell Canada Enterprises, (2006) *Corporate Responsibility and KPIS,* website: http://www.bce.ca/ ; consulted in June 2006.

Bell Canada Enterprises, (2006) *Workplace Practices,* website: http://www.bce.ca/ ; consulted in June 2006.

Bell Canada Enterprises, (2005) *2004 Annual Report,* website: http://www.bce.ca/en/investors/financialperformance/corporatefinancial/bec/; consulted in June 2006.

Bell Canada Enterprises, (2004) *2003 Annual Report*, website: http://www.bce. ca/en/investors/financialperformance/corporatefinancial/bec/; consulted in June 2006.

Bell Canada Enterprises, (2003) *2002 Annual Report*, website: http://www.bce. ca/en/investors/financialperformance/corporatefinancial/bec/; consulted in June 2006.

Bell Canada Enterprises, (2002) *2001 Annual Report*, website: http://www.bce. ca/en/investors/financialperformance/corporatefinancial/bec/; consulted in June 2006.

Coase, R.H. (1994), "Adam Smith's View of Man", Essay on Economics and Economists, Chicago, University of Chicago Press.

Cross, P., Ghanem, Z., (Jan. 2006), "Multipliers and Outsourcing: How Industries Interact with each other and effect GDP", *Canadian Economic Observer*, Ottawa, Statistics Canada, cat. 11-010-XIB.

Crowther, D., (2005), "Corporate Social Reporting: Genuine Action or Window Dressing?" in Crowther, D., Jatana, R., (ed.) *Representation of Social Responsibility*, vol.1, Hyderabad, India, ICFAI University Press, pp.140–160.

Crowther, D., Rayman-Bacchus, L., (ed.), (2004 a), *Perspectives on Corporate Social responsibility*, England, Ashgate Publishing Company.

Crowther, D., Rayman-Bacchus, L., (2004 b) "Introduction: Perspectives on Corporate Social Responsibility", Crowther, D., Rayman-Bacchus, L., (ed.), (2004), *Perspectives on Corporate Social responsibility*, England, Ashgate Publishing Company, pp.1–20.

Crowther, D., Rayman-Bacchus, L., (2004 c) "The Future of Corporate Social Responsibility", Crowther, D., Rayman-Bacchus, L., (ed.), (2004), *Perspectives on Corporate Social responsibility*, England, Ashgate Publishing Company, pp.229–249.

Dupuis, J., P., (1990), « L'individu linéral, cet inconnu : d'Adam Smith à Friedrich Hayek », *Perspectives historiques*, 73–125.

Duxbury, L., Higgins, C., (2003) *The 2001 National Work-Life Conflict Study*, Canada, Health Canada.

Eraly, A. (1988); *La structuration de l'entreprise. La rationalité en action*, Bruxelles, Institut de sociologie, Éditions de l'université de Bruxelles.

Ford Motor Company, (2006), *2005 Annual Report*; website: http://www.ford.com/ en/company/investorInformation/companyReports/annualReports/default.htm, consulted in June 2006.

Ford Motor Company, (2006), *Standard of Corporate Conduct*; website: http://www. ford.com/ , consulted in June 2006.

Ford Motor Company, (2005), *2004 Annual Report*; website: http://www.ford.com/ en/company/investorInformation/companyReports/annualReports/default.htm, consulted in June 2006.

Ford Motor Company, (March 2004), *Corporate Governance Principals, website:* http://www.ford.com/ , consulted in June 2006.

Ford Motor Company, (March 2004), *Code of Business Conduct and Ethics for Members of the Board of Directors*, website: http://www.ford.com/, consulted in June 2006.

Friedman, M. (1970) "A Friedman Doctrine: The Social Responsibility of Business is to Increase its Profits in Summer C., O'Connell, J. and Peery, Newman; (1977), *The Managerial Mind*, Illinois, Richard D. Irwin, Inc., 1964, 1968, 1973, pp.573–576.

Heilbroner, R. and Milberg, W., (1995), The Crisis of Vision in Modern Economic Thought, New York Cambridge University Press.

Herzberg, (1966) *Work and the Nature of Man*, Cleveland, Ohio, World.

Kanungo, R. (December 2001) « Ethical Values of Transactional and Transformational Leaders » in Canadian Journal of Administrative Sciences, Canada ASAC, vol. 18, no.257–265.

Kanungo, R. and Mendonca, M. (December 2001) « Ethical Leadership and Governance in Organizations: A Preamble » in Canadian Journal of Administrative Sciences, Canada ASAC, vol. 18, no.241–243.

Kemp, K. (2002) "Purchasing Power Parities and Real Expenditures United States and Canada, 1992–2001", Income *and Expenditures Accounts Technical Series*, Ottawa, Statistics Canada, cat. 13-604-MIB.

Kotter, J. (2002) *What Leaders Really Do*, Boston, Harvard Business School Press, 1947.

Kotter, J. and D. Cohen, (2002) *The Heart of Change: Real-Life Stories of How People Change Their Organizations*, Boston, Harvard Business School Press.

Marshall, K. (2006) "On sick leave", in *Perspectives on Labour and Income*, Ottawa, Statistics Canada, cat. 75-001-XIE, vol.7, no.4.

Maser, K., Dufour, T., (2001) *Les avoirs et les dettes des canadiens. Perspectives sur l'épargne au moyen des régimes de pension privés*, Ottawa, Statistics Canada, cat. 13-596-XIF.

Maslow, A.H. (1976), *The Farther Reaches of Human Nature*, New York, Penguin.

Maslow, A.H. (1972), *Vers une psychologie de l'être*, Paris, Fayard.

Peter, T. and R. Waterman; (1983) *Le prix de l'excellence*, Paris, Gallimard.

Porter, M. (1985); *Competitive Advantage. Creating and Sustaining Superior Performance*, NY, The Free Press.

Rousseau, J.J. (1712–1778) (1994 ed. a), *Du contrat social*, Paris, Bordas.

Rousseau, J.J. (1712–1778) (1992 ed. b), *Discours sur l'origine et les fondements de l'inégalité parmi les homes. Discours sur les sciences et les arts*, Paris, Flammarion.

Statistics Canada, (Jan. 2006), *Canadian Economic Observer*, Ottawa, Statistics Canada, cat. 11-010-XIB.

Tabi, M., Langlois, S., (Feb. 2003), « Quality of Jobs added in 2002 », *Perspectives on Labour and Income*, Ottawa, Statistics Canada, vol.4, no.2, cat. 75-001-XIE.

Chapter 3

Preventing Alcohol Consumption During Pregnancy: Do Time Orientation Perspective and Skepticism Matter?

Yaromir Munoz Molina

Introduction

The prevalence of alcohol consumption during pregnancy remains a great public health problem. Each year, in the United States alone, more than 40,000 babies are born with some degree of alcohol related problems and the lifetime health care for each one was estimated in 2003 at $ 800,000. The U. S. Department of Health and Human Services (1998) reported that more than half of women age 15–44 drank alcohol while pregnant.

Furthermore, researchers at the Hospital for Sick Children (SickKids) and St. Michael's Hospital, in Canada, have calculated that the annual cost of fetal alcohol spectrum disorder is upwards of $344 million a year[1] (Kyskan and Moore, 2005). In the United Kingdom, it was reported in 1997 that 66% of women drank alcohol while they were pregnant (Kyskan and Moore, 2005). Moreover, in the United Kingdom, the percentage of women exceeding the old "sensible limits" of 14 drinks per week increased from 10% in 1988 to 17% in 2002 (IAS, 2005).

The most severe consequence to the fetus caused by drinking during pregnancy is Fetal Alcoholic Syndrome (hereinafter FAS), which is characterized by growth retardation and developmental abnormalities in the central nervous system generating severe impacts including mental retardation (Hankin, 2002; Kyskan and Moore, 2005; to better review see Cone-Wesson, 2005). FAS is the single most preventable cause of birth defects (Bratton, 1995).

In order to prevent this, many health care organizations and government agencies are working on this challenge as part of their responsibility toward the social well-being. To achieve this goal, printed warning-labels on every alcoholic beverage container have been required to communicate health risks to both drinking while driving and pregnant women (Mackinnon et al., 2000; Warren and Foudin, 2001) among others preventable risky behaviours.

---

1   Source: www.nofas.org; this website offers wide information about FAS and the efforts to prevent it.

Given that most of the information about FAS originates in the USA, which is the only country that has recognized it as a social concern (Kyskan and Moore, 2005), little is known about it in other countries. Researchers have found that social conditions play an important role linking alcohol consumption, smoking, poverty, and FAS (Hankin, McCaul, and Heussner, 2000). As argued by Armstrong and Abel (2000) FAS is undeniably concentrated among disadvantaged groups because poverty is characterized by other factors such as smoking and poor diet increasing the risk. In this sense, the presence of FAS in under developed countries could be worse than in the USA because alcohol consumption is also high, poverty is higher, people are less educated, gathering information is not easy and promotion campaigns to prevent it do not exist.

This chapter aims to offer an overview about warning-labels' effectiveness on drinking during pregnancy and explore two notions that could potentially help to understand this apparent contradiction: women notice the warning-label but it is not enough to move them forward a protective behaviour. These notions are skepticism (Obermiller and Spangenberg, 1998) and time orientation perspective (Gonzalez and Zimbardo, 1985; Hornik, 1990; Bjögvinsson and Wilde, 1996).

Given that having a baby requires planning and health care attention, it implies that the primary motivations lie in the future. Therefore, the time orientation perspective (Gonzalez and Zimbardo, 1985; Bjögvinsson and Wilde, 1996) could be a useful theory to understand why drinking during pregnancy remains a prevalent behaviour.

Furthermore, some research has shown that when women have previous experience in alcohol consumption, it produces favorable attitudes toward alcohol (Hankin et al., 1993; Morris, Swasy and Mazis, 1994), creates defensiveness against warning-label (Hankin et al., 1998; MacKinnon et al., 1999), and diminishes the perceived risks (Testa and Reifman, 1995). These aspects could be thought as a source of skepticism regarding warning-label as an ineffective tool of prevention.

As far as we know, time orientation and skepticism have not been included as variables that could affect effectiveness of the warning-labels. Three main questions have not been considered to date: First, does skepticism affect effectiveness of warning-labels? what is the effect of time orientation perspective on attitude toward both the warning-labels and toward alcohol consumption? What is the relationship between prior experience in alcohol consumption, skepticism and time orientation perspective? This chapter offers some arguments and some research propositions based on the literature review to contribute to the discussion.

Background on Drinking During Pregnancy

Because of a consensus among various government agencies for protecting people and preventing risks related to alcohol use, warning-labels have been required on every alcoholic beverage container since 1989 in the USA. There is evidence that few countries have recently adopted a similar strategy (for a complete review see: Kyskan and Moore, 2005). The warning-label addressed to pregnant women reads:

Government Warning: (1) "According to the Surgeon General, women should not drink alcoholic beverages during pregnancy because of the risk of birth defects".

Some research has been done under the assumption that this strategy may serve as a prevention process (Graves, 1993; Glasscoff, and Felts, 1994; DeCarlo, 1997; Mackinnon et al., 2000). The main purpose of this research has been to establish the warning-labels' effectiveness on prevention (DeCarlo, 1997; Andrews, Netemeyer, Durvasula, 1990, 1993; Hilton, 1993; Hankin and Janet, 1993; Laughery, Young, and Vaubel, 1993; Hankin, Sloan, and Sokol, 1998). Although 87% of individuals notice the presence of alcohol warning-labels (Mackinnon and Lapin, 1998), their effectiveness is highly questionable (Hankin et al., 1998). Heavy drinkers, who are the main target of this preventive measure have either not been reached by the labels (Hankin et al., 1993; Mackinnon and Lapin, 1998) or have become habituated to them (Andrews and Netemeyer, 1996).

The concentrated period of research effort was from 1989 to 1995. After 1995, the amount of research diminishes considerably and some questions about the impact of warning-labels on behaviour remain unanswered, for instance, the link between warning-labels and intention to avoid alcoholic beverages (Mackinnon and Lapin, 1998).

A second legislative strategy oriented to increase public awareness of FAS is the use of warning-posters provided for some states in the United States. Fenaugthy and Mackinnon, (1993) reported immediate effects when the warning-poster appeared. For example, awareness of the poster was increased and more women recalled clearly the message. Moreover, beliefs about the link between pregnancy, alcohol consumption and birth defects were increased.

A third strategy has been promoted by some health agencies involving useful mechanisms to promote health care among women asking for help. This strategy promotes FAS information and related news using websites. These pages are in English and include a wide range of health care organizations who are working to prevent this issue. They offer answers to questions such as: "How can I prevent fetal alcohol syndrome?" The answer given is: "the thing you can do is stop drinking when you are thinking about getting pregnant. If you get pregnant, quit drinking alcohol and drink other beverages like water or fruit juices".[2] Moreover, some agencies use a lifelike FAS manikin designed for a nurse/consultant specializing in FAS education to give clearer information.[3]

Nevertheless, researchers pointed out that when individuals have a history of chronic heavy alcohol use, there is a correspondingly favorable attitude toward alcohol (Hankin et al., 1998; Mackinnon et al, 1999). Thus, they cannot stop it because addictive behaviour has complex physiological mechanisms uncontrolled by them. It is important to note that we did not find any research published regarding the persuasive effects of the strategy of the website's messages.

---

2   Source http://familydoctor.org/068.xml. Consulted March 18, 2006.
3   Source: http://www.realityworks.com/ consulted March 11, 2006.

Research regarding warning-labels has mainly focused on measuring awareness of the warning, recall of their content, beliefs about drinking during pregnancy (Hankin et al., 1993; Mackinnon and Lapin, 1998), perceived believability and attitudes toward the warning (Andrews et al., 1991), cognitive response as mediator between warning and attitudes (Andrews et al., 1993), and perception of risk (Snyder and Blood, 1992). Despite its importance, little research has explored the positive or negative effects of the warning-label on behaviours (Mackinnon and Lapin, 1998; Mackinnon et al., 2000).

Social research has widely recognized that attitudes and behaviour are central cues in persuasive communication. Thus, some studies included attitudes and their links with behaviour in the context of warning research (Greenfield and Graves, 1993; Kaskutas, 1993, Hankin et al., 1993; Andrews et al., 1993; Mackinnon and Lapin, 1998). They included attitudes toward the warning-labels and attitude confidence as dependent variables and concluded that intentions and behaviours remained unchanged in heavy drinkers. Conversely, this link is stronger in the case of occasional or nonusers who felt more confident about their attitudes toward the warning-labels.

Similarly, intentions to avoid alcohol consumption were measured by Mackinnon and Lapin (1998). They also found that nondrinkers were significantly more likely to agree that they would avoid alcohol in the future in order to avoid health problems. Therefore, the warning-labels' effectiveness has been stronger on nondrinkers.

It is not surprisingly that after being less exposed to the warning-label, lighter drinkers or abstainers had reduced their reported alcohol consumption and regarded the alcohol as more harmful (Hankin et al., 1993). In contrast, heavy drinkers, who were more exposed, had not been affected, and some women among them felt that their fetuses were invulnerable to the alcohol effects. Three reasons can explain this: First, some research showed that habituation affects negatively warning-label's effectiveness (Hankin et al., 1998; Mackinnon et al., 1999). Second, defensive attitudes adopted by heavier users (Andrews et al., 1991; MacKinnon and Lapin, 1998) lead them to ignore or discount the warning-label. Third, some people tend to seek immediate gratification in their alcohol consumption desire, which involves necessarily a present-oriented perspective.

Moreover, older drinkers do not seem to be concerned by the warning-label (Hankin et al., 1998; Mackinnon et al, 1999). These researchers identified three conditions affecting warning effectiveness outcomes in the case of risky drinking among pregnant women. First, previous experience of alcohol consumption generates favourable attitude about the use of alcohol as a means of relaxing or escaping (Morris et al., 1994). Second, women who had experienced at least one previous health pregnancy outcome viewed prenatal alcohol consumption as less dangerous. Third, the role played by unemployment rate (Hankin et al., 1998; Cone-Wesson, 2005).

In summary, although the results of some studies are consistent with the aim of the prevention campaign promoted by Tom Donalson, executive director of the National Organization of FAS in the USA, who said, "Our goal is to raise awareness about the dangers of drinking during pregnancy", their effectiveness on changing behaviour is less consistent. It is clear that awareness is rising in many people, but their intentions for reducing alcohol consumption remain unchanged.

A Critical Review of Past Research

The first element to point out is that the warning-label ("women should not drink alcoholic beverages during pregnancy because of the risk of birth defects") is unclear about specific health hazards. Consequently, women are obliged to figure out what kind of birth defects their baby may face. When the hazard is not presented concretely, the message may be ignored or discounted because of the effort and information needed to figure it out.

Although previous studies have demonstrated that prior alcohol consumption experience affects negatively the effectiveness of the warning-label (Hankin et al., 1993; Mackinnon and Lapin, 1998), prevention campaigns do not consider these results in their strategies. Therefore, the second element to point out is the evidence that there is a need for a prevention campaign that is addressed to women who have not yet developed chronic alcohol-related experiences.

Another element to point out is the assumption that increasing awareness by providing information allows people to take preventive actions (Fenaughty and Mackinnon, 1993). Nevertheless, the link between information and behavior has not yet been demonstrated. For instance, people are aware of the existence of Aids and yet they continue to have risky sex (Rothspan and Read, 1996). People are aware that drunk driving is dangerous and yet they continue doing it (Mackinnon et al., 2000). We ought to recognize that awareness based on information is an important (Kalsher, Clarke, and Wogalter, 1993), but insufficient condition for encouraging new behaviour.

It is also important to consider the amount of alcohol consumed and the moral panic (Armstrong and Abel, 2000). The policy response in the USA rested on the unproven premise that any amount of drinking in pregnancy posed a threat to the fetus (Armstrong and Abel, 2000; Hankin et al., 2000). There is some evidence supporting that women can drink alcoholic beverages during pregnancy but limiting the amount per week. The British Royal College of Obstetricians and Gynecologists (1996) demonstrated that no adverse effects on pregnancy outcome have been proven with a consumption of less than 120 grams of alcohol per week.

The last point is dealing with the quality of the measures of alcohol consumption. Hankin et al. (2000) point out that previous studies suffer from selection bias. Most previous studies collected data only on users of services. It implies that non-users of health services are uncovered by the data collection. Researchers also used the self-report mean to obtain frequency and amount of alcohol consumption, but self-report can be biased by participants to avoid social recrimination. So research is needed to improve the reliability of the data.

Framework for Theoretical Propositions

The Warning-label

The beverage warning-label currently used contains a cognitive message whose purpose is that women become aware about the birth defects. It is supposed that the warning-label convey a clear message about birth defects due to drinking during pregnancy. We consider that it would be important to modify the warning wording by using some emotional statement. Given that rational warning statements have generated habituation, we consider that emotional warning statements could affect positively the comprehension and perceived risks among heavy drinkers.

Perception of Risk

Researchers suggested that non-drinkers perceived greater risks associated with alcohol consumption (Mackinnon and Lapin, 1998). Thus, perception of risk is related to some events that could happen because of the specific behaviour such as drinking while pregnancy. Some research argued that risky drinkers have developed habituation against the warning and defensiveness behaviour (Hankin et al., 1998; Mackinnon et al., 1999).

Creyer et al. (2002) did an experiment to show that promoting a new warning (Alcohol is a drug) leads to greater perceptions of risks than the standard USA warning. Thus:

P1: Providing new warning-label (using emotional statement) will have a greater positive impact on perceived risks among heavier drinkers' pregnant women.

Alcohol Consumption Experience

Alcohol consumption experience promotes favourable attitude toward alcohol (Hankin et al., 1998). Previous research on warning-labels showed that alcohol consumption experience affects negatively the warning-labels believability (Hankin et al, 1993; Mackinnon and Lapin, 1998). Furthermore, women who were classified as drinkers were more likely to view drinking in moderation as personally beneficial and not harmful to the unborn child (Morris et al., 1994). Others found that many women may recall examples of women who consumed alcoholic beverages during pregnancy, yet gave birth to normal children (Morris et al., 1994; Warren and Foudin, 2001), and perhaps they have themselves had pregnancies resulting in healthy outcomes (Testa and Reifman, 1995).

Women with greater alcohol consumption experience felt that they were invulnerable (Hankin et al., 1993) and therefore may consider that the warning-label are not believable because of people rarely derogate themselves as a source. Thus:

P2a: Previous alcohol consumption experience and positive pregnancies outcomes diminish directly the perception of risk and tends to disbelieve traditional warning-label.

P2b: Previous alcohol consumption experience does not affect the believability of emotional warning statement.

P3: Previous alcohol consumption experience affects positively skepticism toward the current warning-label (rational statement).

Skepticism

Obermiller and Spangenberg (1998) have developed a scale to measure consumer skepticism toward advertising claims. They define skepticism as the tendency toward disbelief of advertising claims. According to the Oxford Dictionary (1982), a skeptic is a person who is inclined to question the truth of facts, inferences, etc.

In marketing, skepticism research has focused on skepticism toward advertising claims (Ford, Smith and Swasy, 1990); Obermiller and Spangenberg, 1998, 2000), adolescent skepticism toward TV advertising (Boush, Friestad, and Rose, 1994), and skepticism toward environmental claims in marketers' communications (Möhr, Eroglu, and Scholder E., 1998).

Highly skeptical individuals were more negative in response to informational appeals than for emotional appeals of advertising, and were more negative in response to informational ads compared with less skeptical individuals (Obermiller et al., 2005). They further point out that information appeals were ineffective with participants who were highly skeptical toward ads. It means that the perceived believability of the information appeals was lower than emotional appeal. Given that the warning-label is characterized by informational appeal, we consider that skeptical individuals will believe it less than non-skeptical. Thus:

P4: Skepticism affects positively the warning-label believability diminishing its effectiveness.

P5: Skepticism toward the warning-label will be negative when the warning is an emotional statement.

Time Orientation Perspective: Present and Future

Researchers suggested that nondrinkers had a greater concern about their health condition. It implies a future time orientation (Bjögvinsson and Wilde, 1996) because they sought to avoid health problems. Time orientation perspective is an important variable affecting human behaviour (Klineberg, 1968; Trommsdorf, 1983).

The social science literature has shown that individuals differ based on time orientation perspective. In general, two main time-orientation perspectives have been identified: future time orientation (FT), and present time orientation (PT) (Gonzalez and Zimbardo, 1985; Amyx and Mowen, 1995). The former has been associated with high achievement and goal orientation (Gjesme, 1979), low impulsivity (Trommsdorf, 1983), and ability to delay gratification (Klineberg, 1968; Gonzalez and Zimbardo, 1985); whereas the latter (PTO) includes people who are less goal directed, more impulsive, plan less (Amyx and Mowen, 1995) and oriented to immediate gratification (Hornik, 1990).

For example, having a baby is not merely a present action; it concerns the individual's future and may imply planning behaviours as a response to a clear ideation of the future (Bjögvinsson and Wilde, 1996). Heavy drinking is a behavior rooted in the past and it concerns more to the individual present as a tendency to gain gratification immediately (Gonzalez and Zimbardo, 1985; Hornik, 1990; Amyx and Mowen, 1995).

Although the research about time orientation above mentioned were done in sales setting sexual behaviors, and smoking behavior we call to take this notion to apply it in warning-labels setting. We suggest integrating it as a variable that potentially affects the perceived risk and the perceived believability of the warning.

The degree of impulsivity is a primary distinction between FT and PT (Amyx and Mowen, 1995). We agree that impulsivity seeks immediate gratification, that is, people who drink daily need immediate gratification and they are not willing to delay it, so PT people are more impulsive than FT.

Following this perspective, women with a high degree of impulsivity combined with a low delay of gratification produce a strong tendency to enjoy the present time (Gonzalez and Zimbardo, 1985). Moreover, PT women prefer to avoid unpleasant consequences in the present, and the timing of losses influence risk taking (Amyx and Mowen, 1995). We suggest that unpleasant consequences in the present can be considered as negative effects of personal situations that bring women to drink during pregnancy (e.g., unemployment, affective troubles, etc.). Therefore:

P6: PT orientation women are more impulsive when it comes to drinking during pregnancy than FT women because they are seeking immediate gratification.

P7: to PT orientation women, the perception of risk of drinking while pregnant is lower than to FT orientation women.

P8: PT orientation pregnant women are more willing to drink during pregnancy to avoid unpleasant consequences in the present than FT orientation pregnant women.

Conversely, when women have a low degree of impulsivity and a high delay of gratification, their orientation is toward the future. Therefore, they are able to pay attention to the warning-labels to postpone the alcohol consumption during pregnancy even when they have had prior alcohol consumption experience. These women may be aware of receiving a gain if they stop drinking, so they feel there is a compensation. In this sense, the present and future imply a trade off between losses and gains.

P9: FT orientation women will have a higher perception of risk for drinking during pregnancy than PT women, even if they have prior alcohol consumption experience.

P10: Emotional warning execution will have a positive impact on both PT women and FT women.

Final Comments

The focus of this discussion is to understand the role of time orientation perspective and skepticism on the warning-label research. The central cue in our framework is the perception of risks, which may cause favourable attitudes toward warning-labels, and therefore coherent behaviour to avoid alcohol consumption would be expected. It means that if women feel themselves and their unborn children are in danger they will restrict alcohol consumption during pregnancy. We intend to show that both time orientation perspective and skepticism are two dimensions that could affect negatively the effectiveness of warning-labels on attitudes and behavior.

Limitations

There are at least two limitations in our framework. First, prevention to this kind of behaviour should involve a long-term campaign, so time is required to observe the affective-warning effectiveness and if habituation toward this warning can be developed as has been evidenced in the case of traditional warning-labels (e.g. warning-labels addressed to drinking during pregnancy and drinking while driving).

Second, much research has pointed out that obtaining reliable data on women's drinking during pregnancy is very difficult (Hankin, 2000, 2002; Hankin et al., 2000; Warren and Foudin, 2001) because it is gathered through self-reported consumption and women may bias the information they give. We are not sure that women will give reliable data in this concern and we have not found any different way to obtain better data.

Managerial Implications

We suggest including time orientation perspective and skepticism into the warning-label research. These variables can be useful to understand the weak effectiveness concerning the strategy of warning-labels addressed to prevent drinking during pregnancy behaviour. We consider that including these variables will allow to clarify some particular psychological mechanisms underlying the perceived risks among pregnant women. Based on this knowledge, health agencies can draw different communications tactics to achieve better outcomes. Moreover, it will allow agencies do not spend huge sums of money for efforts whose results will not be significant.

The time orientation perspective will allow managers to understand what priorities women have; in this case, PT orientation women would pay less attention to the warning and new strategies would be needed to increase their effectiveness. Public health care agencies may prepare prevention campaigns based on personal interaction (second and third forms of prevention which include personal interviews), and universal prevention could retain beverage warning-labels as a support but make some changes to the nature of the warning-labels.

We believe that prevention should begin when women are younger in order to be better aware of the birth risks they might face. It is also important that clearer messages about birth defects be addressed to adults women even as they gain alcohol consumption experience. Therefore, it is important to include this subject as part of a "healthcare course" within the educational process. We know that non-users are able to avoid alcohol consumption and they perceive more associated risks; thus, younger women and non-users as well as heavy drinkers should be the targets of prevention campaigns while modifying the content of the warning (Mackinnon et al., 2000) to gain novelty and maybe greater effectiveness.

There is another related aspect. Many households in Europe and in others developed countries adopt children from less developed countries.[4] The data related to FAS in those countries are not yet well known. Regarding social responsibly and the health agencies involved, it is important to extend our knowledge to help those countries identify and prevent this issue because nobody wants a baby affected by FAS.

Future Research Suggestions

It would be important to include the significant others in order to regard the effects this dimension could have on attitudes and behaviour. Subjective norm is a variable included in the theory of reason action proposed by Fishbein and Ajzen (1975). As they argued, subjective norm can affect intentions and intentions directly affect behaviour.

Although socioeconomic status and unemployment conditions are not incorporated as variables in our model, we guess that they play an important role as personal factors (deTurck et al., 1995). We suggest measuring them in order to assess their relationships with time orientation people, perception of risk, and attitudes.

As indicated earlier, much research on the warning-labels have measured cognitive dimensions such as awareness, beliefs, and perception of risk induced by warning-labels. Nevertheless, there is a lack of studies related to testing the effects of clearer hazards that could happen as a consequence of drinking during pregnancy. For example, we advocate using a new concrete hazard message: "Alcohol may produce mental retardation", or putting a poster with a child who was born with FAS (showing physical features) using this warning sentence "Alcohol may produce mental retardation. You can avoid it".

Following Gordon and Doyle (1987), it would be interesting to explore what kind of beliefs are associated with stopping drinking when women start pregnancy in the case of heavy drinkers. Women might have fears about the secondary health effects of abstinence.

Conclusions

We have reviewed some research about alcoholic beverage warning-label addressed to drinking during pregnancy. We found that knowledge is lacking in terms of including time orientation perspective and skepticism as variables that could help to explain the weak warning effectiveness. These variables would have a direct effect on perception of risk. In our analysis, we propose that both time orientation and skepticism are individual characteristics that could have implications for beverage warning-labels effectiveness.

We advocate that drinking during pregnancy prevention should begin when women are younger and before they are in pregnant because prior experience of alcohol consumption may cause habituation. We believe that prevention implies a

---

4   http://kidshealth.org/parent/medical/brain/fas.html browsed in March 11, 2006.

complete long-term program. We hope that our discussion will contribute to thinking more effectively about prevention and some important gaps in the knowledge surrounding.

References

Andrews, J. Craig, Richard G. Netemeyer, and Srinivas Durvasula (1993) "The Role of Cognitive Responses as Mediators of Alcohol Warning Label Effect," *Journal of Public Policy & Marketing*, Vol. 12 (1), 57–68.

Andrews, J. Craig, Richard G. Netemeyer, and Srinivas Durvasula, (1993) "Effects of Consumption Frequency on Believability and Attitudes Toward Alcohol Warning Labels," *The Journal of Consumer Affairs*, Vol. 25 (2), 323–37.

Amyx, Douglas, and John C. Mowen, (1995) "Advancing Versus Delaying Payments and Consumer Time Orientation: a Personal Selling Experiment," *Psychology & Marketing*, Vol. 12 (4), 243–64.

Armstrong, Elizabeth M., and Ernest L. Abel, (2000), "Fetal Alcohol Syndrome: the Origins of a Moral Panic," *Alcohol and Alcoholism,* Vol. 35 (3), 276–82.

Björgvinsson, Thröstur and Gerald J.S. Wilde, (1996), "Risky Health and Safety Habits Related to Perceived Value of the Future," *Safety Science,* Vol. 22, No 1–3, 27–33.

Bratton, R. (1995), "Fetal alcohol Syndrome: How Can You Help Prevent it?" *Post Graduate Medical Education,* Vol. 98 (5), 197–00.

Boush, David M., Marian Friestad, and Gregory M. Rose, (1994), "Adolescent Skepticism Toward TV Advertising and Knowledge of Advertiser Tactics," *Journal of Consumer Research,* Vol. 21 (June), 165–75.

Cone-Wesson, Barbara, (2005), "Prenatal Alcohol and Cocaine Exposure: Influences on Cognition, Speech, Language, and Hearing," *Journal of Communication Disorders,* Vol. 38, 279–302.

Creyer, Elizabeth H., John C. Kozup, and Scot Burton, (2002), "An Experimental Assessment of the Effects of Two Alcoholic Beverage Health Warnings Across Countries and Binge-Drinking Status," *Journal of Consumer Affairs,* Vol. 36 (2), 171–02.

DeCarlo, Tomas E. (1997) "Alcohol Warnings and Warning Labels: An Examination of Alternative Alcohol Warning Message and Perceived Effectiveness," *The Journal of Consumer Marketing*, Vol. 14 (6), p. 448.

DeTurck, Mark A., Gerald M. Goldhaber, and Gary M. Richetto, (1995) "Effectiveness of Alcohol Beverage Warning Labels: Effects of Consumer Information Processing Objectives and Color of Signal Word," *Journal of Products & Toxics Liability,* Vol. 17 (3), 187–95.

Fenaughty, Andrea M, and David P. MacKinnon, (1993) "Immediate Effects of the Arizona Alcohol Warning Poster," *Journal of Public Policy & Marketing*, Vol. 12 (1), 69– 78.

Fishbein, M. and I. Ajzen, (1975) *Belief, Attitude, Intentions and Behavior: An Introduction to Theory and Research*, Addison-Wesley, Boston, MA.

Ford, Gary T., Darlene B. Smith and John L. Swasy, (1990), "Consumer Skepticism of Advertising Claims: Testing Hypotheses from Economics of Information," *Journal of Consumer Research,* Vol. 16 (March), 433–41.

Gjesme, T. (1979) "Future Time Orientation as a Function of Achievement Motives, Ability, Delay of Gratification, and Sex," *The Journal of Psychology*, Vol. 101, 173–88.

Glasscoff, Mary A. Michael Felts W. (1994) "The Awareness Level of Pregnant Women of Alcoholic Beverage Health Warning Labels," *Wellness Perspectives*, Vol. 10 (2).

Gonzalez, A. and P. Zimbardo, (1985) "Time Perspective: A Survey Report," *Psychology Today,* 19 (3), 21–26.

Gordon, T. and J.T. Doyle, (1987) "Drinking and Mortality: The Albany Study," *American Journal of Epidemiology,* Vol 125, 263–70.

Graves, Karen L. (1993) "An Evaluation of the Alcohol Warning label: A Comparison of the United States and Ontario, Canada in 1990 and 1991," *Journal of Public Policy & Marketing*, Vol. 12 (1), 19–29.

Greenfield, Thomas K. and Karen L. Graves, (1993) "Alcohol Warning Labels for Prevention," *Alcohol Health & Research World*, Vol. 17 (1).

Hankin, J.R., I.J. Firestone, J.J. Sloan, J.W. Ager, A.C Goodman, R.J. Sokol and S.S. Martier, (1993), "The Impact of the Alcohol Warning Label on Drinking During Pregnancy," *Journal of Public Policy & Marketing*, Vol. 12 (1), pp. 10–18.

Hankin, Janet, Mary E. McCaul and Janet Heussner, (2000), "Pregnant, Alchol-Abusing Women," *Alcoholism: Clinical and Experimental Research,* Vol. 24 (8), 1276–86.

Hankin, Janet R., James J. Sloan, and Robert J. Sokol, (1998) "The Modest Impact of the Alcohol Beverage Warning Label on Drinking During Pregnancy Among a Sample of African and American Women," *Journal of Public Policy & Marketing*, Vol. 17 (1), 61–70.

Hankin, Janet R. (2002) "Fetal Alcohol Syndrome Prevention Research" *Alcohol Research & Health World*, Vol. 26 (1), pp. 58–65.

Hilton, Michael (1993) "An Overview of Recent Findings on Alcoholic Beverage Warning Label," *Journal of Public Policy & Marketing*, Vol. 12 (1), 1–9.

Hilton, Michael and Lee Kaskutas, (1991) "Public Support of Warning Labels on Alcohol Beverage Containers," *British Journal of Addiction*, Vol. 86, 1323–33.

Hornik, Jacob, (1990), "Time Preference, Psychographics, and Smoking Behavior," *Marketing Health Services,* Vol. 10 (1), 36–46.

Institute of Alcohol Studies, (2005), "Women and Alcohol" IAS Fact Sheet, www.ias.org.uk

Klineberg, S.L. (1969) "Future Time Perspective and the Preference for Delayed Reward," *Journal of Personality and Psychology*, Vol. 8 (3), 253–57.

Kyskan, Christina E. and Timothy E. Moore (2005), "Global Perspectives on Fetal alcohol Syndrome: Assessing Practices, Policies, and Campaigns in Four English-Speaking Countries," *Canadian Psychology,* Vol. 46 (3), 153–65.

Laughery, K.R., S.L.Young, K.P. Vaubel and J.W. Brelsford, (1993) "The Noticeability of Warnings on Alcoholic Beverage Containers," *Journal of Public Policy & Marketing*, Vol. 12 (1), 38–56.

Kalsher, Michael J., Steven W. Clarke and Michael S. Wogalter, (1993) "Communication of Alcohol Facts and Hazards by a Warning Poster," *Journal of Public Policy & Marketing*, Vol. 12 (1), 78–91.

Kaskutas, Lee A. (1993) "Changes in Public Attitudes Toward Alcohol Control Policies Since the Warning Label Mandate of 1988," *Journal of Public Policy & Marketing*, Vol. 12 (1), 30–37.

MacKinnon, David P., R.M. Williams-Avery, Kathryn L. Wilcox and A.M. Fenaughty (1999), "Effects of the Arizona Alcohol Warning Poster," *Journal of Public Policy & Marketing*, Vol. 18 (1), 77–89.

MacKinnon, David P. Angela Lapin (1998) "Effects of Alcohol Warnings and Advertisements: a Test of the Boomerang Hypothesis," *Psychology & Marketing*, Vol. 15 (7), 707–27.

Mackinnon, David P., Liva Nohre, Mary Ann Pentz and Alan W. Stacy, (2000), "The Alcohol Warning and Adolescents: 5-Years Effects," *American Journal of Public Health*, Vol. 90 (10), 1589–94.

Möhr, Lois A., Dogan Erouglu and Pam Scholder Ellen, (1998), "The Development and Testing of a Measure of Skepticism toward Environmental Claims in Marketer's Communications," *The Journal of Consumer Affairs*, Vol. 32 (1), 30–55.

Morris, Louis A., John L. Swasy and Michael B. Mazis, (1994), "Accepted Risk and Alcohol Use During Pregnancy," *Journal of Consumer Research*, Vol. 21 (June), 135–44.

Obermiller, Carl and Eric R. Spangenberg, (1998), "Development of a Scale to Measure Consumer Skepticism Toward Advertising," *Journal of Consumer Psychology*, Vol. 7 (2), 159–86.

Obermiller, Carl and Eric R. Spangenberg, (1998), "On the Origin and Distinctness of Skepticism toward Advertising," *Marketing Letters*, Vol. 11 (4), 311–22.

Obermiller, Carl and E.R. Spangenberg, and D.L. MacLachlan (2005), "Ad Skepticism," *Journal of Advertising*, Vol. 34 (3), 7–17.

Rothspan, Sadina and Stephen J. Read, (1996) "Present Versus Future Time Perspective and HIV Risk among Heterosexual College Students," *Health Psychology*, Vol. 15 (2), 131–34.

Snyder, Leslie B. and Deborah J. Blood, (1992) "Caution: Alcohol Advertising and the Surgeon General's Alcohol Warnings May Have Adverse Effects on Young Adults," *Journal of Applied Communication Research*, February, 37–53.

Testa, Maria and Alan Reifman, (1995), "Individual differences in Perceived Riskiness of Drinking in Pregnancy: Antecedents and Consequences," *Journal of Studies on Alcohol*, (July), 360–67.

The British Royal College of Obstetricians and Gynaecologists (1996) *Guideline No. 9: Alcohol Consumption in Pregnancy*. Royal College of Obstetricians and Gynaecologists, London.

Trommsdorff, G. (1983) "Future Orientation and Socialization," *International Journal of Psychology*, Vol. 18, 381–06.

Warren, Kenneth, R. and Laurie L. Foudin (2001) "Alcohol-Related Birth Defects – the Past, Present, and Future," *Alcohol Research & Health*, Vol. 25 (3), 153–60.

U.S. Department of Health and Human Services, (1998), "Substance Abuse and Mental Health Statistics Source Book," Rocville, MD: Substance Abuse and Mental Health Services Administration.

Chapter 4

Reflection about the Structuration of Organizations: The Capacity of Responsibility of Human Agents and Conditions of Absence

Jacques-Bernard Gauthier

Introduction

The current chapter falls within the continuity of debates that lead a particular field of study which some call "the Theory of Organizations".

> A *theory* is an explanation, that is, it is an attempt to explain a segment of experience in the world. The particular thing that a theory explains is called *the phenomenon of interest*. In organization theory the primary phenomenon of interest is the organization. However, organization can be defined in many different ways, for instance, as a social structure, a technology, a culture, a physical structure, or as a part of an environment. Organization can also be studied in terms of the central issues and recurring themes of organizing including control, conflict, decision making, power and politics, and change. (Hatch, 1997, p. 9)

In this way, contrary to its given name, the field of study of *the* theory of organizations is composed by a wide range of theories of organizations. These theories draw their sources from diverse fields, among which sociology (Hatch, 2006). Taking an interest in matters of the relationship individuals/society, a science like sociology suggests a conceptual framework out of which, some authors and researchers in theory of organizations, inspire themselves in order to study the link individuals/ organization. Being sociology characterized by a multiplicity of currents of thought, the relationship individuals/society is broached in different ways (Delas and Milly, 2005). Two perspectives are usually taken into account: a (structuro-) functionalist approach and an interpretative approach.

The traditional approach, known as (structuro-) functionalist is positivist by nature (Donaldson, 2003). In that sense, the nature of social reality (and a fortiori the organization's nature), as well as the structures that make it up, are objective. This principle underlies, among others, the proposals of the influence of the structure over the individual, the social environment determining the individual, etc. (Burrell and Morgan, 1979; Giddens 1979, 1984): "Organizations are objectively real entities operating in a real world. When well-designed and managed they are systems of decision and action driven by norms of rationality, efficiency and effectiveness for stated purposes" (Hatch, 2006, p. 14).

Opposing the traditional movement, and under the name of interpretativism, we find another movement described by Burrell and Morgan (1979) as anti-positivist. The latter movement suggests, among other things, that the organization (and its structures), following the example of society, is a product of the action of the individuals, that social structures are internal to people (subjective nature of the social reality), that the individual controls entirely its social environment, that the individual is its own master, etc. (Burrell and Morgan, 1979; Giddens 1979, 1984; Hatch and Yanow, 2003): "Organizations are continually constructed and reconstructed by their members' symbolically mediated interaction. Organizations are socially constructed realities where meanings promote and are promoted by understanding of the self and others that occurs within the organization context" (Hatch 2006, p.14).

Thus, on the one hand, it suggests the influence of society and its structures over the individual and, on the other hand, structures are seen as sorted out practices emerging from the action (Giddens 1979, 1984). In proposing the Theory of Structuration, Giddens (1979, 1984) wishes to exceed the dualism individuals/society in favour of a duality: the structure and the action (the individual, to be specific) are assumed to be each other in a dialectical relation. Giddens (1979, 1984) gives the name of duality of the structure to this dialectical relation. Giddens' (1979, 1984) subject of study is society and not the organization. Despite everything, we can readily consider the extent of the influence of its Theory of Structuration over the field of the Theory of Organizations as we go in detail through various management journals.

Furthermore, the responsibility of the firm or of the organization[1] is a subject to reflect upon and to which, more and more, numerous authors are looking into. Several among these authors will compare the firm to a legal entity, attached to principles of responsibility, as if the responsibility of the firm was one thing and the responsibility of the individuals bound to the firm was another. In this particular way of seeing the responsibility of organizations, we find the essentials of the objectivation elements, taken from the traditional perspective described above.

Jonas (1998), a philosopher who has been studying about responsibility at length, defines it as an ethical mediation that is held between two ontological areas, the human freedom and the content of worth of the Being: responsibility is a capacity of the human being. Consequently, it cannot be an object of different nature nor independent from an individual, its actions, and the power and influence of those actions over the whole reality.

Willing to go past the dualism individual/organization for a duality, Éraly (1988), inspired by Giddens' structurationist work, defined the organization as "(…) a localized and enduring social nature, composed by keeping in mind a given aim, a structured whole of actions and relatively hierarchical interactions, differentiated and interdependent in comparison with resources and purposes".[2] (p.9). The organization is conceived as the outcome of human activities, where those activities are themselves conditioned by the organization.

---

1   We utilize equally each of both terms.
2   Free translation from the text published originally in French.

On the basis of combining the points of view of both Jonas (1998) and Éraly (1988), we can imagine that when the responsibility of the firms is cited, it is not the firm as a legal entity the one to which the reference is made, but to the ability of being responsible held by the individuals affiliated to the firm. Given the influence of Anthony Giddens' Theory of Structuration over the field of the Theory of Organizations, the present chapter will be organized around Giddens' human agent's capacity of responsibility.

In the first section, we will go through the main elements of the Theory of Structuration. During this review, the capacity responsibility is situated in comparison with the other abilities of Giddens' human agent and in relation to the structural elements that compose the social reality. In its spatio-temporal geography, Giddens (1979, 1984) makes of the co-presence a significant condition of the interactions between human agents. In the second section, the co-presence is defined and linked up with the absence. As far as the responsibility is considered, the definition of the co-presence and its connection with the absence will raise some questions. These questions will be dealt with in the second section as well. Finally, in the last section, we will examine feasible alternatives in order to restore to the human agent its capacity of responsibility in conditions of absence.

The Main Elements of the Theory of Structuration

Inspired by the (structural-) functionalist approaches, Giddens (1984) developed a notion of a social system, which is composed of structures and agents or actions.[3]

> Social systems involve regularised relations of interdependence between individuals or groups, that typically cans be best analysed as *recurrent social practices*. Social systems are systems of social interaction; as such they involve the situated activities of human subjects, and exist syntagmatically in the flow of time. Systems, in this terminology, have structures (…). Structures are necessarily (logically) properties of systems (…). (Giddens 1979, pp. 65–66)

To the concept of system, structure and agent, Giddens (1979, 1984) adds the duality of the structure. The concepts of structure, agents/actions and duality of the structure are the mainstay notions of the Theory of Structuration (Giddens 1984).

The Structure and Structures

The structure is a set of "rules and resources([4]), recursively implicated in the reproduction of social systems" (Giddens 1984, p.377). According to Giddens

---

3   Giddens uses in an undifferentiated way the words actor and agent. On the other hand, in *Central Problems in Social Theory*, Giddens (1979) does not make any distinction between the notions of *action* and *agent*. In other words, the actions cannot be imagined in an independent way from the agents, nor the agents from their actions.

4   During the sub-section dedicated to the principle of the duality of the structure, we specify what Giddens (1979, 1984) understands as rules and resources.

(1979, 1984), the structure sustains itself in a 'virtual order': it transcends space and time. It is only under the way of updated mnesic traces in the action of the agents that the structure can be present in a given spatio-temporal context (Giddens, 1979, 1984; Rojot, 1998). Consequently, a social system does not have a structure, but it has structural properties: "As I shall employ it, 'structure' refers to 'structural property', or more exactly, to 'structuring property', structuring properties providing the 'binding' of time and space in social systems. I argue that these properties can be understood as rules and resources, recursively implicated in reproduction of social systems" (p. 66). Giddens (1984) organizes into a hierarchy the structural properties in accordance with their spatio-temporal extent: "The most deeply embedded structural properties, implicated in the reproduction of societal totalities, I call *structural principles*" (Giddens 1984, p. 17). In this way, comparing various societal totalities, returns, to a comparative analysis of the structural principles, among others. Nevertheless, the degree in which the structural principles are rooted seems to vary from a societal totality to another. In fact, following Seyfarth (2000), it is possible to conclude, that in the case of the organization defined as a societal totality, the structural principles are less profoundly rooted than those analysed by Giddens (1984) in *The Constitution of Society*. At last, Giddens (1979, 1984) gives the name of *institutions* to the practices that possess the greatest spatio-temporal extent within the societal totalities.

The Agents and the Actions

Giddens (1979, 1984, 1993, 1998) conceives the action as a continuous stream of conduits containing events experienced by an agent:[5] "I shall define action or agency as *the stream of actual or contemplated causal interventions of corporeal beings in the ongoing process of events-in-the-world*" (Giddens 1993, p. 81). Regarding their actions, individuals are capable of reflexive monitoring (see Figure 1). In other words, the individual has the potential of situating the action in relation to himself (acting self); he has the capacity to supervise, to monitor all the angles of the physical and social contexts in which he interacts (Giddens 1979, 1984, 1998; Rojot, 1998). In addition to the reflexivity as a characteristic of the concerned agent, Giddens adds the rationalization of the action (see Figure 4.1).

On the one hand, the rationalization of the action is closely linked to its reflexive monitoring of action (Éraly 1988; Rojot, 1998). In this sense, rationalization of the action is referred as the fact that "(...) actors – also routinely and for the most part without fuss – maintain a continuing 'theoretical understanding' of the grounds of their activity" (Giddens 1984, p.5). In other words, the agents have the capacity of explaining (regardless of the fact that they have to do it or not) what they do, while they are doing it (Rojot, 1998). On the other hand, to this first meaning of the concept

---

5   For Giddens, both the actions and the agents form the two sides of the same coin. In fact, in *Central Problems in Social Theory*, Giddens (1979, p.56) presents the characteristics of the action under the way of a model that he names: "stratification model of action". In *The Constitution of Society*, he gives to the same stratification, the name of "stratification model of agent" (Giddens 1984, p.5).

of rationalization, Rojot (1998), following Giddens, specifies a second meaning: justify in a discursive way the reasons of the actions. The reasons discursively put forward by the agents have nothing to do with the capacity of rationalization that they mobilize during the reflexive monitoring of their actions.

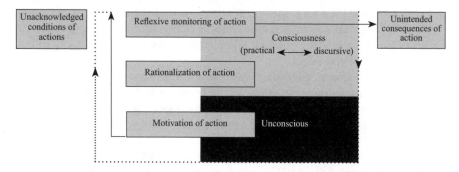

Figure 4.1   The stratification model of the action and the agent's strata of the psyche (Giddens, 1979, 1984)

Even if the agent is a potentially knowledgeable individual, Giddens (1984) emphasizes that this knowledgeability is limited. What is done by the agent has a range that eludes his power. A single action can produce non-intentional consequences that entail a series of unforeseen events. On the other hand, actions that are involuntarily coordinated between the agents may entail desired or undesired consequences. The consequences of actions have the potential of constituting the context in which subsequent actions will unfold: "This consequences influence in return the conditions of future accomplishment of these repetitive actions, in such a way that they may occur again in a context that resembles the one where they were initially carried out"[6] (Rojot, 1998, p.7). At last, agents are only rarely conscious about the motives driving their behaviours: "Unconscious motivation is a significant feature of human conduct (…)" (Giddens 1984, p.6).

Giddens (1984) distinguishes the motivation of the reflexive monitoring from the rationalization of the action. While reflexive monitoring and rationalization are directly concerned with the way in which the agents carry out their actions in a regular basis, the motivation of the action refers to the potential consequences of the actions. Contrarily to reflexive monitoring and rationalization, motivation is not part of all the actions that the agents carry out: "Motives tend to have a direct purchase on action only in relatively unusual circumstances, situations which in some way break with the routine ([7]). (…) Much of our day-to-day conduct is not directly motivated" (Giddens 1984, p.6).

---

6   Free translation from the text published originally in French.

7   According to Giddens (1984), the routine "(…) is integral both to continuity of the personality of the agent, as he or she moves along the paths of daily activities, and to the institutions of society, which *are* such only through their continued reproduction" (p.60).

We insist, during the action, motivations reside in the unconscious (see Figure 1). Giddens (1984) gives to the concept of unconscious a different meaning that the one proposed by the Freudian School. It contains the foundation of the actions for which the agent does not possess any knowledge and he cannot express: "(…) the existential anguish, the seeking of an ontological security and the desire to conserve the self-identity are the main motives (unconscious) of the action (…)"[8] (Lamont, 1993, p. 437). As ontological security, Giddens (1990) refers to the confidence that agents place in the extension of their self-identity as well as the constancy of both their natural and social worlds.

To the unconscious, Giddens (1984) adds the discursive consciousness and the practical consciousness. In doing so, he proposes to replace the triade of the Freudian psychoanalysis of the self, the ego, the superego and the id, by flowing strata: the discursive consciousness, the practical consciousness and the unconscious (see Figure 4.1).

The discursive consciousness forms the reservoir of knowledge, feelings, etc., that the agent can verbalize. The justification of actions, second aspect of the rationalization of action emphasized before, mobilizes the implementation of the agent's discursive capability. Regarding the practical consciousness, it contains what the agent knows how to do, but is incapable of expressing in a discursive way (Rojot, 1998); it is the main habitat of the reflexive monitoring of the action. The practical consciousness contains two analytical elements: mutual knowledge and common sense. Mutual knowledge refers to interpretative schemes. It is on the basis of interpretative schemes that individuals, on the one hand, arrange their perceptions, and, on the other hand, give meaning to the social life in which they participate. Concerning the analytical element of common sense, it refers to beliefs engaged into daily actions. The agent utilizes its common sense "(…) to explain why things are the way they are, or why they occur in the way they do in the natural and social world"[9] (Rojot, 1998, p.11).

The Duality of the Structure

Éraly (1988) emphasizes that the main interest of the theoretical reasoning that Giddens pursuits for the organizations theory lies on the idea that action and structure are the facets of a unique social reality: the rules and the resources of a social system, whose structural properties are at the same time the conditions and the outcome of the human conduct (Éraly, 1988; Giddens 1979, 1984, 1998; Rojot, 1998).

According to some authors, Giddens lacks preciseness when he defines the notion of rules (Bailyn, 2002). Having said that, when Giddens talks about rules, it is clear to Bailyn (2002) that he is referring to Wittegenstein's "knowing how to go on". Consequently, the rules of social life are defined as the "techniques or generalizable procedures applied in enactment/reproduction of social practices" (Giddens 1984, p.21). Two types of rules are distinguished: interpretative and

---

8   Free translation from the text published originally in French.
9   Free translation from the text published originally in French.

normative: "Interpretative rules govern the way actors interpret the world in which they live. They constitute the cognitive aspect of social structure. Normative rules regulate the legitimization of actions" (Berends, Boersma and Weggeman, 2003a, p. 1040). The rules of interpretative nature form the structures of *signification*, and the normative rules, those of *legitimation*. To these two dimensions of the structure, Giddens (1979, 1984) adds a third one, closely linked with the notion of power.

Power is the capacity that the agent possesses to gather resources in order to, on the one hand, see to it that the other agent's action achieves the expected results, and, on the other hand, to intervene on the events in order to change their course (Giddens 1984). The resources that power mobilizes form the structures of *domination*. The first line on Figure 4.2 refers to the rules and the resources that compose the three dimensions of the structure.

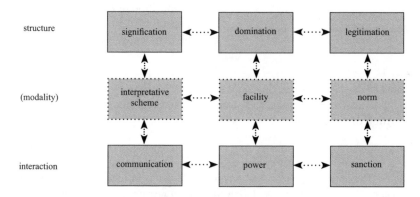

Figure 4.2   The dimensions of duality of structure (Giddens 1984: 29)

Giddens (1979, 1984) classes the resources that form the structures of *domination* under two categories (see Table 4.1): the allocative resources and the authoritative resources. Allocative resources bring together the "material resources involved in the generation of power, including the natural environment and physical artifacts (...)" (Giddens 1984, p. 373), whereas authoritative resources are associated with "non-material resources involved in the generation of power, deriving from the capability of harnessing the activities of human beings (...)" (Giddens 1984, p. 373).

The last line on Figure 4.2 highlights three interaction elements. Concerning these three elements, Lazar (1992) states:

> It is not a question of a typology of interactions, but a matter of presenting the diverse dimensions of social practices, combined in different ways. The communication of significations, while interacting, is not separated from the exercise of power or from the context of normative sanctions. These three elements are included in every social practice.[10] (pp. 412–413).

---

10   Free translation from the text published originally in French.

Table 4.1   **Resources that constitute the structures of domination, classified in allocative resources and authoritative resources (Giddens 1984, p. 258)**

Allocative Resources	Authoritative Resources
1. Material features of the environment (raw materials, material power sources)	1. Organization of social time-space (temporal-spatial constitution of paths regions)
2. Means of material production/reproduction (instruments of production, technology)	2. Production/reproduction of the body (organization and relation of human beings in mutual association)
3. Produced goods (artifacts created by interaction of 1 and 2)	3. Organization of life chances (constitution of chances of self-development and self-expression)

Giddens (1979, 1984) refers the modalities, core aspects of the structure duality, to the mediation of interaction and structure inside the process of production and reproduction of social aspects.

> Firstly, human communication involves the use of interpretative schemes which are stocks of knowledge that human actors draw upon in order to make sense of their own and others' actions. They thereby produce and reproduce structures of meaning which are termed structures of signification. Secondly, human agents utilise power in interaction by drawing on facilities such as the ability to allocate material and human resources; in so doing, they produce and reproduce structures of domination. Finally, human agents sanction their actions by drawing on norms or standards of morality and thus produce and reproduce social structures of legitimation. (Walsham and Han, 1991, p. 78).

On Figure 4.2, the arrows between the lines mark the recursive nature of the duality of the structure, while the arrows between the columns indicate the interdependence of the three aspects of the duality of the structure during the production and reproduction of the social aspects (Cohen, 1989). In order to illustrate the interdependence between the interpretation schemes (modality of the first column) and the norms (modality of the third column), Giddens (1984) resorts to the idea of responsibility in the sense of *accountability*.

> To be 'accountable' for one's activities is both to explicate the reasons for them and to supply normative grounds whereby they may be 'justified'. Normative components of interaction always centre upon relations between the rights and obligations 'expected' of those participating in a range of interaction contexts. Formal codes of conduct, as, for example, those enshrined in law (in contemporary societies at least), usually express, some sort of claimed symmetry between rights and obligations, the one being the justification of the other. But no such symmetry necessarily exists in practice, a phenomenon which it is important to emphasize, since both the 'normative functionalism' of Parsons and the 'structuralist Marxism' of Althusser exaggerates the degree to which normative obligations are 'internalized' by the members of societies. Neither standpoint incorporates a theory of

action which recognizes human beings as knowledgeable agents, reflexively monitoring the flow of interaction with one another. (Giddens 1984, p. 30).

Giddens' agent is potentially capable of a responsibility that goes beyond simple 'accountability'. Following Jonas (1998) "man is the only being that we know who may have a responsibility; if he may have responsibility, he has it. The capacity of responsibility means being placed already under its command: power itself entails duty within it".[11] (p. 76). Even if Giddens (1979, 1984) has never been truly interested in the agent's capacity of responsibility, it seems possible to build up links between the conscience (both discursive and practical), the reflexive monitoring of the action, the rationalization (typical features of Giddens' agent) and the capacity of responsibility as understood by Jonas.

> The capacity of responsibility – capacity of ethical order – is based on the ontological faculty of the human being to choose, knowingly and deliberately, between the alternatives of the action. Responsibility is therefore complementary to free will. It is the burden of freedom proper to an active subject: I am responsible for my action as such (as well as its omission), regardless if there is somebody who asks me to be accountable for it sooner or later[12] (Jonas, 1998, p.76).

In this way, on the grounds of the features in which Giddens' agent bases its knowledgeability, the agent possesses as well the capacity of responsibility, having for objective any *being* affected by its actions. It is important to emphasize that according to Jonas, responsibility takes an ethical meaning if the being has any worth, and because of this value, the *being* possesses a right over the human agent: "in front of a being of indifferent value, I can answer to everything, which amounts to saying that I do not need to answering anything"[13] (Jonas, 1998, p. 78).

From an organizations' structural analysis point of view, the above means that in a daily basis, individuals making part of organizations are knowledgeable agents and, given that they are knowledgeable, they are capable of being responsible. Consequently, when the organizational actor[14] begins an interaction involving clients, shareholders, colleagues, citizens who share the same environment as the organization, etc., he is capable of being responsible (capacity of ethical order) towards those from whom he recognizes a value that calls him to duty. The interaction that we just referred, and which is made up of the three elements that form the last line on Figure 4.2, is located in a time-space frame.

---

11   Free translation from the text published originally in French.

12   Free translation from the text published originally in French.

13   Free translation from the text published originally in French.

14   Giddens (1984) uses in an indistinctive way the terms actor and agent. This practice meets the common use that "(...) reserves the first to individuals considered as autonomous and the second to 'individuals' acting by forces beyond themselves or that they ignore" (Free translation) (Rojot, 1998, p.6).

Time, Space and Regionalization

The spatio-temporal nature of Giddens' social interaction is established from the coordination of the agents' activities occurring in numerous places on a daily basis. The locale refers to the space that agents use as interaction frame. It can be a country, a province, a city, a neighbourhood, a firm, the workshop of a factory, etc. The physical characteristics of a place, as well as the families of actions that it lodges, allow the agent to define the locale and recognize it: "A 'house' is grasped as such only if the observer recognizes that it is a 'dwelling' with a range of other properties specified by the modes of its utilization in human activity" (Giddens, 1984, p. 118).

A locale is regionalized. It is not only located in an area but also it is divided, cut into zones, according to a set routine of social behaviour. In this way, the interactions of an agent in a region of space such as his office can be different from those of another area in the same place, as it is the case of a conference room. The regions of space accommodated in a locale are separated by physical or symbolical frontiers. This distinction between the regions favours the concentration of interactions. Giddens (1984) gives the name of regionalization to "(...) temporal, spatial or time-space differentiation of regions either within or between locales (...)" (p. 376).

Combined both with the co-presence of actors and with the communication established between them, the properties of a locale, give a 'contextuality' to the interactions that occur in it. In this way, by definition, contextuality implies exchanges between co-present human agents, during which, it is highly likely that the capacity of responsibility has a potential of being mobilized. To this reciprocity between individuals in a context of co-presence, Giddens (1984) gives the name of social integration.[15] But, the notion of co-presence, how should it be understood?

The Co-presence and the Absence

Giddens (1979, 1984) defines the co-presence on the same meaning as Goffman (1963):

> The full conditions of co-presence, however, are found in less variable circumstances: persons must sense that they are close enough to be perceived in whatever they are doing, including their experiencing of others, and close enough to be perceived in this sensing of being perceived. In our walled-in Western society, these conditions are ordinarily expected to obtain throughout the space contained in a room, and to obtain for any and all persons present in the room. On public streets (and in other relatively unobstructed places) the region of space in which mutual presence can be said to prevail cannot be clearly drawn, since persons who are present at different point along the street may be able to observe, and be observed by, slightly different set of others. (pp. 17–18).

In other words, co-presence is the condition in which agents interact among each other, meeting face to face (Zhao, 2003). To this condition of co-presence, Giddens (1984) adds however the following point: "Although the 'full conditions of co-presence'

---

15   The term *social* should be understood in the restrictive sense of encounters that either take place or are or were cancelled (Giddens, 1984; Giordano, 1998).

exist only in unmediated contact between those who are physically preset, mediated contacts that permit some of the intimacies of co-presence are made possible in the modern era by electronic communication, most notably the telephone" (p. 68). In doing so, Giddens (1984) introduces the feeling of *being together* in a media covered environment.[16]

Summarizing, to Giddens (1984), co-presence is a condition of interaction that mobilizes the physical aspects of agents. In the same way, co-presence is perception and feeling, the feeling of being perceived, or even more, the feeling of *being together*. Within the framework of a different approach than the one followed by Giddens (1984), Zhao (2003) felt the need to clarify the confusion surrounding the notion of co-presence by proposing instead a bidimentional conception of it: "I regard human co-presence as consisting of both the physical conditions in which human individuals interact and the perception and feeling they have of one other. Whereas the physical conditions constitute the mode of co- presence, perceptions and feeling constitute the sense of co-presence" (p. 446).

In the organization, the great majority of interactions takes place in a context of co-presence as understood by Giddens. However, there are situations during which individuals exercise their behaviour through absence. They are alone attending to their own affairs without the presence (physical or mediated) of a colleague, or even of a client. In other cases, they have to make decisions that potentially may cause an impact on future clients, or even on their own future descendants. While Giddens (1979, 1984) discusses prolifically about co-presence, he treats the absence very vaguely. We have nevertheless picked out some indications about the definition of the notion of absence that he holds, by taking his reflections on *time, space and regionalisation.*

Giddens (1984) structures his conception of time-space around the spatio-temporal geography of Hägerstrand: "In stressing the corporeality of the human being in structured time-space contexts, Hägerstrand's ideas accord closely those I (Giddens) have sought to elaborate (in structured theory)" (pp.116–117). For Hägerstrand (1982), the term *corporeality* refers to the physical aspects of the body. For every human agent, the corporeal structures constitute a constraint: because of the architecture of the body, certain actions are impossible, and at the same time, they are a means of action. Relying on the support of Hägerstrand's geography, Giddens (1984) gives a great importance to the role played by corporeality in the constitution of a locale: "The constitution of locales certainly depends upon the phenomena given pride of place by Hägerstrand: the body, its media of mobility and communication, in relation to physical properties of the surrounding world" (p. 118). The importance granted to corporeality in the constitution of interaction frames, linked to the corporeal beings at the core of the conception of the agent or of the action, allows to understand clearly that Giddens' agent acts (and consequently lives in the locale) by means of his body – therefore physically. This premise is on

---

16   Since the publication of *The Constitution of Society*, the world of information and communication technology has known numerous innovations. In this way, due to technology, the feeling of presence can be exercised while individuals are in separated locations, or even more, while they interact through virtual space (the Internet).

the other hand supported by the principle of packing together in the Hägerstrand's[17] time-space for which Giddens takes his time to clarify.

From the above we understand that Giddens' agent is absent of an interaction frame if he does not act physically there; in other words, if he does not live in the locale physically. Furthermore, it is under these conditions of absence that Giddens (1984) bases the system integration: "System integration refers to connections with those who are physically absent in time or space" (p. 28). Amazingly, this conception of absence is not linked with the one of co-presence presented before. Even if it is possible to pick out two aspects of the giddensian co-presence (mode and sense), only the physical dimension is used to understand the absence. Wrongly, it could have been possible to believe that Giddens' agent is absent from a time-space encounter, if he is not there physically, or even more, if the agents living in a locale do not experiment any perception or do not experience any feeling of presence towards themselves.

As far as the responsibility arena is concerned, the theory of structuration raises, among others, these two questions. In order to develop an organization theory supported by the theory of structuration, does it mean to postulate that human agents will use their capacity of responsibility towards an alter-ego only with the condition of co-presence? In which way, the capacity of responsibility will be mobilized in a context of absence?

We would like to remind that the capacity of responsibility, which we formerly made reference to, is of ethical order, and that ethics are based on an ontological foundation. Aside the links he forged, with Goffman's and Hägerstrand' works, Giddens (1984) develops an ontology in which the presence of the agents' bodies plays a capital role: the body is an important medium to the constitution of social reality (and, to be specific, of organizational reality).

From all that we have picked out since the first section of the present chapter, we infer that Giddens' agents who form an organization are pictured as responsible towards clients, shareholders, colleagues, citizens who share the same environment as the organization, etc., as well as for the cases where they recognize their values and where they are physically present. I have a moral responsibility towards the alter-ego given that its presence mobilizes inside of me my own responsibility (as ethical capacity): there is someone, *there, facing me*, whose physical presence *reminds me* that I have to take into consideration his well-being. I have to measure my actions upon his own reality.

In conditions of absence, as understood by Giddens (1984), there is not a body to remind the agent the existence of the alter ego. The absentee cannot solicit anything concerning himself, hence he depends upon the capacity of responsibility of the present agent. Even though he is the only one who occupies a locale, the agent can show he is responsible, but this responsibility comes down to his *accountability*. In this sense, the responsibility shown by Giddens' agent in context of absence, does not

---

17   "The limited 'packing capacity' of time-space. No two human bodies can occupy the same space at the same time; physical objects have the same characteristic. Therefore, any zone of time-space can be analysed in terms of constraints over the two types of objects which can be accommodated within it." (Giddens, 1984, p. 112).

fall in the order of its ethical faculties, but rather, as we have previously emphasized, in the order of the structure, and more precisely, of a particular configuration of interpretation rules and norms to which we give the name of 'code of conduct'.

We mentioned that structural properties are both the conditions and the results of actions localized in the time-space. Properties extensively stretched in the time-space,[18] are called structural principles. Structural principles are the result of the agents' behaviours over numerous time-spaces and structural properties are the result of localized actions that are justified by structural principles (Fuchs, 2003). In this way, in a given time-space, by the intervention of structural principles, absent agents can have an impact on the conduct of present agents. In other words, there is a system integration. Even if there is no other agent physically present with him, these rules of interpretation and these norms (the conduct code) have a strong chance of conditioning the behaviour of an individual simply because it is possible that sooner or later, he may be held accountable for his actions towards the absent agents.

If the unconscious and the non-intentional consequences of actions limit the potential knowledgeability of Giddens' agents, it appears that the capacity of responsibility, as an ethical capacity, is restricted to contexts of co-presence (physical). As a result of that, choosing the theory of structuration as a conceptual architecture of the organization reverts to inscribe our reasoning in the traditional ethical systems: " To Jonas, the specific universe of traditional ethics is limited to the immediate environment of the restricted range action, in a short time and shared by contemporaries (…)"[19] (Homs, 2006).

On the previous paragraphs we have been discussing about the absentees. How did Giddens (1984) imagine the absent agents? Ancestors, individuals who live in other locales, future and potential human beings? It is difficult to answer this question. Obviously, the actions our ancestors came up with, as well as those lead nowadays by individuals that live in a different time-space than ours, have the potential to constitute an order of interpretation rules and norms, a conduct code, in the basis of which we have potentially explained and justified our actions. Our late predecessors took part in their time to the construction of conduct codes, among others, to establish guidelines for today's responsible acts. We conceive nowadays configurations of interpretation rules and norms that will condition the behaviour of future descendants.[20]

For Jonas (1998), the ethical faculty, which is the capacity of responsibility, contains all conditions: the presence as well as the absence. For the particular case of future and potential alter egos, Jonas (1998) bases the capacity of responsibility on the ethics of the future. Contrarily to the traditional ethical principles that we find in Giddens (1979, 1984), ethic in a jonasian (1998) future does not appoint a configuration of interpretative rules and norms, nor a conduct code that has been conceived today for our future descendants, "(…) but a nowadays ethics that is

---

18   This extent varies from one author to another.

19   Free translation from the text published originally in French.

20   This participation of past and present agents to the constitution of conduct codes could have been conscious or not, intentional or not.

concerned by the future of our descendants and that it intends to protect it from the consequences of our present actions"[21] (p.69).

In which way is it possible to restore the human agent's capacity of responsibility, and its ethical faculties, in conditions of absence?

The Capacity of Responsibility and the Conditions of Absence

In this section, we lead a '*re*conceptualization' on two planes: the human agent and the conditions of absence.

The Re-examined Concept of Human Agent

Emirbayer and Mishe (1998) propose a conception of the agent different from Giddens' (1979, 1984), given the importance they attached to temporality.

> What (…) is human agency? We define it as *the temporally constructed engagement by actors of different structural environments—the temporal-relational contexts of action— which, through the interplay of habit, imagination, and judgment, both reproduces and transforms those structures in interactive response to the problems posed by changing historical situations.* (p. 970).

This definition incorporates three processes that characterize the human agent: iteration, projection and practical evaluation.

The iterational element refers to the routine process during which the agent integrates into his ordinary run of things, schemes of thought and action that he selected from his past (Emirbayer and Mishe, 1998). Through the integration of elements from the past to the present, the agent chooses to reproduce existing structures (Hatch, 2006). Furthermore, thanks to the projection, "(…) the possibilities of the future signal creative options that allow for the intentional or even planned reconfiguration of existing structure." (Hatch, 2006 p.125). In short, the practical-evaluative element, "it entails *the capacity of actors to make practical and normative judgments among alternative possible trajectories of action, in response to the emerging demands, dilemmas, and ambiguities of presently evolving situations.*" (Emirbayer and Mishe, 1998, p. 971). On the basis of these judgments of practical and normative order, agents can adopt conducts that will reproduce the existing structures, or even more, that will favour their changes (Hatch, 2006). Emirbayer and Mishe (1998) have identified the practical-evaluative dimension of the human agent, among others, following critical analyses of different philosophical systems (Aristotle, Kant, Dewey, Arendt, Habermas). These critical analyses have been focused over numerous fundamental matters, some of which are of ethical order. The practical-evaluative dimension of agency forms, without a doubt, the home of the capacity of ethical order, which is the moral responsibility. In this sense, contrary to Giddens (1979, 1984), Emirbayer and Mishe (1998) clearly identify the ethical

---

21   Free translation from the text published originally in French.

capacities as a faculty of human agents.[22] As a whole, these three processes "(...) help to set structuration in motion by permitting agents to reach both backward and forward in time to structure their present activities" (Hatch, 2006, p. 125).

The works of Emirbayer and Mishe (1998) go further than a simple redefinition of the human agent. They are seen as a new theory of structuration, which following the example of Giddens, emphasizes mostly on the human agent (Hatch, 2006). In terms of responsibility and absence, what are the implications of Emirbayer and Mishe (1998) in the new theory of structuration?

As well as in a situation of presence, in conditions of absence of the alter ego, the Emirbayer and Mishe's (1998) agent is capable of being responsible on the frame of an ethical nature. In fact, since he has planning capacity, the agent is able to asses the consequences that his behaviour produces upon the reality of the absent alter ego.[23] This goes even further. By combining these three processes previously presented, the agent can correct in the present, the potentially disastrous consequences of a past action upon the reality of the absent alter ego.

The Emirbayer and Mishe's (1998) Theory of Structuration, following the example of Giddens (1979, 1984), has the social aspect as its main subject of study. Nevertheless, it is possible to make a list of authors and researchers who appeal to these two theories of structuration in order to have a better understanding of a variety of constructs linked with the organizations. Contrarily, the influence that Emirbayer and Mishe's (1998) Theory of Structuration has on management works amounts to a lesser degree. In fact, in journals and reviews identified as having a greater influence on the field of management, we have made a list of some articles that deal, or even more, that are inspired on the Emirbayer and Mishe's (1998) theory. However, in those same journals and reviews, we were able to make a list of dozens of articles that deal with Giddens' works (1979, 1984). Given the importance that authors and researchers in management[24] seem to grant to Anthony Giddens' Theory of Structuration, instead of choosing a new conception of the human agent (and at the same time a new theory of structuration), it appears to us that it is important to reflect on the conditions of absence in which Giddens' agent mobilizes his capacity of responsibility.

---

22   Certainly, the matter about the link between the Jonas' ethics and what emerges form the critical analyses of Emirbayer and Mishe (1998) is laid down. However, to dwell on details, would take us away from our initial objective: the structuration as a theoretical foundation of the organization.

23   The alter ego is not only a contemporary being, but also a future and potential descendent. It implies that he is capable of being concerned by the future and wishes to protect it for the descendants from the consequences of his present action.

24   Tahai and Meyer (1999) have identified seven journals that influence the most the field of management: Strategic Management Journal, Academy Management journal, Journal of Applied Psychology, Organizational Behaviour and Human Decision Process, Academy of Management Review, Administrative Sciences Quarterly, and Journal of Management.

Some Reflections about the Presence and the Absence

Goffman (1963), from whom Giddens (1984) borrows the notion of co-presence, has lead his observations on the social organization of meetings, among others, with patients of a psychiatric specialized hospital centre. By the same token, during his psychiatric clinic experiences, Janet (1928) has lead reflections on presence and absence. The conclusions drawn by Janet and Goffman, as a result of their experiences, are nonetheless different. We see in Janet a conceptual way from which it is possible to remedy Giddens' (1984) balance problem between co-presence and absence.

During his psychiatric clinic experiences, Janet (1928) noticed that some persons who were set in conditions where perception was impossible, said to having felt physical presence. He concludes that "(...) presence is not a perception, it is something else linked to perception but it is not (...)"[25] (p. 123). It is a feeling, the feeling of presence. Janet (1928) distinguishes clearly the feeling of presence from perception: "(...) there are some cases where the feeling of presence exists without perception; there are other cases where the feeling of presence disappears even though under complete perceptive conditions"[26] (p. 121). In the latter case, there is a feeling of absence. For Giddens, the feeling of presence is mediated (by a technique) whereas for Janet, it has no need for mediation in order to have the feeling of presence.

The feeling of presence identified by Janet (1928) is not exclusive to people affected with psychiatric problems. It is common in certain situations to experience the feeling of the presence of an individual who is situated in another time-space. For us, this feeling of presence is not unusual simply because it rekindles the consciousness of the alter ego. The consciousness of the alter ego is defined as what the agent living in a society knows or feels of the alter ego's reality. Among other things, the social agent knows that some individuals live in other time-spaces. He feels, at the same time, the potential of future descendants and of their reality.

Even if the alter ego is absent, the agent can have the feeling of presence, simply because he knows or feels about the absentee's reality. On the basis of this knowledge, the human agent has the capacity, if he desires it, to appeal to his ethical faculties in order to adopt responsible conducts towards the alter ego, regardless if the alter ego is present.

Is it possible to acknowledge the fact that Giddens' agent may experience feelings of presence that are not mediated by any kind of technique? In other words, without having to question Giddens' description of the individual, is it possible to recognize the consciousness potential of Giddens' agent alter ego and consequently, the exercise of a responsibility of ethical order towards the absent?

Given that Giddens' agent is first of all a social agent, he possesses, without a doubt, the consciousness of the alter ego. May the feeling of presence of the alter ego be exercised in conditions of absence? In all likelihood, as it is the case for the

---

25   Free translation from the text published originally in French.
26   Free translation from the text published originally in French.

majority of the human beings. Presenting the facts differently[27] consists in granting as true two propositions, which may seem amazing, about the conduct of social agents in conditions of absence. First proposition: in conditions of absence, Giddens' agent is unable of having a non-mediated feeling of presence, and consequently, he has no consciousness of the alter ego. He thinks he is alone in the world and he thinks he is the centre of the universe – there are no duties but those towards himself. As corollary to this premise (second proposition): in each one of the experiences of presence, Giddens' agent has the potential to living an experience comparable to Piaget's' Copernicus revolution.[28] In other words, the agent becomes aware that his body is no longer the centre of the world, but an object among other objects that are now related between each other, either linked by causality or by spatial relations, the whole in a coherent space that encompasses them all.

Immersed in conditions of presence and absence, as understood by Janet (1928), Giddens' agent is capable of being responsible when he rests on a particular configuration of interpretation schemes and norms. For instance, on the basis of the conduct code of his organization, an employee is able of justifying his behaviour towards another employee who is right there facing him. In these same conditions of presence and absence, Giddens' agent is equally capable of being responsible when he rests on his ethical faculties. For example, a manager who is conscious of future descendants and their potential reality, can decide to choose a method of production, which is less polluting in order to protect tomorrow's environment, today.

Conclusion

During the study of the leading management journals and reviews, we noticed the constant influence that Anthony Giddens' (1979, 1984) Theory of Structuration exercises on the conceptual architectures of the organization, even if the organization is not the main subject of Giddens' reflections.

Organizational theories inspired by Giddens' (1979, 1984) works highlight the dependent relation between the organization and the individuals: the organization is the result of human actions; simultaneously, human actions are conditioned by the organization. In a structurationist perspective, some authors associate responsibility to the firm when it is not in the organization order, but in the nature of the individuals, who constitute the organization: human agents have the capacity of responsibility.

Giddens (1979, 1984) attaches a lot of importance to conditions of co-presence as a context of interactions of individuals. These conditions of co-presence limit the scope of the capacity of responsibility of an ethical nature in Giddens' agents. This

---

27   To our understanding, it is what Giddens (1984) appears to do.

28   During the sensori-motivity period, first stage of the individual's development in Piaget, the most fundamental and quick changes are occurring. Using again Piaget's words, it is a matter of a real Copernican revolution: "(…) during the first year and half or so, a Copernican revolution takes place, in the sense that now the child's own body is no longer the centre, but has become an object among other objects, and objects now are related to each other by either causal relationships, or spatial relationships, in a coherent space that englobes them all" (Evans, 1973, p.16).

capacity of responsibility is exerted towards people who are physically present, who are possible to be perceived, or even more, to people in touch via a technological device (e.g. the telephone), towards whom we experience a feeling of presence. In a situation of absence, responsibility only takes the aspect of accountability. It is possible to establish a link between the limit of the scope of Giddens' agent's responsibility and the traditional ethical principles. We believe it is possible to go past the traditional ethical principles implicit to Anthony Giddens' Theory of Structuration by re-examining the conditions of presence and absence in the light of Janet's (1928) observations.

Janet (1928) picks out situations in which people have felt the presence of a being who is objectively absent: a non-mediated feeling of presence by any kind of technique. In this sense, in a giddensian structuration perspective of organizations, the feeling of presence has the potential to rekindle again in the agent the consciousness of the alter ego. In a situation of presence, or when feeling a presence mediated by a specific technique, the alter ego's consciousness falls on his contemporaries and their reality (for example, a client on the phone, a colleague facing us, etc.). In the cases of a non mediated feeling of presence, the alter ego's consciousness affects both his contemporaries and its reality as an inhabitant of another region of space (for example, the citizen who lives in the same neighbourhood than the organization, a future client, etc.) as well as a future being and his potential reality (future children and having as well a feeling of their environment). For the whole of these conditions of feeling of presence, the capacity of responsibility of Giddens' agents rests on uniting the reflexive monitoring of the action with the rationalization (two capacities of the agent that have as home the giddensian consciousness), the alter ego's consciousness and his ethical faculties. From that moment, the responsibility shown by the agent simultaneously has an accountability nature as well as an ethical nature.

This chapter does not claim to having considered from all angles the matter of responsibility broached in the field of organization theory. It humbly proposes a first thought about a possible link to be established between Anthony Giddens' Theory of Structuration – for which authors and researchers in the organization science seem to have a certain interest, and Hans Jonas' works. We simply hope to pass on to others the desire for exploring possible links between the fields of both organization theory and philosophy, in order to create new prospects about organizations.

References

Bailyn, S. J. (2002). Who Makes the Rules? Using Wittgenstein in Social Theory. *J Theory of Social Behaviour, 32*(3), 311–329.

Berends, H., Boersma, K., and Weggeman, M. (2003a). The Structuration of Organizational Learning. *Human Relations, 56*(9), 1035–1056.

Berends, H., Boersma, K., and Weggeman, M. (2003b). The structuration of organizational learning. *Human Relations, 56*(9), 1035.

Burrell, G. and Morgan, G. (1979). *Sociological Paradigms and Organisational Analysis.* London: Heinemann.

Cohen, I. J. (1989). *Structuration Theory. Anthony Giddens and the Constitution of Social Life.* New York: St. Martin's Press.

Delas, J.-P. and Milly, B. (2005). *Histoire des pensées sociologiques* (2ème ed.). Paris: Armand Colin.

Donaldson, L. (2003). Organization theory as a positive science. In H. Tsoukas and C. Knudsen (Eds.), *The Oxford handbook of organization theory* (pp. 39–62). Oxford: Oxford University Press.

Emirbayer, M. and Mische, A. (1998). What is agency? *American Journal of Sociology, 103*(4), 962–1023.

Eraly, A. (1988). *La structuration de l'entreprise. La rationalité en action.* Bruxelles: Éditions de l'Université de Bruxelles.

Evans, R. I. (1973). *Jean Piaget the man and his ideas. Transl. by Eleanor Duckworth.* New York: Dutton.

Fuchs, C. (2003). Structuration Theory and Self-Organization. *Systemic Practice and Action Research, 16*(2), 133.

Giddens, A. (1979). *Central Problems in Social Theory.* Berkeley: University of California Press.

Giddens, A. (1984). *The Constitution of Society.* Cambridge: Polity Press.

Giddens, A. (1990). *The consequences of modernity.* Stanford, Calif.: Stanford University Press.

Giddens, A. (1993). *New Rules of Sociological Method* (2 ed.). Standford: Standford University Press.

Giddens, A. (1998). *Conversation with Anthony Giddens. Making Sense of Modernity.* Cambridge: Polity Press.

Giordano, Y. (1998). Une reconsidération par la théorie de la structuration. *Revue de gestion des ressources humaines, 26–27*, 20.

Goffman, E. (1963). *Behavior in Public Places. Notes on the social organization of gatherings.* New York: The Free Press.

Hägerstrand, T. (1982). Diorama, Path and Project. *Tijdschrift voor Economische en Sociale Geografie 73*, 323–339.

Hatch, M.J. (1997). *Organization Theory. Modern, symbolic and postmodern perspectives.* Oxford: Oxford University Press.

Hatch, M.J. (2006). *Organization Theory. Modern, symbolic and postmodern perspectives.* (Second ed.). Oxford: Oxford University Press.

Hatch, M.J. and Yanow, D. (2003). Organization theory as a positive science. In H. Tsoukas and C. Knudsen (Eds.), *The Oxford handbook of organization theory* (pp. 63–87). Oxford: Oxford University Press.

Homs, C. (2006). *Hans Jonas et le principe responsabilité*, Website : http://www.decroissance.info/Hans-Jonas-et-le-principe, consulted in april 2006.

Janet, P. (1928). *La durée* (Vol. I). Paris: Collège de France.

Jonas, H. (1995). *Le principe responsabilité une éthique pour la civilisation technologique.* Paris: Flammarion.

Jonas, H. (1998). *Pour une éthique du futur.* Paris: Rivages.

Lamont, M. (1993). Fierté, honte, identité de soi et frontières symboliques. In M. Audet and H. Bouchiki (Eds.), *Structuration du social et modernité avancée. Autour des travaux d'Anthony Giddens.* (pp. 437–441). Québec: PUL.

Lazar, J. (1992). The Competence of the Actors in Structuration Theory. *Cahiers Internationaux de Sociologie, 39*(93), 399–416.

Rojot, J. (1998). La théorie de structuration. *Revue de Gestion des Ressources Humaines, 26–27*, 5–19.

Seyfarth, B. (2000). Structuration Theory in Small Group Communication In M.E. Roloff (Ed.), *Communication Yearbook* (Vol. 23, pp. 341–379). New York: Sage.

Tahai, A. and Meyer, M.J. (1999). A revealed preference study of management journals' direct influences. *Strategic Management Journal, 20*(3), 279–296.

Walsham, G. and Han, C.K. (1991). Structuration Theory and Information Systems Research. *Journal of Applied Systems Analysis, 17*, 77–85.

Zaho, S. (2003). Toward a Taxonomy of Copresence. *Presence, 12*(5), 445–455.

Chapter 5

Suffering as a Quest for Adaptation

Pierre-Paul Morin

Suffering as a Quest for Adaptation

Some words are not usual in business literature. One of them is love, another one is suffering. Most organisational development literature would rather use words like respect and strain as their equivalent. One of the reasons for that seems to be that strong emotions are usually considered incompatible with proper business behaviours. Once described as "sicknesses of the soul", emotions have been and are still often identified as weaknesses in a working environment. Some authors discuss the virtues of acting rationally, without emotions, as if this could be studied outside of the concept of emotions. Yet one may wonder, if this totally rational behaviour could really be observed, if the lack of emotion then displayed could not be classified as coldness or ruthlessness, an emotional definition nevertheless. Even taking moderate emotions into consideration may again be perceived by many as a mistake or at least as embarrassing (Ashkanasy, Härtel, Zerbe, 2000). If managers are strong, they will be able to take "tough decisions" often associated with the suppressing of their own emotional judgement. Strong employees will also be able to discard their feelings and take on challenging or even dangerous tasks.

Emotions and reason are indeed most of the time described as opposing functions, as if rationality necessarily excluded emotions. Yet, many contemporary authors now find emotions to be essential to taking *rational* decisions (Ashkanasy, Härtel and Zerbe, 2000; Lazarus, 1993; Lurie, 2004). The implied hypothesis is that emotions can be rational as well. They can be the predictable expression of the consequences of behaviours, as examined through conscious and unconscious values and beliefs. But how predictable can they be? Is this the true measure of what is called rationality? Is it possible to rationally seek to create a work environment in which positive emotions will be sought? Can this be an important aspect of managing a business? How can managers achieve this if they do not include emotions in their decisions?

In a world of "emotional intelligence" (Goleman, 1997), the ability of managers to relate to their fellow workers in a way that fosters their commitment and loyalty has become an essential skill. In order to do that, dealing rationally with empowering emotions already appears like a challenge for most managers. Dealing with negative emotions such as pain and suffering can be even more difficult. But, can the negative side of suffering be useful to organisations? Can it be helpful to foster adaptation and implement change?

When does Stress become Suffering?

The words used to designate suffering vary from one discipline to the other. Even though this is somewhat of a rough generalisation, the word suffering is used more often in the psychology or psychiatry field. When individual suffering comes from a pathological problem to adapt, it is called an adjustment disorder finding links in the field of sociology as well. Business literature very seldom refers to suffering. It refers more readily to stress, or eventually strain, the suffering part of stress.

Based on vocabulary alone, the interpretation of similar concepts take on different perspectives and are treated differently, in separate networks. Suffering is generally described as an individual concern. It also has a social, value loaded significance. It is something that should be avoided if possible and should not be tolerated for too long if it happens. Maybe this is why this word is not used in a working environment. The word strain seems more acceptable as the urgency or the seriousness of the problem seems to be more... manageable.

These differences in interpretation have deep consequences. If someone is *strained* at work while *suffering* on a personal basis, the solution to the problem will be sought in different networks, irrespective of the source of the problem. This may eventually create a disconnection between the organisation and the personnel, two realities that should be inseparable. It therefore becomes possible for suffering persons to seek a meaning to their working lives in the network of psychology or psychiatry, while the organization does not provide an acceptable answer to them. There can be many explanations to this. But many times organisations will propose to find a meaning to working life in reaching corporate goals, looking for a solution to reduce stress and strain in motivation and re-engineering programs. These programs typically have a low success rate both in their ability to improve business performance or to decrease stress and strain.

The abundance of literature available on stress reflects the importance of this concern. (Selye, 1974, Lazarus, 1993, Vakola and Nikolaou, 2005). All over the world, for at least the last thirty years, numerous studies have indicated not only a significant level of stress to be experienced by both workers and managers, but this level as being significantly on the rise (Vakola and Nikolaou, 2005). Those studies also show the cost of stress to be measured in billions of dollars each year (Perrewé and al, 2004). But, something less visible in the same context, stress also impacts individual, family and societal well-being, thereby increasing social costs even more. So, it is safe to say that excessive stress, or suffering, has become a major social issue.

Even though life would not be possible without some stress, it is now accepted that there are desirable and optimal levels of stress. Selye, 1974 and Lazarus, 1993 have been pioneers in studying this phenomenon. They have found that one cannot take action if a certain level of stress is not present. They also describe a level of stress at which performance is maximized. They found that when this level is exceeded, performance decreases and that, if stress is encountered for too long, permanent consequences will happen. They have also described concepts such as individual ability to cope with stress. Their work clearly demonstrates that certain people have a lower threshold than others. All these considerations clearly affect the management and the overall performance of organizations.

That eventually raises the question of the level of stress generated in one's specific job, versus the level of stress tolerated by one individual. Is the problem with the stressor or the stressee, or is it the match between the two? Over the years many attempts were made to measure the relative importance of stressors. One of the most renowned works is that of Holmes and Rahe, developed in 1967, but still referred to extensively today. It proposes standardized levels of stress for individuals based on specific life events. Examples of such would be the death of spouse or the loss of one's job. Stress levels for all relevant events are then added to give a total stress level. Interestingly these measurements, as we have seen, ignore the individual ability to resist stress and present stress on a universal scale. The same thinking is applied to organizations. For example, the National Institute of Occupational Safety & Health, from the US Department of Health and Human Services,[1] has come up with scales of what specifically creates stress in a work environment. Not only do they seem to have the same limitations as the individual model in terms of their inability to include individual stress tolerance level, but they also describe stressors in a generic way, referring to "heavy workloads" or "lack of support from peers" without giving a more specific measurement for these. So, at this point, organisations still have very few benchmarks to deal with stress and strain. They have to rely on their "intuitive" ability to detect it, and finding the causes does not seem any simpler.

Other research focuses on people's attitude or personality. Rathus, 1985, Friedman and Rosenman, 1974, and Matthews, 1982, have worked with the concept of personality types, referred to as Type A or Type B. Their work this time reflects the individual interpretation of stressors, linking them with the consequences on their health. Type A personalities are more concerned about time and performance than Type B personalities; they are generally more worried and have a different outlook on life. They are believed to incur a higher risk of a heart attack (Freidman and Rosenham, 1974). Again, the link between the stressor and the stressee is not attempted. Not only is this approach of little practical help but this also opens the question as to the social responsibility of organizations hiring Type A or Type B staff in specific jobs as well.

So, at this time, it seems very difficult to predict or even to analyse when stress crosses the frontier from being a business concern to being an individual problem. Or, if one was to cross the boundaries of language and disciplines, he may ask the question: when does stress become suffering?

An attempt to answering that question can be found in the organization's ability to detect individual stress symptoms and act appropriately on them. Because otherwise, as stress increases, or as one's ability to cope with it decreases, what business literature calls strain takes on another reality called suffering.

---

1   See its WebSite: http://www.cdc.gov/niosh/homepage.html, consulted in June 2006.

Suffering as a Symptom

Suffering is a state interpreted as a breech of integrity, a sense of powerlessness in the face of threats (Marcoux, 2005). Suffering is something that patients would describe as "touching their interior" not only their body (Wright, 2005). It is associated with a loss of control. As we continue making a link between suffering and stress, research shows that stress levels are usually inversely proportional to the perception of control. Therefore, suffering happens when someone has lost hope of finding personal or collective resources to face a threatening situation, thereby losing control over his destiny. For the person who suffers, the condition is generally easily detected: it is uncomfortable, it hurts. The state of suffering for an individual is not subjective, it is observable objectively. But the causes of that state can be subjective, because not everyone is affected by specific stressors on one part, and the level of stress created by those stressors can vary significantly on the other part. This may be one of the reasons why stress and suffering go so often undetected or ignored.

Suffering is a warning that something is going wrong. Physical suffering, pain, is useful to detect illnesses, or to indicate danger. Without pain, animals and humans would all undoubtedly be wounded... or even dead. So pain is very useful as a sign to indicate potential damage to oneself. It is a symptom of an inability to adapt to an unsuitable environment: the food is too hot, the load is too heavy, the shock is too big. From a psychological point of view, the same principles prevail. Suffering is a reaction to grief, loss, dreams unfulfilled, failures and mistakes, as interpreted through desires and expectations, through values and beliefs. It is also a reaction to unacceptable workloads, long hours, injustice, role conflict and so on. As for physical pain, it also indicates a need for adaptation or retreat.

Suffering is an invitation to act, to change, so that the person suffering is relieved from this state (Cunningham et al., 2002). Small suffering, as well as small pain, may not trigger immediate action. The reaction has a chance to get filtered by the intellect. The person gets a chance to choose the proper reaction, including no reaction at all. Intense suffering or pain usually triggers immediate reaction, referred to as reflex, many times not governed by rationality. Not only does one usually stop what one is doing but also may choose an inappropriate reaction.

Slowly increasing or recurring suffering, even if intense, may not trigger a reaction either. One gets used to the suffering and does not realize it has reached critical levels before the consequences are irreversible. This is another failure to take appropriate action. After the fact suffering indicates that one has exceeded the limits of his/her adaptability. It can only trigger action in the future. It may not be a sign of required adaptation but the sign of adaptation taking place.

So, suffering as an invitation to act, needs to be detected, understood and interpreted correctly. Even if many sufferings will trigger appropriate reactions, some have to be purposely ignored because they are not threatening, some because the adaptation or the remedy will take time to act, some because the cause cannot be cured. Moreover, some sufferings will not lead to appropriate actions. But all sufferings need to be recognized, diligently and competently assessed.

So why not get trained to recognize suffering?

Suffering as an Illness

As we have seen, research shows that not all individuals have the same threshold to stress and suffering. Also, this threshold typically varies with age and/or circumstances. When the resistance to stress is unusually low, or abnormally low, individual suffering may be pathological. In businesses, this condition is often hard to diagnose correctly. An employee may complain about a seemingly unimportant aspect of the work while not disclosing a potential major problem. Just as a properly identified symptom is an invitation to act, change and adapt, adjustment disorders, as they are called, should be treated on an individual basis. Ignored suffering, in this context, usually leads to increased levels of distress and eventually to the individual losing the ability to perform the work.

Suffering as a Learning Opportunity

We have defined suffering as a request for adaptation. The need for adaptation comes from an inappropriate match between the subject and its environment. For correct action to be taken, one has to be able to properly assess boundaries and then determine what the matching conditions are. This is an opportunity to become conscious one's limits, both in the sense of recognizing what they are and in the sense of knowing how far they can be extended. This is precious knowledge as it will keep one from getting involved in conditions where suffering would be experienced again. This would also foster consciousness for the conditions for which one is adapted and able to perform; and experience pleasure, the other side of suffering.

So, suffering is also an opportunity to learn. As the environment changes and as people themselves change, the ability to adapt is linked very closely with the ability to learn. If one detects it early, people can learn how to constantly probe their limits with the possibility to stay within the pleasurable, productive range. Senge, 1990, refers to this as creative tension and applies it to whole organisations. Much of what is true for individuals holds for learning organisations as well. This includes the difficulty that humans and organisations have to understand the long term consequences of short term actions and to learn from something that has not completely happened yet. In other words, today's solutions may very well create tomorrow's problems.

One example of how one can prepare now for long term potential problems would be to learn how to act "assertively". Such behaviour will lessen the uncertainty associated ambiguity in organisations (Tidd and Friedman, 2002). As change, role conflict and other challenges arise, adopting an active and assertive attitude increases adaptability and reduces stress. Along the same lines, the development of "political skills" has been proven empirically to improve one's ability to exercise perceived and actual control on the situation, reducing stress and suffering as well (Perrewé and al, 2004). Adopting the opposite attitude leads, as expected, to the opposite result. Therefore, with an early detection of suffering, preventive measures can help increase one's ability to avoid further occurrence.

People will naturally try to avoid suffering. Typically individuals will perform tasks for which they feel comfortable, staying away from those that present a risk of failure (Armenakis, Stanley and Mossholder, 1993). One way of doing this is to rely on experience. They have tried it before, and it hurts. When people do that, they make a link between the suffering and its source. They also make mistakes: they thought the problem was the temperature, but it was the acidity level. They thought the problem was the lack of money, but it was over-protection. So, another precious skill is that of being able to properly match the cause and the consequence. This in turn should limit unnecessary avoidance behaviours, fostering improved risk-taking abilities, while limiting potentially destructive actions.

Suffering as an Opportunity for "Tempering the Soul"

Stress and the need for adaptation cannot always be controlled. There are many instances in personal or working life when the only possible strategy is coping. As the rate of change in organisations keeps increasing, the ability to cope with increasing stress becomes essential to a successful career. In society, people have found ways to get prepared for higher stress. All kinds of strategies can be used: meditation, healthy food, plenty of sleep, exercise and so on. There is no doubt that they all help.

Initiations are yet another example of such preparation. On the first days of your arrival at university, you are introduced to this new life by participating in playful yet stressful games that, most of the time, replicate the challenges that you will eventually be confronted with. In many civilisations there are still tough initiations to adult life as well. Mentoring or, to a lesser extent coaching, are ways that organisations use to achieve the same result. The objectives of such experiences are to reduce the threshold to suffering at which one will take action or to improve the ability to cope.

One other consequence of such preparation can also be to give people an opportunity to determine what level of suffering is worth the result expected or obtained. In the popular, arguable statement "no pain, no gain", there is an implied option of how much suffering needs to be sustained to achieve specific results. Being given this choice will increase one's level of perceived control and confidence level as well. This should then reduce the stress level, a circular pattern.

As one's competency to withstand higher stress levels increases, one may seek more responsibilities or take more risk. Typically, this behaviour will be recognised by one's colleagues and will foster empowering social support, increasing even further their ability to take on challenging situations.

Suffering as a Degenerative Experience

It appears that, over a lifetime, humans and animals have a finite potential to adapt (Selye, 1974). When this limit is exceeded, performance decreases, illness can happen (Siegall and McDonald, 2004). This is to say that one's ability to adapt must be used carefully, for purposes that are worth the effort. If suffering is an opportunity for tempering the soul, too much suffering will eventually deplete the "adaptation reserve" and increase vulnerability. The expected result of this vulnerability is retreat and isolation, in an attempt to lower the need for further adaptation, in a degenerative spiral.

Systems theory tells us that the world is interconnected and constantly changing. Organisations have to adapt. Very often, managers are given the role of change agents. They are expected to foster change without creating harmful disruptions in the functioning of the organisation. This can sometimes be a heavy burden. If the expected change happens to cause unbearable stress to some of the members of the group, there will be a strong temptation for managers not to take responsibility for individual suffering of others and put on those members' shoulders the burden to either adapt or leave. Especially when this behaviour is seen as part of acceptable institutional values, it may eventually lead to unbelievable excesses. This refusal to take responsibility as a group member, which is also true for fellow workers not reacting to injustice (Lurie, 2004), keeps them impervious to their own suffering, as if they were not concerned and as if the same immersion in suffering cannot happen to them.

Vulnerability to this degenerative process also increases as individual motivation reaches levels that do not reflect that of the group. "Over-motivated" individuals become potential victims of their commitment to the organisation as their emotional involvement makes them a target for high stress and low control of their social environment.

Suffering as a Catalyst to Collective Change

If one subject has been researched even more than stress, it is change. Over the years, change has taken over tradition as a universal reference. There is plenty of evidence that the rate of change is increasing rapidly in modern organisations. As an illustration of this new reality, a majority of North-American companies are now in the process of at least one major change initiative and many of them have three or more going on (Vakola and Nikolaou, 2005). This has reached a point where the change model that suggests a refreezing stage to its process is being challenged, as the refreezing does not seem to take place before the next change is introduced.

Just as individuals have a finite potential to adapt, groups and organisations seem to have the same limitations. Constant change programs have been proven to adversely affect business performance and customer satisfaction (Valoka and Nikolaou, 2005).

The need to change arises from unmet internal or external objectives. Recent research indicates that readiness to change in organisations is a function of individual perception of their own ability to change as well as their ability to contribute to overall change (Cunningham et al., 2002). This model is preferred to the traditional one suggesting that change will happen when the anticipated benefits clearly outweigh the expected costs and risks. Under those circumstances, as we have discussed earlier, the reaction may very well be one of coping with the situation and the suffering. This is to say that increased suffering will not trigger change as effectively as empowering individuals and groups to change. It is by using suffering as a symptom of a need for adaptation and creating an empowering context to change that the readiness for change can be improved.

We have seen that change and adaptation cause stress and potential suffering just as stress and suffering, used as a symptom, can foster change and adaptation, in a circular pattern (Michailidis and Georgiou, 2005). But symptoms have to be interpreted competently. It seems relatively easy to detect individual suffering and treat it in the separate network of health institutions. A more challenging task is to properly identify which part of this suffering originates from the collective functioning of the organisation, as the result of collective conflicts and injustice, in an effort to alleviate its source (Nyberg and Harrison, 2002).

The sense of injustice and many conflicts arise from the feeling of not being treated fairly, in comparison with others. As nobody can work for oneself without working for others as well (Grimaldi, 2002), the more people contribute to others, the more rewards they get back. This last statement will be true only if the result of their work is accepted and valued by others. This is quite obvious when applied to a commercial operation. It should also be quite obvious when applied to a workgroup. It is not enough to contribute; the contribution must be valued by others.

So, contributions may be optimised for individuals but may not fit in the system, in order for it to function optimally. In many instances, quantitative research in the western world represents reality in terms of linear, causal relationships. Many times, a perspective including reciprocal or circular relationships would open new fields of understanding. One illustration of this would be to consider that when individuals suffer, the whole group is affected. This model would fit other research showing that participation reduces resistance to organisational change (Armenakis, Stanley and Mossholder, 1993). Information, in participative organisations, is shared between stakeholders and risks and fears as well as expected benefits can be processed by the group. This way, individual readiness to change can support collective readiness and vice versa (Rutherford, 2004).

Individual contributions may also fit one sub-system but not fit the others. This is referred to as role conflict. Role conflict increases stress because expectations created in different sub-systems may be hard to reconcile. In the last few years, it has become the subject of extensive research and publications. Originally focused on the conflict parent/worker, role conflict research in organisations now includes many other complex issues. An example of such is the salesperson confronted with the need to offer customers the best value for their money while being under pressure to maximise profits for the company. Another one would be a marketing department requesting an extensive product line while production people ask for the opposite. Not all those conflicts could or should be avoided. Maintaining equilibrium between opposing forces is indeed part of what fosters adaptation. If prices are too high, the business will eventually go to the competitors. If the line of product is either too large or too small, the business will suffer. As a matter of fact, under many circumstances, conflict can be beneficial to both individuals and organisations, especially when performing non-routine tasks (Jehn, 1995). Moreover, the temptation to deal with such "useful" conflicts openly will not result in their reduction but, on the contrary, will lead to their escalation, to the point where productivity will suffer. The challenge becomes here to maintain the "proper level of ambiguity" and avoid what can be described as "extreme conflict" (Nygaard and Dahlstrom, 2002).

Suffering as a Change Inhibitor, as the Result of an Expression of Power

Just as adaptation disorder is a pathology, excessive use of power can be one as well, called psychopathy. It is characterized by a lack of sensibility and empathy for others and for oneself.

When suffering is wrongfully ignored or even created by management, after an initial urge to change, further changes are usually inhibited unless they are motivated by clear incentives from the environment. The use of power in organizations typically results in denial and distancing from suffering, making the required adaptation more superficial and short-term.

The tendency to ignore the consequences of abuses of power can be explained. The necessity to produce short-term results is sometimes overwhelming, on one hand. The tendency to make others responsible for the consequences of one's actions is also a form of self-protection, on the other hand. Why indeed should someone suffer from someone else's suffering if he/she is not the cause? Also, it is easy to ignore those that do not have power or are in difficulty (Frank, 1995). Usually their message is either weak or unclear, or both. Therefore, once organisations begin using power as their preferred relational model, it becomes very difficult to break the cycle.

The use and abuse of power in relationships will typically generate a sense of unfairness or injustice (Adelson, 2005). Not only are these two stressors, but they lower people's confidence in their ability to manage change competently (Judge and Colquitt, 2004). This in turn reduces the organisation's ability to adapt and, eventually leads to major disruptions.

Some authors, having perceived the role of suffering as a motivator to change, suggest to deliberately "create pain" (Nadler and Tushman, 1989). They even suggest "multiple intense exposures" to painful experiences in an effort to create the energy required to unfreeze the system. We believe, even though this strategy may prove to be successful in the short term, that its long term effects on the group will not create the desired results, as the group will quickly realise what is happening and go to a coping strategy, thereby considerably increasing its resistance to change. We also believe that such conduct would be unethical in most organisations.

Suffering as an Invitation to Define Ethics and Values

There seems to be little doubt on what causes physical pain, on an individual basis. And identifying the source is most of the time fairly easy, especially over a long period of time. It may not be that easy with psychological suffering. The source is often hard to find or changing. Or, it may be the result of a "preferred" interpretation. Literature identifies as one of the greatest source of suffering the breach of group values and beliefs by one of its members (Wright, 2005). It may be perceived as a lack of integrity or an injustice. It may also be perceived as a failure of the group to properly teach and influence the members. In all cases, the consequence is a sense of disempowerment and group performance is affected. On the opposite, if a climate of trust is created and if values are clearly stated and followed over a long period of time, stress decreases and the group can handle more complex and challenging tasks.

Ethical conduct can be defined as knowing the difference between right and wrong (Rand, 1964). It is based both on group consensus and on personal values. The group agrees on values and beliefs, and on rules (Seijts and O'Farrell, 2003). Individuals then decide if they are to comply or not. So people get to assess all behaviours and compare them to the perceived rules and/or to their own values. It is invariably a matter of interpretation. "Richard is such a jerk, he is always against anything that will challenge his own comfort", can also be interpreted as: "Richard is so smart, he makes sure that changes take into account the human side of things". One scenario leads to frustration and suffering, the other one leads to action and empowerment. The change required is therefore a reflexive change in social roles.

Sometimes ethical conduct is so narrowly defined that so called "inspirational leaders" are said to be unethical because they appeal to emotions rather than reason in their relationships (Michie and Gooty, 2005). The underlying assumption there is that a leadership based on emotions would eventually become immoral, unable to distinguish between right or wrong and that leadership based on reason would be able to do so. But, there seems to be little evidence to support such a statement. We can even imagine a context of extreme pressure to increase profits, for example, where managers could rationally be tempted to exploit both employees and customers in order to reach their targets. In this case, it looks as though emotions and the acknowledgement of suffering would help in maintaining an ethical behaviour. So, in a situation where there is a choice between behaving productively and ethically, the leader will eventually have to abide by the consensual set values and beliefs set by the group. As a matter of fact, the ability to correctly diagnose what these are and actively and openly support them will create, as we have seen, a climate of trust. This climate is essential to lowering the stress and ambiguity levels that, in turn, increase productivity and adaptability. Productive leaders may just be ethical leaders as well.

When some members of a group experience suffering, there is a point at which such suffering becomes unbearable and triggers change. Sensitivity to suffering, as defined by values and beliefs, regulates that limit. Sometimes, shame and guilt become motivators (Gilbert, 2003; Lurie, 2004). They can be so powerful that people will take vigorous actions to avoid them. In a context where people eventually compete for social recognition, shame is a symptom of a potential breach in one's own opinion of what is acceptable behaviour. Guilt is concerned with others being negatively affected by one's behaviour. Both are driven by the fear of rejection. Being able to recognise and take into account shame and guilt may indeed be useful in increasing people's ability to integrate values such as courage, compassion and tolerance.

Some authors refer to the ethics of listening (Frank, 1995). This perspective proves to be useful in the development of participative behaviours, the building of trust and the early detection of symptoms of suffering. They can be part of the set of values and beliefs that influence positively the ability of organisations to adapt.

Suffering as a Breach in Values

At the beginning of the 21st century, suffering is taking a new meaning. In many parts of the world, a shift in societal values has made happiness become compulsory (Bruckner, 2000). It is so because of what looks like almost total freedom and limitless possibilities. Individuals should find no reasons not to live happy and very active lives, sometimes even extreme lives, as they hold in their fate in their own hands. This quest for perfection takes place in a context where individual rights are heavily protected and promoted. This typically leads to individualism and, in many instances as well, to intolerance to others. But it also leads to intolerance for short term stress and for suffering. And, as the possibility of suffering may not be taken upon oneself, its responsibility must be attributed to others, leading to further isolation and to more stress and suffering.

As suffering becomes perceived as a social injustice, it appears like a problem to solve (Biron, 2005). This changes the perspective on its usefulness, its inevitability and its social role. Suffering becomes outside of people, leaving emotions to the individuals who, as we saw, cannot take responsibility for it, in a circular pattern. This eventually opens the way to a sense of powerlessness, to despair and violence.

Conclusion

Suffering is one of our main adaptation tools. It can be used as an advance warning of an even greater suffering. It can be used as information on what does not fit. One can learn from it for future actions as well. It can be a catalyst to collective readjustments and foster organisational adaptation. It is also potentially destructive. So, there is a need to consider and properly diagnose the causes and consequences of suffering. Suffering being inevitable, there is also a need to maintain "acceptable" levels and kinds of suffering.

Managers and employees can be trained to recognise suffering. They can be encouraged to gain control over situations that threaten their well-being. Information and power can be shared in an effort to create a climate of trust. This active search for participation will in turn enhance individual and collective confidence in handling change. But, even with every effort made to enhance adaptation ability, the rate of change has to take into account the ability of the organisation to integrate values and beliefs that "fit" the changing environment.

Suffering is part of being human, still. It is an opportunity for people to share this condition. It is an opportunity to help, support, love our fellow humans. It is an opportunity to give a meaning to our lives, as all humans will eventually suffer and die. There is a possibility for suffering to create freedom and justice. Many times, it is in moments of intense suffering that people can demonstrate friendliness, courage, loyalty. Sometimes, collective well-being is a cause worth suffering or even dying for.

References

Adelson, N., « La souffrance collective : une analyse anthropologique de l'incarnation d'injustice », *Revue Québécoise de Psychologie*, Vol. 26, No. 2, 2005.

Ashkanasy, N., Härtel, C., Zerbe, W., *Emotions in the Workplace: Research, Theory, and Practice*. Quorum, Westport, 2000.

Armenakis, A., Harris, S., Mossholder, K., "Creating readiness for Organizational Change", *Human Relations*, Vol. 46, No. 6, 1993.

Biron, L., « La souffrance des intervenants : perte d'idéal collectif et confusion sur le plan des valeurs », *Revue Québécoise de Psychologie*, Vol. 26, No. 2, 2005.

Bruckner, P., *L'euphorie perpétuelle. Essai sur le devoir de bonheur*. Éditions Grasset et Fasquelle, Paris, 2000.

Cunningham, C., Woodward, C., Shannon, H., MacIntosh, J., Lendrum, B., Rosenbloom, D., Brown, J., "Readiness for organisational change: A longitudinal study of workplace, psychological and behavioural correlates", *Journal of Occupational and Organizational Psychology*, Vol 75, 2002.

Frank, A.W., *The wounded storyteller: Body, illness, and ethics*. The University of Chicago Press, Chicago, 1995.

Freidman, M.I., Rosenham. R.H., *Type A behaviour and your heart*. Knopf, New York, 1974.

Gilbert, P., "Evolution, Social Roles, and the Differences in Shame and Guilt", *Social Research*, Vol. 70, No. 4, 2003.

Goleman, D., *L'intelligence émotionnelle*, Robert Lafond, Paris, 1997.

Holmes, T.H., Rahe, R.H., "The social readjustment scale", *Journal of Psychosomatic Research*, Vol. 11, p. 213–218, 1967.

Jehn, K.A., "A Multimethod Examination of the Benefits and Detriments of Intragroup Conflict", *Administrative Science Quarterly*, 40, 1995.

Judge, T., Colquitt, J., "Organizational Justice and Stress : The Mediating Role of Work-Family Conflict", *Journal of Applied Psychology*, Vol. 89, No. 3, 2004.

Lazarus, R.S., "From Psychological Stress to Emotions: A History of Changing Outlooks", *Annual Review of Psychology*, 1993, 44:1–21.

Lurie, Y., "Humanizing Business through Emotions: On the Role of Emotions on Ethics", *Journal of Business Ethics*, 49:1–11, 2004.

Marcoux, H., « La réflexion éthique : une source de soulagement pour le clinicien souffrant », *Revue Québécoise de Psychologie*, Vol. 26, No. 2, 2005.

Matthews, K.A. and al, "Unique and common variance in structured interview and Jenkins Activity Survey measures of the Type A behavior pattern", *Journal of Personality and Social Behavior*, 42, 1982, pp 303–313.

Michailidis, M., Georgiou, Y., "Employee occupational stress in banking", *IOS Press*, Work 24, 2005.

Michie, S., Gooty, J., "Values, emotions, and authenticity: Will the real leader please stand up?", The Leadership Quaterly, Vol. 16, 2005.

Nadler, D., Tushman, M., "Organisation Frame Bending: Principles for Managing Reorientation" *The Academy of Management Executive*, Vol. 3, No. 3, 1989.

Nyberg, B., Harrison, R., "Being an Agent of Organizational Healing" *The 2002 Annual: Volume 2, Consulting*, John Wiley, San Francisco, CA, 2002.

Nygaard, A., Dahlstrom, R., "Role Stress and effectiveness in Horizontal Alliances", *Journal of Marketing*, Vol 66, April 2002.

Perrewé, P., Zellars, K., Ferris, G., Rossi, A.M., Kacmar, C., Ralston, D., "Neutralizing Job Stressors: Political Skill as an Antidote to the Dysfunctional Consequences of Role Conflict", *Academy of Management Journal*, Vol. 47, No. 1, 2004.

Rand, A., *The Virtue of Selfishness: a New Concept of Egoism*, Signet, New York, 1964.

Rathus, S., *Psychologie générale*, HRW, 1985.

Rutherford, M. D., "The effect of social role on theory of mind reasoning", *British Journal of Psychology*, Vol 95, 2004.

Seijts, G., O'Farrell, G., "Engage the heart: Appealing to the emotions facilitates change", *Ivey Business Journal*, Jan/Feb 2003.

Selye, H., *Le stress sans détresse*, Les Éditions La Presse, Montréal, 1974.

Senge, P. *The Fifth Discipline*, Doubleday, New York, 1990.

Siegall, M., McDonald, T., "Person-organization value congruence, burnout and diversion of resources", *Personnel review*, Vol33 No. 3, 2004.

Tidd, S., Freidman, R., "Conflict Style and Coping with Role Conflict: an Extension of the Uncertainty Model of Work Stress", *The International Journal of Conflict Management*, Vol. 13, No. 3, 2002.

Vakola, M., Nikolaou, I., "Attitudes towards organizational change", *Employee Relations*, Vol. 27 No. 2, 2005.

Wright, L. M., *Spirituality, Suffering and Illness, Ideas for Healing* F.A. Davis, Philadephia, 2005.

Chapter 6

Psychoanalysis and the Myths of Corporate Communication

David Crowther and Ana Maria Dávila Gómez

Introduction

Although there are many theories concerning the formation of personality and the way this formation affects behaviour in organisations, one large body of thought is concerned with psychoanalysis. Psychoanalysis is well known and it arouses strong feelings for most people: some reject it absolutely while others think that it provides insights which are not apparent elsewhere. Among academics some hold that it is coherent body of theory while others claim that it is not theory at all as the explanations it gives are untestable. Here we do not enter this debate but rather look at the perspective it offers upon behaviour in organisation, through a focus upon corporate communications and the associated myths surrounding behaviour in organisations. In this chapter we do this through the lens of semiology.

The Origins of Semiology

Semiology, or semiotics,[1] has been defined simply as 'the study of signs' (Guiraud 1975). This description however must be viewed as being overly simplistic. In actual fact semiology can be considered to be the study of the creation of the symbolic and its subsequent signification. Thus semiology has been further defined as 'a science which studies the life of signs within society' (Saussure 1966). Semiotics can therefore be considered to be a study of communication and more particularly the study of communication acts or events – a study of the message itself and its relationship with the recipient of that message. According to semiotic theory therefore communication is determined by the interrelationship between the message itself and the recipient of that message. In this respect therefore, as Derrida (1978) argues, the writer of the message ceases to have any significance once the message has been written, as interpretation is entirely determined by this interplay between the message and its recipient. In other words meaning is in the interpretation of the message by the recipient and the intentions of the writer are therefore irrelevant. This inevitably places a heavy burden upon the recipient of the message in extracting meaning from that message but it also places a heavy burden upon the writer of the message. Thus

---

1   The two terms were created independently. Semiology is the term used by Saussure while semiotics is the term used by Peirce. Effectively the two terms are synonymous.

rather than being irrelevant to the message, the writer of the message is in fact central to the message itself as (s)he must endeavour to ensure that the meaning wished to be imparted is actually the one which is extracted by the recipient rather than any alternative meaning.

In spoken communication[2] this is a relatively simple exercise as the speaker knows something about the hearer, has a general understanding of the context in which the communication is being made, and receives feedback which enables the message to be modified during its transmission. When the message is transmitted in written form, either as text or as pictures, however, the situation is very different as there is no framing context for the message, or rather a different framing context for each reader, and no relationship between the writer and the reader other than the message itself. The message itself therefore becomes the sole form of mediation between the writer and the reader and thereby assumes the dominant role in the communication. This message therefore becomes the totality of the communication act, and the communication event becomes the relationship between the message and the reader of that message. Semiotics therefore is the study of both the communication act and the communication event.

Semiotics has its origins in linguistic theory and a perennial debate since its acceptance within the discourse of communication has been one of whether semiotics is merely a subset of linguistic theory or whether, since its scope is much greater than linguistics and encompasses linguistics within its scope, it is a meta-level of analysis, of which linguistics comprises one subset.[3] In this chapter we focus upon the communication act itself and the way in which it is encapsulated within the myths associated with everyday life. Within this communication act there are two transmission devices, one of which are linguistic and the other of which is non-linguistic. These devices are:

- The natural language used in communication – in the case of the reports considered this is the language of English
- The non-linguistic devices used within the act, comprising pictures, graphs, colours etc which are an integral part of the communication event.

These devices combine within the reports to make the communication act, and thereby the text. As such the text, which is to be semiotically analysed, comprises the complete communication act.

Postmodern analysis of society and its organs (Barnett and Crowther 1998) therefore provides a mechanism for the semiotic analysis of such communication. In

---

2   This is not quite the same if the speakers are apart and communicating by telephone as all feedback must be given by the words used.

3   Hervey (1982) argues that this debate is sterile and that while semiotics can be considered to be simply 'looking in other areas of communication for the properties first encountered in natural languages' it is also 'defined by explicit reference to the non-linguistic'. In this particular chapter this debate is ignored because it is felt not to be relevant to the development of a semiology of corporate communications.

this context Baudrillard (1988) claims that there is a need to break with all forms of enlightened conceptual critiques and that truth in the postmodern era is obsolete, while Fish (1985) claims that truth and belief are synonymous for all practical purposes. This would suggest that the meaning of any such communication becomes whatever it is interpreted to mean. This interpretation will depend upon the perspective of the person performing that interpretation, and the purpose for which that interpretation is undertaken. Thus a postmodern perspective is in perfect accord with the semiotic arguments considered above. This need for interpretation naturally places a heavy emphasis upon the interpretative ability of the receiver of the information as well as presupposing that this receiver understands the language and conventions sufficiently well to be able to extract meaning from this information. It also provides an opportunity for those undertaking the communication to structure the information in such a manner as to facilitate their desired manner of interpretation. Thus corporate communications are carefully constructed and designed not merely to communicate information but rather to construct and communicate the desired image, with that image changing according to who the communication is aimed at.

Approaches to Semiotic Analysis

The roots of semiotics stem from two distinct strands of literature – the linguistic work of Saussure and the philosophical work of Peirce. Each source leads to a slightly different mode of analysis

Saussure (1966) identified a sign as dyadic, having two sides – the signifier and the signified: the signifier being the material object and the signified being its associated mental concept. The inseparability of these two aspects of the sign led to his diagrammatic representation:

Figure 6.1   The Saussurian Dyadic

Thus Saussure's understanding of the process of communication is based upon an assumption of the transfer of mental concepts through the signs produced.

Peirce (1958), on the other hand, developed a triadic theory of the signs based upon the triple relationship of the representamen, the object and the interpretant. In his theory the representamen is the sign itself, the object is that which the representamen stands for and the interpretant is the significate effect of the sign.

Saussurian semiology must necessarily be undertaken in the context of a wider system of meaning external to the sign itself. In this mode of analysis the sign itself is part of a flow of meaning and is interpreted contextually and individually by each individual participating in the communication event. Peircian semiotics on the other hand functions on the basis that each sign is self-contained and able to generate further signs, with associated meanings, from within itself. Thus the Peircian approach has its own internal dynamic associated with both the sign and its interpretation which is often referred to as an unlimited semiosis. Peirce's system of semiotics has been extensively critiqued by Habermas (1971) because of his assumption that every individual is able to produce his own semiotic from the communication event. Thus the semiotic is infinitely variable, as any event would not produce the same semiotic for each individual. He states (1971: 138–9):

> Not every communication, however, is merely the subsumption of the individual under an abstract universal, or what is in principle mute subjection to a public monologue that everyone can produce for himself. On the contrary, every dialogue develops on an entirely different basis, namely that of the reciprocal recognition of subjects who identify one another under the category of selfhood and at the same time maintain themselves in their non-identity. The concept of the individual ego includes a dialectical relationship between the universal and the particular, which cannot be conceived in the behavioural system of instrumental action.

For static signs, such as advertisements, this Peircian method of semiotic analysis provides the most suitable method of interpretation and understanding of meaning. For corporate communication however the sign is not static but is contextual to the organisation, its external environment and its audience. Moreover each individual corporate communication produces not just one sign but rather a multiplicity of signs each of which are contextually dependant upon the other signs produced. It is for this reason that Saussurian methodology is considered to be the most appropriate method of analysis and is used here in order to develop a semiotic understanding of corporate communications.

The semiology of Saussure has been developed extensively by later writers, but one significant analysis has been undertaken by Lacan (1977) who argued that human beings are entirely enmeshed within the sign and its subjectivity, thereby making the separation of the signifier and the signified impossible.[4]

Myth *vs* Ritual

The myth creation role of corporate communication has several aspects but one aspect is the creation of the myth of the unified whole. As Nietsche (1956: 156) states:

> Only a horizon ringed about by myth can unify a culture.

---

4   Lacan developed these arguments further in the context of his psychoanalysis, but this inextricable enmeshment of the person as an individual within the semiotic of any sign is at variance with the argument of Derrida above. The adoption of a Lacanian perspective would necessitate a consideration of the motivations of the actors involved in the semiotic, a point which will be returned to later.

One of the purposes of corporate communication therefore is the creation of the myth of the unified culture of the actors on the semiotic stage – in other word the common cultural bond of identity between the authors of the script and the audience.[5] This is achieved by the creation of a symbolic order which is an autonomous order of reality independent of the things symbolised (Jenkins 1979). The myth itself is a symbolic form (Brandist 1997) which assumes a life of its own. As Cassirer (1955: 5–6) states the specificity of myth lies not in its content but rather in

> the intensity with which it is experienced, with which it is believed – as only something endowed with objective reality can be believed.

Thus myth has the power to present a single viewpoint as directly expressive of the existence of the organisation, which consequently exists in the form presented in the communication. The corporate communication as myth therefore provides an authoritative discourse about the organisation, and as Bakhtin (1981: 342) states

> The authoritative word demands that we acknowledge it, that we make it our own; it binds us, quite independent of any power it might have to persuade us internally; we encounter it with its authority already fused into it. The authoritative word is located in the distanced zone, organically connected with a past that is felt to be hierarchically higher.

Thus a corporate communication replaces the organisation itself as the real through this power assumed from its myth creation role and the organisation becomes in the minds of both the readers and the authors (through the reflective quality of the readership) that which is presented through the corporate communication mechanism. The concept of the corporate communication can therefore be considered to have attained a life of its own through the resurrection of the myth of its origin and authenticity.[6]

In addition to the myth creation role of corporate communication for the individual organisation, Campbell (1949) argues that all myths have an underlying commonality which transcends the individual myth. Thus as far as such communication is concerned the common elements can be seen in the common format of such communications, the common style and the use of common language (often known as the "house style") – natural and non-linguistic – to provide a unified myth concerning the corporation as the authoritative discourse of organisational existence and activity.[7] Thus the history of organisations unfolds through this corporate communicating (Campbell 1976) but unfolds in a manner which is common to all organisations and can therefore be depicted as universal and immutable. This unfolding of history can be seen in the development of corporate annual reports over time (McKinstry 1996) but the mythical role of such reports ensures that, although the image of the

---

5   See Crowther, Cooper and Carter (2001) for a consideration of the symbiotic relationship between the actors on the water company stage.

6   It can therefore be considered to have attained hyperreality through becoming more real than reality (Baudrillard 1981).

7   It is recognised of course that legislation can often enforce content which requires a considerable element of this commonality but it is argued that this is subsumed within the image creation requirements of corporate communications.

organisation changes with the development of corporate reports (Preston, Wright and Young 1997), the image of the organisation remains immutably fixed in the present.[8]

The creation of the myth of organisational existence is an essential step along the road to the creation of the religion which binds the organisation together (Malinowski 1962) and this religion becomes manifest in the rituals of organisational behaviour which will be explored as the other pole of this binarism. Malinowski (1962: 119) defines this in the following terms:

> What is then the fact of a myth? Briefly, that all the principal tenets of religious belief have a tendency to be spun out into concrete stories; in the second place, these stories are never merely accounts of what happened in the past. Every act of ritual, every artistic representation of religious subjects, in the worship of relics and sacred places in short, in all the visual signs of past sensational acts of grace every theme is revivified. The events of the mythological past play also a leading part in moral conduct and social organisation.

One further purpose of myth creation in this context is the reinforcement of organisation boundaries, and hence the restatement of organisational existence. It has been argued (Crowther 2002a) that corporate reporting is essentially for external consumption and that the accounting of organisations, together with all other information systems of those organisations, is directed within the text to this end.[9] External reporting serves the function of providing a statement to the external world that the organisation exists as a discrete entity and the production of the annual report[10] actually is designed to fulfil this role. Moreover the design of the report is carefully considered to make a statement not just that the organisation exists but also to create an image of that organisation. Thus, over time, corporate reports have become more and more full of information, statements from the chairman and others, and pictures of organisational activities.[11] These corporate reports have therefore become more of a symbolic representation of the organisation designed to give to the (by implication) 'discerning' reader the impression that this is an organisation to be interested in, with a dynamic present and an even more interesting future. The legal purpose of reporting past performance thereby becomes less significant as the focus is upon the prospects for the future. These prospects are always suggested

---

8   Levi Strauss (1955) contends that myth is different from language and so the techniques used to analyse myth must be different from those used to analyse language. This point is refuted however through the use of semiotic tools of analysis, which it is argued are equally appropriate to this study when considering the language used in corporate reporting and the myth creation role of such reporting.

9   Corporate reporting for external consumption can be considered as a myth creation mechanism for the redefinition and reinforcement of organisational boundaries which are in reality obsolete for performance determining purposes.

10 It is recognised that this reporting is actually required by law for all public limited companies but argued that this reason has been relegated in importance.

11 That is to say the reports of large UK plc's rather that other companies (public or private). Equally the contrast can be made with foreign companies reporting in other environments. Thus for example the annual report and accounts of VEBA (German company aiming to satisfy the reporting requirements of the USA) contain large amounts of legally required information but nothing else – certainly no pictures and no colour.

to be an improvement upon the present and this provides a means of signalling the importance of the organisation and of its existence.

Despite the assertions of Norris (1990), language creates reality which then becomes truth. Thus, as Barthes (1988) claims, meaning is not in the linguistic structure of a message but in the image created by the recipient of the message. Corporate communication by its nature creates an image of the organisation, the decision making within the organisation and the future of that organisation. This is achieved though the use of the language of the house style and the perceived certainty attached to that language. One of the purposes of such styled communication is to continually recreate the myth of organisational existence as certainty in the uncertain world. This certainty is of course a myth and one important function therefore is to act as a myth creation mechanism for the organisation as a statement of organisational existence as immutable.

One of the purposes of myth making is to remove temporality from the perception of the onlooker (Levi Strauss 1966), who in this case is an external consumer of the information supplied by the organisation. Removing temporality has the effect of conflating the past and present into the present and to make this present contiguous with the future. In doing so the uncertainty of images made through such communications, from one period to the next, is disguised within the omnipresent organisational myth based upon the eternal present. Rationality and predictability through using a house style of communication within the metanarrative myth of organisational immutability therefore seems reasonable within any discourse of organisational reporting. This removal of temporality has the concomitant effect of focusing upon spatiality. As far as spatiality is concerned the organisation seeks to create the myth of itself as omnipresent through the attention given to both the local and the global aspects of organisational existence. This is achieved through the use of appropriate text and image.

Thus the myth of organisational existence is created by this means and this existence is continually recreated as atemporal and omnipresent, but also extremely local. In this manner synchronicity and diachronicity are conflated and subsumed within the myth. Likewise the past is removed in favour of the eternal present and better future as the organisation signals its existence and importance through this mythical role of corporate communication.

This myth of organisation importance is naturally of concern to the authors of the text. If the organisation is important then, by implication, those managing the organisation, ie the authors of the script, must also be important. The form of corporate communication is designed to create an image of the importance and permanence of the organisation, and hence of those managing that organisation. This therefore explains the increased dominance of messages from members of the dominant coalition managing the organisation and particularly the chairman, managing director and increasingly other powerful members of the management team. This message is designed to indicate the need for the organisation to exist as a discrete entity, defined through the reinforcement of the organisational boundary and reinforced through the production of appropriately constructed corporate reports. At the same time such reports demonstrate just how necessary those members of the dominant coalition are to maintenance of the organisation and to its future. The language of the statements from these people tends therefore to be used as a device for corrupting thought (Orwell 1970) through being used as an instrument to prevent thought about the various alternative realities of the organisation's existence, in terms of the multiple representations of the organisation which actually exist throughout out its being.

These realities imply that in a postmodern environment, if the organisational boundary is irrelevant, or even deleterious, to organisation performance, then so too are the managing team of that organisation. Therefore reporting to the external environment must be made to appear the most important function of corporate communicating, with other purposes made subservient to this need in order to demonstrate the need for the dominant coalition of senior managers. Thus the myth of the organisation is extended to the authors of the script and their essential contribution to the success of the organisation (as epitomised by the expensive product of that success, the corporate report) is made into reality (Barthes 1973). Communicating information therefore becomes a defensive instrument, not for the organisation, but for the senior management of the centre, and a means to retain power through using such communication to symbolise the necessity of their continued existence, with the whole control and use of information and systems being directed towards this end.

In binary opposition to myth as far as corporate communication is concerned is ritual. For an individual, ritual is an essential part of personality integration – a process of becoming whole (Perls 1975). Rituals therefore are steps along the way to completion of the whole.[12] So too for organisations are rituals steps to be completed along the way to wholeness. In the case of the organisation however the integration needed is not that of parts of the organisation but that of the various people involved in the organisation into a unified whole, based upon the rituals of organisational religion. This religion, of necessity, becomes institutionalised into the organisation and its culture and forms part of the way in which the organisation conducts itself both internally and in relating to its external environment.[13] As Bocock (1974: 174) states:

> Ritual action can have two sorts of consequences for the society in which it takes place: either it can provide a process whereby people become more attached to the basic way of life and values of the society, or to the major sub-groups within it of which the participants in ritual are a part, or ritual can lead to people making new demands on the way of life in their society, and a desire to see change both in action and in the values the society pursues.

It is naturally not in the interests of the organisation to allow the ritual actions of the organisation to lead to demands for changes. It therefore becomes imperative that the ritual role of corporate activity becomes subsumed within the myth creation role

---

12 These can be considered to be the rites of passage (Beit-Hallahmi and Argyle 1997) which mark the way to that wholeness.

13 This institutionalisation of religion becomes part of the culture of the organisation and socialises the individual who assimilates the cultural givens of the organisation (Dollimore 1984).

and this can be achieved through the institutionalisation of such ritual activity within the organisational religion.

One of the purposes of such ritual behaviour is to remove spaciality from the discourse of organisational activity and to focus attention upon the temporal dimension. Thus organisational existence is legitimated in this manner as a temporal sequence proceeding from one rite of organisational existence to the next in a smooth flow of routinised ritual activity. The use of communication – the monthly review, the quarterly newsletter, the annual report etc – in such a ritual way serves the purpose of an organisational religion and, when used in this way, is essentially inward looking for internal consumption. The rituals, for maximal effectiveness also need to encompass external stakeholders and the corporate reporting ritual serves in this way.[14] This reporting ritual serves to both include these external stakeholders, as audience of the script, within the rituals of organisational religion.

Thus in the corporate reports the authors signal that the organisation is moving forwards to better times. This is achieved through the language and style of the communication which clearly sends the message that the authors of the report are the decision makers for the organisation. At the same time it signals that their knowledge enables them to make the best decisions on behalf of the other stakeholders.

Carl Jung and Analytic Psychology

Further understanding of the psychoanalytic motivation of corporate communications can be derived from a consideration of the Jungian interpretation of behaviour. Although based initially upon the work of Freud, Jung deviated from this interpretation significantly by focusing his concentration upon the understanding of individual behaviour through an understanding of societal behaviour and through the development of his concept of the collective unconscious (Jung 1972). This determines the way in which all people act and, according to Jung, provides a way of acting which is universal in nature and is inherited by all individuals. This way of behaving has existed from time immemorial and can be seen equally in the myths of primitive society[15] and in the behaviour of individuals in present society.

Many of the concepts which Jung developed in his work have become part of everyday speech to such an extent that people use the concepts without being aware of their origins. An example of this is Jung's work in the development and identification of personality types. In this work he laid the foundations of psychometric testing as developed by Eysenck and his concepts of extroversion and introversion have entered common vocabulary. Other work led to his formulation of the concept of the collective unconscious as an impersonal substratum of memory underlying the personal unconscious and common to everyone. In this respect it can be likened to a form of racial memory which is independent of an individual's own experiences. An example of the operation of the collective unconscious is that of the urban myth.

---

14 The inclusion of the press in the reporting rituals of the organisation also serves to include the press into the religious activities of the organisation while at the same time seeking to use them as acolytes in the mediation and promotion of the corporate message.

15 See also Cambell (1949, 1972, 1993).

Legend: A customer who picks up some fried chicken from a fast food outlet discovers that an unusual-tasting piece is actually a batter-fried rat.[16]
Examples:

[Collected by Fine, 1976]
An old lady ordered out for Kentucky Fried Chicken. She was eating along when she noticed teeth; she pulled back the crust and discovered she was eating a rat. She had a heart attack and died, and her relatives sued Kentucky Fried Chicken for a lot of money.

[Collected by Fine, 1977]
There was a wife who didn't have anything ready for supper for her husband. So she quick got a basket of chicken and tried to make her dinner look fancy with the prepared chicken. Thus, she fixed a candle-light dinner, etc. When her and her husband started eating the chicken, they thought it tasted funny. Soon to find out it was a fried rat.

Variations:
1   The name of the fast food outlet varies, but it is nearly always Kentucky Fried Chicken.
2   In most versions the chicken is consumed in a dark place (e.g., a car, a theater, a darkened room).
3   How the rat came to be mixed in with the chicken is usually not explained, although it is sometimes attributed to unsanitary conditions or employee sabotage.
4   A few variants involve other animals, such as a mouse or a cat (the latter in the sabotage versions).
5   The victims who eat the rats are most frequently female, less often male, and occasionally both members of a couple.
6   The rat ingester becomes ill, sometimes requiring hospitalization; in some versions she develops psychological problems (such as giving up eating [solid food] for good) or even dies (from poison in the rat).

There is no evidence that such a thing has ever happened but this urban myth continues to exist. As folklorist Gary Alan Fine writes, "The frequency of attachment of an urban legend to the largest company or corporation is so common as to be considered a law of urban folklore." The myth has no know author but it has entered popular culture to such an extent that it is generally known. So, what does this myth have to say? As our society becomes more urbanised (and frenetic), we become less and less involved with the preparation of our own food, frequently dining out instead of eating at home, grazing a quick meal rather than enjoying a leisurely one, and leaving the food preparation entirely in the hands of others. And these

---

16   Source: www.snopes.com

others are not local restaurateurs we know well, but anonymous corporate fast food franchisees and their faceless employees. The combination of our guilt at abdicating this responsibility and our mistrust of corporations is expressed as fear that fast food entities who don't care about us will serve us tainted food prepared under unsanitary conditions, due to carelessness, laziness, or sheer malice. Women are most often the victim in this legend probably because they are considered more vulnerable than men, but perhaps also because this tale reinforces the notion that women have abdicated their traditional role as the family's meal preparers (with tragic results).

In terms of our behaviour such myths have no obvious effect except that, in psychoanalytic terms, to possibly heighten our sense of guilt at being less than perfect individuals. it certainly does not prevent us buying and consuming fast food. As part of this concept of the collective unconscious however Jung introduced the idea of archetypes which can be used to explain individual behaviour and which form the basis of much of the work of Joseph Campbell. These archetypes are claimed by Jung to provide the source of our attitudes and hence an explanation for our individual behaviour. An example of such an archetype which is commonly used by marketers to make their products appeal is that of the hero – someone who can conquer adversity – with the implication in the advertising that merely purchasing the product being advertised will turn an ordinary mortal into a hero.

Every organisation has of course its own myths similar to this but specific to the organisation. In some respects they act as foils to compensate for the unsatisfactory nature of the working environment but in many respects such myths complete the organisation and bind people with a sense of belonging and participation. For Jung, as for Freud, a basic part of his analytical process was based upon dream analysis and he published extensively on this topic. Jung also considered and defined the process of individuation as the path to individual self knowledge. According to Jung everyone has an innate desire to achieve this self realisation and the prevention of this through external influences (from other people in close contact with the individual or from societal pressures) is the root cause of an individual's dysfunctional behaviour. According to Jung an individual's personality can also be described in terms of the persona and shadow: the persona representing the mask which mediates between an individual and the world and the shadow representing that part of the personality which the individual will not allow him/herself to express. An individual also has both a masculine and a feminine side, labelled animus and anima. For a man the masculine side (animus) is resident in the conscious mind with the anima being present in the unconscious, while for a woman the reverse is the case.

In his later career Jung became extremely interested in and knowledgeable concerning the religions, myths and rituals of primitive societies and as a result, after his break with Freud, he became more concerned with the interpretation of society rather than individual psychology. He used concepts from within these myths and the concepts from his own psychological work for his analysis, viewing societal development as a continuing battle between good and evil. In his later years Jung also became interested in the paranormal and in flying saucers. Much of his later work has a mystical aspect to it and this aspect of his work has led to a resurgence in popularity in Jungian psychology in recent years amongst alternative communities. Indeed the psychology of Jung provides much of the foundations of 'New Age' psychology and spirituality.

Ethics, Psyche and Social Responsibility

An essential part of the motivation provided by the collective unconscious is concerned with the drive for belonging to a society or to a group within that society. This is manifest in such features of society as tribalism, the concept of the nation state, and the existence of a multitude of diverse groups such as local football supporters clubs, the Mothers Union and the Sealed Knot. It also explains the need for identification with and belonging to the organisation by which one is employed as well as the importance of family ties. This belonging (to whatever group or groups one chooses to identify with) is an essential part of the constitution of an individual's sense of identity and is vital in an individual's search for meaning in life. This sense of belonging through identification is naturally enhanced if one can have a significant, and preferably an essential, role in the group to which one belongs. This search for belonging and being needed is a part of every person's search for meaning in life which we will explore in more detail in later chapters.

This need for meaning and belonging is manifest in the mythopoeic imagination (Jung 1953, 1954) and one manifestation of this need leads to the need for the creation of myth (May 1991) and the constitution of self as hero (or saviour) within the group to which one belongs (Jung 1953, Campbell 1949). In its extreme manifestation within a group situation this need for myth creation and the constitution of oneself as hero leads to a situation of groupthink (Janis 1972) and the notion of invulnerability. At a lesser level of intensity it leads the managers of an organisation to both portray themselves to the outside world as essential to the wellbeing of the organisation, and to believe this portrayal themselves. These unconscious motivations driving our behaviour[17] are present in all of us and consequently form one of the underlying themes of individual existence and behaviour (Mitroff 1983).

The collective unconscious provides an important element of the constitution of identity of self which is represented in the drive for belonging. This can be seen in behaviour such as tribalism. It is also reflected in our purchasing behaviour through a desire to imitate others and this is particularly prevalent in teenagers who tend to seek to demonstrate their individuality by their style of dress but often end up looking like others in the same sub-culture. In this context it is interesting to consider the issue of fashion and whether the purpose of following fashion is to raise one's self esteem by purchasing goods which demonstrate out individuality, or which demonstrate our worth by acquiring the correct trappings, or which demonstrate our sense of belonging.

Jacques Lacan: The World as Mirror

Since the development of psychoanalysis by Freud, critiques of this theory have been prevalent in the discourses of social theory and of Marxism. Indeed the intertwining of Marxist and Freudian theory as a means of understanding organisational behaviour and the distribution of power within society is a recurrent theme within many discourses. Thus for example Marcuse (1956) argues that rather than the foundations of civilisation being built upon the subjugation of human instincts in the

---

17 See Bettelheim (1976).

assuagement of guilt it is instead built upon the way in which power is distributed and the consequent suppression of labour. Similarly Habermas (1971: 219) argues that Freudian psychoanalysis is based upon the voluntary self-deception of individuals as part of their anxiety reducing mechanisms, stating:

> The ongoing text of our everyday language games (speech and actions) is disturbed by apparently contingent mistakes: by omissions and distortions that can be discounted as accidents and ignored, as long as they fall within the conventional limits of tolerance.

Habermas (1971) continues this analysis by applying this criticism not just to individuals but also to organisations and argues that institutions are involved in this deception, of themselves and others, when he states (1972: 282):

> Freud comprehends institutions as a power that has exchanged acute external force for the permanent internal compulsion of distorted and self limiting communications. Correspondingly he understands cultural tradition as the collective unconscious, censured in varying measure and turned outwards, where motives that have been split off from communication are driven incessantly about and are directed by the excluded symbols into channels of substitute gratification.

Equally Baudrillard (1993, 1999) is critical of psychoanalysis when he states (1999: 138–139):

> For it is from psychoanalysis (though not only from it, of course) that this inconceivable hallucination of the individual about his own desire proceeds..... it is psychoanalysis which, at the end of the "psychological revolution" of the nineteenth century, succeeded in this mad substitution of an individual psychic economy, of a libido, of one's own desire, and the Oedipal reversals of this desire at the event come from elsewhere, for the initiatory, seductive, and fatal incidence of the other as an event without precedent, for the surprise, for the coincidence of the world and the signs that make you not a subject but a preferred object of election and seduction.

Possibly the most significant critique of psychoanalysis has been undertaken by Lacan who developed an alternative interpretation of Freudian theory which has permeated popular culture. Lacanian interpretations incorporate both structuralist and post structuralist arguments to extend the value of Freudian theory. Its limitations from this perspective can be encapsulated in the work of Harris (1979) who stated that the Freudian attempts to understand pan-human psychodynamic processes were sufficient to understand and explain the similarities but not the differences in such processes. Lacan argues that the formation of the ego is concerned with a fascination with one's own image. For him the external world merely represents a mirror upon which the self is displayed and the concern of the individual is to create a reflection in this mirror. This reflection must of course support that person's desire to see the most flattering reflection, but in such a way that it appears as reality. This is brought about by every person's inherent insecurity and seeking for the ideal self (Lacan 1977, 1988a, 1991) and thus every action which a person undertakes is derived from this motivation. It is accepted however that this motivation may not be overt and may not even be recognised by the individual him/herself. Like Freud therefore Lacan accepts that an individual's motivation may not be transparent even to him / herself but nevertheless that motivation becomes inseparable from the actions undertaken, and those actions have a motivation which is based upon the seeking of personal individuation.

The Lacanian view of personal development can be considered to be a reinterpretation of the Oedipal model promulgated by Freud (1977) in which the focus is less upon the biological aspects of development and more upon the cultural aspects. For Lacan the sense of self arises in the child's misrecognition of itself in the mirror stage of development (Crowther 2002b, 2002c) and in its subsequent insertion in the symbolic order. This insertion of self into the symbolic order originates with the Oedipal crisis and this leads to the division of the subject in language and the origins of the unconscious. According to Elliott this happens because the child finds itself separated from the imaginary world of the maternal body and must learn to represent itself in a world of symbolic meaning. It is argued that this takes place, at least in part, by the acquisition of language. Lacan uses the work of Saussure (1966) to argue that language is a system of signs which refer, not to objects themselves but rather to the psychic representation created by their interplay. According to Lacan therefore the human subject is inserted into the symbolic order of language, attempting the impossible task of representing itself while being at the same time an effect of the Saussurian signifier. Saussure (1966) identified a sign as dyadic, having two sides – the signifier and the signified: the signifier being the material object and the signified being its associated mental concept.

Saussure's understanding of the process of communication is based upon an assumption of the transfer of mental concepts through the signs produced. One significant analysis of Saussure's work has been undertaken by Lacan (1977) who argued that human beings are entirely enmeshed within the sign and its subjectivity, thereby making the separation of the signifier and the signified impossible. This leads to the division of the subject in language because for Lacan the unconscious is not a realm within the subject but rather an intersubjective space between people. Thus Lacan argues that the unconscious is essentially outside the subject and is produced by the subject's insertion into the symbolic order. For him the unconscious is structured like language (Lacan 1988b) and therefore operates in accordance with the relationships which are inherent in language. It therefore is not possible to state that the unconscious belongs to the individual but rather is correct to say that it comes to the individual from outside and is an effect of signification on the subject.

Lacan bases upon this argument his understanding of unconscious desire by arguing that because the subject is divided from itself in language it is continually aware of a sense of absence. By this he means an awareness that as a subject (s)he is not fully present and he refers to this as the 'Thing' of the 'lost object'. He considers that this sense of the 'lost object' produces in the subject a desire for something which will make good this loss, thereby creating the unconscious desire. For Lacan this unconscious desire is doomed to be unfulfilled because it is a fantasy and there is no position of completeness to which it is possible to return. Thus the subject is forever seeking to recapture an impossible position and it is this which motivates its continual identification with the subject positions which the symbolic order make available to it. Thus, according to Lacan, we are continually motivated to invest in the various subject positions of language, in our attempts to recover from our absence from them and to recover a state of completeness in self presence.

For Lacan this notion of unconscious desire also explains human sexuality (Rose 2000) and sexual identity is something which is imposed upon the subject by the presence of absence of the phallus. Sexuality and sexual differentiation is placed in the area of the 'lost object' with each sex being seen by the other as that which can satisfy and complete the person and recover the lost object which is the subject of continual fantasy. This is of course impossible but remains a source of continual striving. Zizek (1992) uses to metaphor of Hitchcock's film Vertigo to explain this by considering the dual person Judy – Madeleine and Scottie's attempts to recapture the ideal person he believes existed. In reality of course there was no such person and when she is finally attained then ' this gift of her person "is changed into a gift of shit"' (p86) as the fantasy is traversed and the Other and absence of the Other are revealed at the same time. Rose (2000: 61) explains this by stating 'As negative to the man, woman becomes a total object of fantasy (or an object of total fantasy), elevated into the place of the Other and made to stand for truth.'

The emphasis upon sexual differentiation in Lacanian theory is based upon the importance given to the Oedipal crisis and the major role ascribed to the phallus by Lacan. For Lacan the phallus is not a biological concept but rather fulfils a symbolic function in the underpinning of culture. An example of this underpinning of culture is in the enforcement of the incest taboo. In the symbolic realm the phallus is that which established communication and representation but in the unconscious the phallus occupies a more prominent position. It represents a point of fixity which overcomes the division of the subject in language and thereby provides a position from which the subject can speak as if author of its own meaning – at least it would fulfil this position if it were possible for it to be reached. Sexual differentiation is central to this process because the taking up of a position with respect to the fantasized phallus also implies making an unconscious identification with one side of the sexual divide. The position taken up is not necessarily related to the biological sex of a person and in this respect Lacan deviates significantly from Freud. It is this treatment of sexuality as distinct from biology which brought about an interest in Lacanian theory by feminist theorists.

Rose (2000) argues that women's articulation to the subject positions of gender made available in the symbolic order are constantly challenged by the unconscious. She argues however that Lacan provides a more specific identification of women's resistance to sexual identity – that of jouissance. For Lacan this does not mean the French meaning of orgasm or pleasure but rather that which is unobtainable, in other words the 'lost object'. Rose suggests that woman equates with jouissance because she is that towards which man's desire is directed. Jouissance therefore provides women with a means to resist a conventional femininity inscribed within the phallic economy and therefore an alternative space from which they can speak as themselves. Lacanian theory has been influential therefore in feminist discourses concerning identity but has not been unchallenged by such people as Irigaray. Nevertheless Lacanian theory is central to feminist studies.

Another area in which Lacan's ideas have been influential is that of cultural studies, and in particularly film studies. One of the most important developments in the subject of language approach to identity was the development of the concept of suture. This concept refers to the way in which the subject, although having no existence outside language, is repeatedly articulated within the positions made available. Thus the subject who is actually absent from language is made to appear, through the process of suture as actually its point of origin. According to Silverman (2000: 76) suture is 'that moment when the subject inserts itself into the symbolic register in the guise of a signifier, and in so doing gains meaning at the expense of being'. Silverman uses the Hitchcock film Psycho to elaborate upon the concept of suture and explain its significance to film studies by showing the relationship between the speaking subject and the viewing subject as mediated by the camera acting as narrator.

Although valuable to film theory the concept of suture has wider application to the subject of language approach to identity because of its utility in theorising the way in which a subject is articulated within the subject positions of language and the wider cultural codes. It can be applied not just to the production of the subject in speech acts but also to help understand the constant failure of identity as it continually appears and disappears from language and from the symbolic realm. In this respect therefore suture provides an account of the way in which the individual is articulated within the subject positions made available in language. In doing so it adds to the repertoire of concepts brought into the arena of identity using the subject of language approach, which have been derived from Lacanian theory.

Lacan's work is complex but important in the context of psychoanalysis. It is concerned primarily with the ego and with the fascination with one's own image. Lacan argues that the external world is merely a mirror to reflect the self. This reflection becomes reality and therefore we are each seeking to see reality the most flattering reflection and behaving in such a way as to achieve this. In this respect Lacan concurs with the other psychoanalysts we have considered in suggesting that we all suffer from inherent insecurity which drives us to search for ideal self.

The Drive for Individuation

Psychoanalytic theory is quite complex but, in terms of corporate communication, it can be summarised as being about a search for the ideal self. This has been termed as a seeking for the reintegration of conscious and unconscious and as a concern for the guilt complex which we all possess. This becomes manifest in our striving for a reduction of anxiety which we feel. We do this in order to increase our self respect and at the same time to gain respect from others.

As described before, as individuals that we are, even though many times we put in a lot of effort to belong to a group that differs from other groups, we experience the need to be different and unique even in the very heart of our own group. In these terms, and following Lacans' formerly exposed theory, there are various ways of communicating our inner self to others in ways that are not necessarily verbal. Others perceive our uniqueness not only by means of our language, but also by our corporal movements, our appearance, our gestures and reactions to interactions initiated by others, etc.. In this sense, messages inside organizations cannot always be codified under normalized signs (as a written code).

Every interaction has a uniqueness that is given by the personality of the actors. Even if at the core of the interaction an accord of a mutual code of exchange (e.g. English as verbal code) takes place, there may be different interpretations of a same word depending on the code attributed by each actor given the uniqueness of its own context, which has been elaborated through time by history, personal experiences and moreover by nationality and regionalism (point that is increasingly important nowadays in an context of globalization dynamics). As such, d'Iribarne (1998) explains how in an encounter between people from France and Sweden, the fact of utilizing a neutral language does not imply that people will understand the words in the same context. Hereby, we enter the field of meanings and significance attached to social and individual patterns that have been constructed over time in different parts of the world (as referred before by Freud's and Jung's explanations).

Each individuals taking part in any organizational communicative action has at the same time a social interest (by acceptance, power imposition or sharing of corporate values) and an individual component (either if its motives remain in the unconscious or if they have been consciously identified). The simple fact of belonging to a group sharing certain social values, yet at the same time having a unique individual component, makes us all different, and in this sense, an individuation process takes place. The importance of this aspect in organizational communicative action is that personality and individuality serve us to mobilize between different groups and at the same time to be recognized by other either as followers (of certain norms or simply by allegiance or convenience) or protesters (looking to establish other norms).

Therefore, corporate reports may show to the external world a homogeneous image of the organization as an entity, but they cannot explain the diversity and heterogeneous aspects of groups and individuals therein. As explained before, some managers act by blindly following orders without analysing the consequences because of a childhood trauma with authoritarian parents and early educators, or speculate and construct organizational images that will allow them hierarchical progress and community acceptance. In this sense, managerial actions conducted in order to construct corporate reports also express a sign of the representation that others have of some managers' conduct. Hence, actions and motives behind them also constitute a part of the puzzle of the communicative action. The problem is that the true reality may appear clear in the eyes of the people working inside the organization, but in some cases, real motives are concealed to some people of the community. Therefore, we trust our governmental instances in legislating and regulating organizations by means of imposing new rules and audits.

Even if it is very difficult to unveil the inner motives of powerful individuals inside organizations, there is however, the results of the actions that many times are not documented by written material (either an official report, a public statement on the web or in the media). For us, these results are the consequences of the actions and as such, they obey to previous decisions and reflections occurred in the minds of those who give orders and have power in organizations. Therefore, when managers act, they have a conscience that tells them that their actions may produce some consequences for the community. As such, a process of reflection takes place in the conscience, but not necessarily a process of inner discovery of the reasons of why, even though knowing beforehand that a decision may bring disastrous consequences for some, and yet they still take the decision. It is here where unconscious motives of the past drive impulses.

As explained by Winnicott (1965), a reflection that includes a specific concern for others implies in the individual to have lived a childhood or an adolescence with episodes in which s(he) learned by example of others that type of concern. We also show here that learning something, in this case a value, a virtue (concern), was communicated from the parent to the child not totally by verbal explanations and language codes, but mostly by observation of the action, its motives and its consequences. Observing compassion and concern for others makes realize that a comfort is experienced by the other person. In this way, the value of an action is internalized, remains in the unconscious and triggers and alerts later in life, when, for instance, the grownup child, today's manager, needs to make decisions affecting the well-being of others (community or employees). This reminds us about the need for good educators demanded by Pestalozzi (1746–1827) and Dewey (1975). There is a need to generate in future directors the willingness to well conduct themselves and the need for inner and social reflection.

In the same way, past experiences that were not necessarily so pleasant may trigger the wish of revenge in the future, against either society, or other people in the organization who need to suffer what the manager suffered during childhood or adolescence. For instance, a bad example of incoherence observed in parents when verbal communication was very clear in explaining how to behave with morals, but the action observed by the child in the parent was a contradiction of the well-codified speech. As a child observes inconsistencies of these kinds, s(he) identifies, interprets and internalizes for future actions that it is not so bad to be incoherent between words and actions, because if the parent had this type of behaviour, and mostly everything went well for s(he) in life, it must be the same for him or her to apply at this stage of life.

As such, the dominant positivist theory in management (leadership) that exhorts managers to apply an effective communicative action in order to convince others to be followed (e.g. employees), or accepted (e.g. by means of corporate reports to community) are incomplete, impositive and not real. They do not show the psychoanalytical component that we describe in previous points, taking into account that its complexity not only includes social ties and values, but also individual motives, and individuation desire of uniqueness. These theories are also incomplete because they try to explain the whole communicative action and the leadership task ignoring the psyche of the public (community and employees) who have interpretations of actions and reports, not only by means of analysing words or the corporate image, but also by means of introspection of the organization's history, the behaviour of directors, the actions of powerful individuals inside and the consequences of these organizational actions. In this way, even though many times corporate reports or internal communiqués are accepted by employees and the community, as it is many times taken for granted by shareholders and managers, the interpretational reality that remains in the mind of the people is many times very different from what reports show. Employees and members of the community have also a psyche, a history, and a different individuation and social process, as well as managers and shareholders have.

In this way, communicative action, and more important than all, its results, should include perception and its interpretation in individuals' minds (i.e. what Merleau-Ponty (1965) explains as phenomenology of perception, or what Husserl (1859–1938) qualifies as phenomenology and truth construction) as a result of gestures, history, observable actions and non-objective facts. It should also include the relativeness of conception of ideas regarding the particularity of each individual's context interacting in the same language but with diversity of origins.

References

Bakhtin M M (1981), *The Dialogic Imagination*; trans M Holquist and C Emerson; Austin, University of Texas Press.

Barnett N J and Crowther D (1998), "Community identity in the 21st Century: A Postmodernist Evaluation of Local Government Structure" in *International Journal of Public Sector Management*, 11 (6/7), 425–439.

Barthes R (1973), *Mythologies*; trans A Lavers; London; HarperCollins.

Barthes R (1988), *The Semiotic Challenge*; Oxford; Basil Blackwell.

Baudrillard J (1981), *For a Critique of the Political Economy of Signs*; St Louis; Telos.

Baudrillard J (1988), in M Poster (ed); *Jean Baudrillard: Selected Writings*; Cambridge; Polity Press.

Baudrillard J (1993), *Symbolic Exchange and Death*; trans I H Grant; London; Sage.

Baudrillard J (1999), *Fatal Strategies*; trans P Beitchman and W G J Niesluchowski; London; Pluto Press.

Beit-Hallahmi, B. and Argyle, M. (1997), *The Psychology of Religious Behaviour, Belief and Experience*, London; Routledge.

Bettelheim B (1976), *The Uses of Enchantment*; London; Penguin.

Brandist C (1997), "Bakhtin, Cassirer and symbolic forms"; *Radical Philosophy*, 85, 20–27.

Campbell J (1949), *The Hero with a Thousand Faces*; Princeton, N J; Princeton University Press.

Campbell J (1972), *Myths to Live By*; London; Souvenir Press.

Campbell J (1976), *Creative Mythology* Vol 4: The Masks of God; London; Penguin.

Campbell J (1993), *The Mythic Dimension: Selected Essays 1959–1987*; New York; HarperCollins.

Cassirer E (1955), *The Philosophy of Symbolic Forms Vol 2: Myth*; trans R Manheim, New Haven, Connecticut; Yale University Press.

Crowther D (2002a), *A Social Critique of Corporate Reporting*; Aldershot; Ashgate

Crowther D (2002b), Psychoanalysis and auditing; in S Clegg (ed), *Paradoxical New Directions in Management and Organization Theory*; Amsterdam; Benjamins.

Crowther D (2002c), The psychoanalysis of on-line reporting; in L Holmes, M Grieco and D Hosking (eds); *Distributed technology, distributed leadership, distributed identity, distributed discourse: organising in an information age*; Aldershot; Ashgate (2002).

Crowther D, Cooper S and Carter C (2001), Regulation – The Movie: a semiotic study of the periodic review of UK regulated industry; *Journal of Organizational Change Management, 2001* Vol 14 No 3 pp 225–238.

Derrida J (1978), *Writing and Difference*; trans A Bass; London; Routledge & Kegan Paul.

Dewey, J. (1975), *Moral Principles in Education*, copyright 1909, Southern Illinois University Press U.S.

d'Iribarne, P. (1998), "Comment s'accorder – une rencontre franco-suédoise", in P. d'Iribarne et coll., *Cultures et mondialisation*, Paris, Seuil, chap. IV, p. 89–115.

Dollimore, J (1984), *Radical Tragedy*; Chicago: University of Chicago Press.

Fish S (1985), Is there a text in this class?; in W T J Mitchell (ed); *Against Theory*; Chicago; University of Chicago Press.

Freud S (1977), *On Sexuality*; trans A Richards; Harmondsworth; Pelican.

Guiraud P (1975), *Semiology*; London; Routledge & Kegan Paul.

Habermas J (1971); *Knowledge and Human Interests*; trans J J Shapiro; Boston, Mass; Beacon Press.

Harris M (1979), *Cultural Materialism*; New York; Random House.

Hervey S (1982), *Semiotic Perspectives*; London; George Allen & Unwin.Husserl, E. (1859–1938), *The idea of phenomenology*, trans. by William P. Alston and George Nakhnikian, The Hague : Nijhoff, 1964, reprinted 1968.

Janis I. L. (1972). *Victims of Groupthink*; Boston; Houghton Miffin.

Jenkins A (1979), *The Social Theory of Claude Levi – Strauss*; London; Macmillan.

Jung C G (1953), *Psychology and Alchemy*; trans R F C Hull; London; Routledge.

Jung C G (1954), *The Development of Personality*; trans R F C Hull; London; Routledge.

Jung C G (1972), *Four Archetypes*; trans C F Baynes; London; Routledge.

Lacan J (1977), *Ecrits: a selection*; trans A Sheridan; London; Tavistock.

Lacan J (1988a), *The Seminars of Jacques Lacan Book II: The Ego in Freud's Theory and in the Technique of Psychoanalysis 1954–1955*; trans S Tomaselli; New York; Cambridge University Press.

Lacan J (1988b), *The seminar of Jacques Lacan Book III The Psychoses 1955–56*; trans R Grigg; London; Routledge.

Lacan J (1991), *The Seminars of Jacques Lacan Book I: Freud's papers on Technique 1953–1954*; trans J Forrester; New York; W W Norton & Co.

Levi Strauss C (1955), *The structural study of myth; Journal of American Folklore.* 28, 428–444.

Levi Strauss C (1966), *The Savage Mind*; London; Weidenfeld & Nicolson.

Malinowski B (1962), Myth as a dramatic development of dogma; in I Strenski (ed) (1992); *Malinowski and the Work of Myth*; Princeton, N J; Princeton University Press.

Marcuse H (1956), *Eros and Civilisation*; London; Routledge & Kegan Paul.

May R (1991), *The Cry for Myth*; New York; W W Norton & Co.

McKinstry S (1996), Designing the annual reports of Burton plc from 1930 to 1994; Accounting, *Organizations and Society*, 21 (1), 89–111.

Merleau-Ponty, M., (1965), *Phenomenology of perception*, trans. by Colin Smith, New York, Humanities Press, 1965, 1962.

Mitroff I I (1983), *Stakeholders of the Organisational Mind*; San Francisco; Jossey-Bass.

Nietsche F (1956), *The Birth of Tragedy*; New York; Doubleday.

Norris C (1990), Lost in the funhouse: Baudrillard and the politics of postmodernism; in R Boyne and A Rattansi (eds), *Postmodernism and Society*; Basingstoke; Macmillan, pp 119–153.

Orwell G (1970), *Collected Essays, Journalism and Letters Vol 4*; Harmondsworth; Penguin.

Peirce C S (1958), *Collected papers Vol 5*; P Weiss, C Hartshorne and A Burks (eds); Harvard, Harvard University Press.

Perls F S (1975); *Theory and technique of personality integration*; in J O Stevens (ed), Gestalt Is; Moab, Utah; Real People Press.

Pestalozi, 1746–1827, *The Education of Man – Aphorisms*, trad. Heinz and Ruth Norden, Philosophical Library , New York 1951.

Preston A M, Wright C and Young J J (1996), *Imag[in]ing annual reports; Accounting, Organizations and Society*, 21 (1), 113–137.

Rose J (2000), Feminine sexuality; in P du Gay, J Evans and P Redman (eds), *Identity: a reader*; London; Sage, pp 51–68.

Saussure F de (1966), *Course in General Linguistics*; (trans W Baskin); New York; McGraw-Hill.

Silverman K (2000), Suture: the cinematic model; in P du Gay, J Evans and P Redman (eds), *Identity: a reader*; London; Sage, pp 76–86.

Winnicott, D. (1965), *The maturational processes and the facilitating environment: studies in the theory of emotional developments*, NewYork, International University Press.

Zizek S (1992), *Everything you always wanted to know about Lacan but were afraid to ask Hitchcock*; London; Verso.

Chapter 7

Caring Principle and Practices in Corporate Social Responsibility

Jelena Debeljak, Mirna Koričan, Kristijan Krkač and Andrijana Mušura

Caring, Negligence, and Harm Principles in Corporate Social Responsibility

Among the many different kinds of events there are human actions of caring, such as for example a parent taking care of child, or a manager taking care of her / his business. We can, and in fact statistically we ordinarily do, understand actions as morally right or wrong in the light of their consequences concerning all relevant actions an reactions. This fits in neatly between:

- The grounded idea of market economy which says that a market economy is essentially directed toward the future i.e. future profit; "Capitalists, then, are people who make bets on the future. The essence of capitalism is a psychological orientation toward the pursuit of future wealth and property." (McCraw 2000, Debeljak and Krkač 2006),
- And pragmatist ethics principle which says that consequences of our actions are viewed, not from the present action to them as actualizing in the future (like in Mill), but rather viewed from the future world that one is produced by performing certain action with its consequences (like in Dewey).

So, both our morality and the economy depend in fact on our present hopes regarding the future facts which still don't exist (see Kagin, Krkač and Mušura 2005) and yet they are a criterion of morally right and wrong in terms of a better future world that we want to produce by performing certain actions or whole standard practice, like in pragmatist ethics. Caring seems to be, among other things, a kind of (legitimate) interpretation (narrative) of our motives or intentions, and the most of all of consequences of our actions (everyday, ethical, economic, and legal).

Caring is an everyday and also a legal term. Care is exercise of caution and prudence in one's conduct so as to avoid causing injury or loss. Care can be ordinary care (due care, or reasonable care), or utmost care (extraordinary care). In legal terms negligence is a type of malpractice. Malpractice is negligence or other failure of a professional such as a doctor, lawyer, manager, or accountant, to live up to reasonable professional standards in the performance of services for a client. Negligence is conduct involving an unreasonable risk of injury or loss to others, or the conduct that falls short of the degree of care that a reasonable person would have exercised in the same circumstances.

Care	Failure to exercise care
↓	↓
Ordinary	→ Negligence
Extraordinary	→ Breach of fiduciary duty
	→ Malpractice

"To take care" of X by Y, as it were, means for Y to execute actions by which X will perform properly, and without which X will not perform properly or even not perform at all; meaning that X will suffer certain loss, injury, harm, or damage. On the other hand "to act with care" means something rather different, i.e. to act with something which seems to be added to the act itself and which can serve as explication, not of the action itself, but to some extent as explication of the manner in which the action is performed. So, "to act with care" means in fact "to act with special care", not just "to take (regular, necessary and sufficient) care". But there is some kind of ontic difference, namely between:

• Taking care as performing an action properly or *lege artis* regarding the standard procedures of a profession,
• And "acting with care" is a narrative which is the best story about what one as a professional does in terms of producing a better world – compared to the present status of it – by certain action and its consequences, in a situation where one is doing something more than "taking care", and which can be conceived as something added to proper performance of an action or of a standard practice of necessary and sufficient care, or ordinary care.
• In other words it can be said that "caring" as covering value determined by our actions as future benefit from their consequences, is essentially manifest "in the stories which are told about, told by, and told to" ourselves, others, firms or organizations (Crowther and Jatana 2005: 125–165). What is more, it is a "myth of acting with care" which seems to prove it useful, and moreover it is used in practice.

But regarding this ontic difference, there is nothing caring, non-caring, or careless in or about our actions (there is no caring "aboutness" of human actions). Caring is the way of "seeing" human actions, i.e. caring is a way of talking about them, not the way of performing an action as a part of practice. There is no ontic power of acting with care, or caring action, as something added to *lege artis* performance, but nonetheless in any type of action or whole practice we can describe what it would be to act with sufficient or reasonable care or on the other hand with relevant lack of care. Caring can exist in the mind of the performer of an action as the motive, goal, or emotion, and also it can exist in the mind of the person to whom the action is directed to as the benefit, but it cannot exist in action itself. For example:

(a) Washing hand properly, and
(b) Washing them with regular care,

in fact means the same thing because both (a) and (b) can be described in terms of the certain procedure of washing hands in order to make them sufficiently clean for a given purpose. So in fact there is no normative addition in (b) as an act compared to (a), although there can be and in fact there is a certain narrative addition to the very act of washing hands in terms of explicating the motive for washing hands (for example to a child) or explicating the purpose or goal as a certain value, (for example hygiene, as health avoidance of illness, etc.) in order to explicate future benefits.

Nevertheless we speak of a person as doing something with care, but that means that the person is performing an action with high motivation, and / or with strong feelings for the benefit of the object to which the action is directed. Maybe it implies a certain kind of altruism but we will deal with this issue later. On the other hand what is lack of care, or malpractice? It seems that it is negligence, and negligence is, as formulated by Judge Learned Hand:

"the failure to take care where the cost of care is less then the probability of the accident multiplied by the loss if the accident occurs". The product of this multiplication is the expected costs of the accident. (Posner 1983:5, referring to US v. Carroll Towing Co. 159F 2d.169 (2d Cir. 1947))

An objective test of negligence says:

"a person who considered a situation thoroughly and took what he genuinely regarded as a reasonable risk would nevertheless properly be found negligent if the jury concludes that a person of ordinary intelligence and prudence in that situation would not have done what the defendant did." (Clapp 1996:171)

So it seems that is easier to understand what is (regular) care in terms of lack of (regular) care or negligence. In other words X is negligent regarding Y if:

(1)   X is choosing between practice α and practice β, and X chooses and performs α rather then β

(2a) and where practice α implies action involving an unreasonable risk of injury or loss to Y and/or others (X is excluded, and where a reasonable person is a person of ordinary intelligence and prudence),

(2b) or the action that falls short of the degree of care that a reasonable person would have been exercised in the circumstances in which X was in time of choosing α and performing α.

Say that X is a manager and Y is a firm in which he is employee, or a customer of the firm, or part of the environment surrounding the industrial region of the firm.

- Then there must be a certain set of rules implicit in an action or, in short, a certain set of procedures, and X is by performing these actions or procedures displaying "care" or X is "taking care" of Y, and by not performing these actions or by performing them only partially or incompletely X is displaying negligence toward Y.

So it seems that care can be standardized in terms of formulating standard procedures of, for example, management of the firm, or at least in terms of standard exceptions of procedures that must be avoided in order not to perform in a negligent manner toward the other stakeholders of the business in question. But in order to connect all these procedures, as it were, as practices that can be described as business practices that are legal and moreover morally correct, we can apply a universal rule to the sphere of business in order to create a general care principle (or in negative terms a "harm principle") for CSR. So, application of the care principle in negative form of negligence and in combination with the harm principle will result in the following principle for moral correctness in terms of CSR:

- In order not to display negligence or any other kind of malpractice as a lack of ordinary care, any business activity should be conducted in such a manner that by itself or by its direct consequences does not produce any kind of irreparable damage or harm (or preferably if it is possible not to damage or harm at all) to any of its stakeholders (social, non-social, internal, or external).

An application of this to the previously stated criterion would be the following: where X is a firm, or its member (for example a manager) and Y is any other stakeholder of the business (employee, customer, owner, environment, etc.), then in terms of business action (relevant to the type of market economy and cultural context of the business) X is negligent regarding Y if:

(1)   X is choosing between business practice α and business practice β, and X chooses and performs α rather then β,

(2a)   where practice α implies action involving an unreasonable risk of injury or loss to Y in such a way that the practice α by itself or by its direct consequences does produce any kind of irreparable damage or harm to Y,

(2b)   or that the business person X or his action is such that it falls short of the degree of care that a reasonable business person would have exercised in the circumstances in which X as a business person was at the time of choosing α and performing α rather then β.

Nel Noddings in "Two Concepts of Caring" considers that neither utilitarianism nor deontology can provide a proper understanding of the feminine approach to morality which is, traditionally, embedded in receptivity, relatedness and responsiveness. In that sense, characteristic terms of her theory are:

- Natural caring – a moral attitude upon which ethics should be based – 'a longing for goodness [rather than moral reasoning] that arises out of the experience or memory of being cared for' – comes out from her elementary point that care is basic in human life – referring to that relation in whom we respond as one caring out of love or natural inclination. (N. Noddings, "The Ethics of Care and Education").
- Ethical caring – arises out of natural caring. It is 'a state of being in relation, characterized by receptivity, relatedness and engrossment', the relation in which we meet the other morally.
- Sympathy – feeling with 'the affective state of attention in caring'.
- Receptive attention – an essential characteristic of a caring encounter – explains that this encounter is beneficial for both the carer and the cared for.
- A caring person – 'one who fairly regularly establishes caring relations and, when appropriate maintains them over time' (ibid).
- Caring for – direct encounters in which one person cares for another – refers to a special attribute of relations, and as such, theoretically stands above "caring about".
- Caring about – more generally, refers to a virtue, and takes us to a more public realm. "May be foundation of justice" (Noddings, "Two Concepts of Caring").

These concepts will be used in the next section so it seems that these definitions are quite important.

Ethics of Care and CSR

One may hear that the 21st century is a century of women. Why? What is so fresh about this *different kind of voice*? It has not been very highly esteemed in the history of mankind and only in recent history awakes. What sort of "holes" does the lack of typically female contribution produce, that one can sense if one takes a closer look? In the scientific area of moral philosophy, the 'different voice' or 'women's way of knowing' has grown into a syntagm by the name of *the ethics of care*.

In the light of women and work problems, we will try to provide some guidelines that are helpful in giving a proper answer to the questions asked, by starting with a short background of care ethics, introducing some relevant theorists' thoughts and current discussions, and ideas on the sources of prejudices in western society regarding sexual discrimination and its leftovers.

The ethics of care is defined as moral reasoning that derives from a concern for others and a desire to maintain thoughtful mutual relationships with those affected by one's actions.

It emerged in the late 1970s, in the context of Carol Gilligan's interviews with women facing abortion decisions. Gilligan gave the basic arguments and set the grounds for the ethics of care. Versus Kohlberg's theory of gradient development of morality, Gilligan introduced ethics of care as a "different voice", a different moral approach, and not just one of Kohlberg's stages of moral development.

The ethics of care fits more to women's psychology, since it emphasizes intimacy, caring and personal relationships, while male psychology sees morality more as a matter of justice and principle. A traditional approach to morality and ethics matches better the male way of thinking, while the ethics of care opens doors for a new way of observing moral situations coming from a female perspective.

Virginia Held propounds the ethics of care to be an alternative to the dominant approaches of Kantian moral theory, utilitarianism, and virtue ethics. She is arguing that female traits should not be underrated in explaining human morality and behaviour. It is social definitions that need to be changed, not women themselves. Ultimately, the culture of feminism could provide a fresh perspective on – even solutions to – contemporary social problems.

She is not the only one who sees the ethics of care, or female way of thinking, as beneficial and needed in this context. As Paul Tournier, at the end of the 1970s, pointed out, nowadays society lacks what are known as typically female approaches. In his opinion, the business environment is the area that needs it the most.

"The concern of the ethics of care is the responsibility of the individual to respond to another, or in other terms, acting out of care for the other person" (Gilligan, 1982). This is distinct from conceptions of morality as justice in that it does not attempt to follow impartial rules or ensure impartial treatment. It focuses on responsiveness to another's needs. It also includes caring for oneself in a nurturing rather than a self-maximizing way. Few scholars urged extensive incorporation of the ethics of care into business ethics research. For example, surveying ethics education for accountants, Sara Reiter indicated the need for cases with real individuals in concrete situations; Thomas White distinguished its potential involvement to a better understanding of how women manage organizations; John Dobson and Judith White further suggested that a "feminine oriented relationship-based value system complements the essential nature of the firm as a nexus of relationships between stakeholders"; Jeanne M. Liedka noticed strong relations between the ethics of care and Freeman's stakeholder theory – as some scholars noted, for stakeholder theorists, the interdependence is between groups; for care theorists, it is between and among the individuals who comprise those groups. Ethics of care is also consistent to the 2nd formulation of Kant's Categorical Imperative to always treat persons as ends, and not merely means. That means treating each person as a concrete rather than a generalized other. It is also observed as reversing Kantian priorities – by Nel Noddings, ethical caring comes after the 'natural' caring – it arises from the 'natural', what makes the ethical caring an instrument in 'establishing or restoring' the natural care.

Care Theory by Nel Noddings

As Noddings explains, "it is physically impossible to 'care for' all of humanity, strangers who have not addressed us directly, or those unknown others at a great distance." (*ibid*) According to her, we learn to care through our experience of being cared for. Caring about must be seen as instrumental in establishing the conditions under which caring can grow; it can help in establishing, maintaining, and enhancing caring. Those who care about others in the justice sense must keep in mind that the objective is to ensure that caring actually occurs. Caring about is empty if it does not culminate in caring relations. She argues that the ethics of care reveals the old distinction between *is* and *ought* as a pseudo problem.

Caring is a moral attitude "informed by the complex skills of interpersonal reasoning, that neither without its own forms of rigour nor somehow less professional than the calculated skills of formal logic" (N. Noddings, "The Ethics of Care and Education"). Expressions usually used in the language of the care ethics are: experience, relation, female traits – love, caring, emotion.

Virginia Held finds experience to be the central category of feminist thought: "It is not the constructed experience of mere empirical observation, as various giants in the history of modern philosophy and as analytic philosophy tend to construct it. Feminist experience is the experience with which art, literature and science deal. Is the lived experience of feeling as well as thought, of acting as well as receiving impressions, and of connectedness to other persons as well as self." (Held, "Feminist Moral Inquiry: The Role of Experience") And further on, she points out that, by now, for feminists, it is not the experience of what can be thought of as women as such from which we learn and by which we test our moral views. It is the experience of actual woman with no regard to her cultural background, outward appearance the society is infatuated with nowadays, colour, sexual orientation, status or prestige, feminist men and other aspects. Contrary to the predominating theory of liberal individualism in the society today, Held cites, caring is partly emotional. It involves feelings and requires high degrees of empathy to discern what morality recommends in our caring activities.

If we try to consider the possible implication of the care ethics to business ethics and social responsibility, the thought is developing through several distinctive features. The ethics of care emphasize the maintenance of relationships and their numerous commitments. In the corporate environment there's an increasing demand for business to be attentive to its many stakeholders, particularly customers and employees, in caring ways. As organizations attempt to build such relationships, important for sustainable business, they must define the responsibilities of initiating and maintaining care. The ethics of care may be able to facilitate an understanding of these responsibilities.

> Lack of love, care and understanding of the people and the pressure of internal politics coupled with work pressure have caused high absenteeism and, in extreme cases, high staff turnover. People have emotions and I am very sure that love can attract love and lack of love and kindness can attract dislike and dissatisfaction. (Gyatso, 1990, by Perspectives on Corporate Social Responsibility: Management by Love and Kindness p. 220)

The ethics of care observes women's lives and perspectives as informative and instructive. An increasing number of women and minorities taking on a significant role in management creates a greater need for that. Modern corporations and companies follow the trend of investing in what they recognize as their most important capital – people, employees. This is a realm for care as well. Studying it and expanding its possibilities helps better understand the importance of quality relationships inside the corporations and those that stretch throughout its walls – relationships with other stakeholders, like investors, customers, society and environment. The only way to be sure that taken actions are morally correct, is to be sure that there are certain root habits and routines in business or in short "organizational culture."

Judging by what has been said about care ethics so far, this is a moral theory perfectly suitable for estimation of mutual relationships among people. Perhaps they are even the most important for ethics / morality since most ethical / moral wrongdoings are done by neglect or omission to do a good deed, and not by bad / evil deeds (Krkač 2006) It is possible to observe the ethics of care as a certain universal, alternative approach. In the business arena, that kind of observation brings us once more to the conclusion, to follow the advice of some of the most successful businessmen, who *loved* what they were doing, and that caring attitude brought them success. For them business was not just a mere means in the pursuit for profits They were treating it guided by a caring ethics – nourishing it as it was a child or a plant one wants to grow. Success means showing the care for what one is doing, and everything and everyone involved. "If wealth is your only goal in life, you shall never accomplish it" (Rockefeller). This is the place of application of the ethics of care and a way of improved morality, since it may as well be a natural position on which (corporate) social responsibility is built. Virginia Held adds,

> Economic activity would be socially supported to serve human well-being rather than to merely increase the economic power of the economically powerful. The ethics of care builds trust and mutual responsiveness to need on both the personal and wider social level. (...) The ethics of care offers a view of both the more immediate and the more distant human relations on which satisfactory societies can be built. (Held, "Feminist Moral Inquiry: The Role of Experience" http://www.janushead.org/5-1/held.cfm)

Pro-social Behaviour, Ethics of Care and CSR

Some authors argue that in *virtue ethics* emphasis is on being a good person rather than simply making justified and fair decisions. When asked to list the attributes that characterize a moral person, Walker and Henning (2004) found that besides being *just* and *brave*, *caring* was central to the moral personality. Caring in different term is love, altruism and empathy. When making a link between ethics of care and corporate social responsibility, we must consider *caring* elements as individual characteristics that promote socially responsible behaviour, defined as discretionary decisions and actions taken by individuals in organizations to enhance societal well-being (Schneider et al, 2005).

One of the key assumptions of underlying socially responsible behaviour is its intrinsic motivation. This means that individual behaviour is motivated by inner motives and satisfaction and not serving just as instrumental good. Pro-social behaviour, understood as intrinsically motivated behaviour, is defined as behaviour that serves for benefiting others. When it is coloured with altruism and empathy, the former being defined as willingness to help another person even in if encountering personal loses and later as capacity of experiencing the feelings, thoughts, and experience of another, pro-social behaviour serves as no instrument (Aronson et al, 2005).

As Schneider et al (2005) see it, from a corporate philanthropy perspective, social and moral engagements are seen as instrumental to making profit but from the *integrated* view, CSR activities are an expression of "who we are" and as such can be an illustration of organizational virtue. The way to delve into the core of organizational social responsibility is to consider an individual that is standing behind a strategic organizational decision to act socially responsible. This individual needs to be pro-socially oriented.

Some research found a high correlation between pro-social behavior and an individual's attitudes toward social responsibility (O'Connor and Cuevas, 1982). Pro-social behavior can be of great importance to organizations, the ones that see themselves and act as socially responsible. Knowing if a potential employee is pro-socially oriented toward people, groups and society as a whole can add to that organization's CSR value from the inside. Elements of the *ethics of care* embedded as motives of pure pro-social behaviour can add intrinsic value to an organization's CSR.

So to conclude, it is unlikely to expect that a person will behave in terms of a corporate social responsible way if he or she is not intrinsically motivated to do so. Even though pro-social behaviour is intrinsic, organizations that promote this kind of behaviour can achieve that this kind of behaviour is shown more often. This pro-social behaviour can be achieved through motivation of the workers in the organization. Also, provided by arguments and lots of evidence, people can conform under the informational social influence and change their opinion and behaviour towards socially responsible behaviour. Informational social influence is influence by others that can lead towards conforming because we use other people as a source of information. So, organizations that have corporate culture which is nurturing the care of others and ethical behaviour are likely to have their workers who will act and promote socially responsible behaviour.

Discrimination, Prejudice and Bias – Background

Unfortunately, a discussion about women still cannot be avoided by the sexual discrimination and bias quandary. Although it may seem like this problem has been worn out by now, unfortunately again, it is only seemingly so. As Anna Fels' research shows, discrimination of today is hidden below the surface.

> "A key type of discrimination that women face is the expectation that 'feminine' women will forfeit opportunities for recognition at home and at work. Being silenced or ignored often remains a baffling and frustrating barrier to women's understanding of how their lives are shaped. This is a 'sin of omission' rather than one of commission, so it's hard to spot. It's not as obvious as being denied the right to vote or access to birth control." (Fels, Anna. "Do Women Lack Ambition?")

These are the inner battles modern society must fight, and can relate to social models that vary from one country to another making the models more or less equally flexible for the sexes, in the way one wishes to organise her / his life. Of course, in "the man's world" they are usually made more flexible for men. We must not forget the commonly used term of "the glass ceiling" which we can explain as an invisible barrier that women can not pass within an organization. Women are usually promoted on the level within the organization which can be near the top of the management, but are usually not promoted in the top level management places. On those top management level places men rule, considering the percentage of the places they have.

Even though we must notice that when talking about managerial skills more and more people are mentioning skills that are considered "soft" and more common in women than men. In the past, organizations were functioning dependant on machines and not so much on human resources. Today, human resources are the most valuable capital that a firm can have and all organizations that are in the top invest a lot into their human resources. To lead a successful company and lead people inside the organization towards a mutual goal a manager has to have soft skills. Women managers are better at the beginning because by nature they have them developed, and if they train other capabilities and knowledge, they can be as successful as a male manager. Some say that 21ˢᵗ century is a century of a woman. The time will show what will happen.

Mobbing in Croatia

Internet portal www.vip.hr reports, the experiences of women, aged 25–45, who were searching for employment, and shows that by the job interview there are a small number of employers for whom experience, motivation and willingness to learn are important. Most of them ask questions about marriage status, the number of children, and possible commitments that would stop a woman from working 'in case of a need'. (www.vip.hr, Zagreb, 06.04.2005. 16:17 (Hina)). The latest news on Croatian National Television (HRT) show women in Croatia being generally 20 per cent less well paid than men for the same work.

The same portal provides information for the EU: the salary difference between the sexes in 2004 was 15 per cent, respectively women were earning 15 per cent less than men in the EU. The difference is smallest in Malta, in Portugal and Belgium, 5 per cent and biggest on Cyprus, Estonia and Slovakia, 25 per cent. This data is quite offensive and disrespectful at the beginning of the third millennium, and does not speak much in favour of the development of human consciousness or knowing.

At least regarding Croatia it can be reliably claimed that mobbing is a big issue. It is also possible to say that the lack of features traditionally recognized as feminine, since they include what the meaning of caring represents in itself, is in question here, too – meaning, traditionally female approaches are viewed as less valuable.

The causes of mobbing, according to psychiatrist Elvira Koić, are unsettled relationships between people, bad organizations, vague business processes and working assignments, and finally, though in the smallest number of cases, psychopathological characteristics of the abuser. Consequences are reflected in the psychological, social and physiological field. Subjects of mobbing in Croatia most often are superior men. (Lider, *MOBBING. How to defend from mobbing?* (in Croatian). November 2ⁿᵈ 2007, pp. 24–29). These dregs of prejudice, now mostly present only in our minds / conscience, need to be swept away, before we pull the curtains down and applaud to one more good show of the World's theatre!

Western civilization is culturally fundamentally Christian. If one searches the Bible on which the Christianity is based, and consequently the largest amount of the western culture, one will not find any justified bias. Christ was the first one in history whose teaching and life example brought women to a righteous level in society. It is only after Him when women started engaging in society and their role was justifiably recognized after the classical period (Gal 3:28: *There is neither Jew nor Greek, slave nor free, male nor female, for you are all one in Christ Jesus.*) The prejudice of *moral weakness* of women was based on the sin of Eve – various interpretations of that story were made by generations of theorists and commentators who could hardly wait to fill in the places where the Scripture keeps silent (for more see Brown, Anne. p. 101, etc.). Concerning the well known hater of women of the church fathers, Erich Fuchs proves it has originated from the influence of stoicism of that time, and Dr. Nodet points on the neurosis of the holy Jerome (Tournier, Paul. p. 94). And until nowadays, a crooked picture of Eve imbues the culture of the west. It has been always said more about the weak sides of a woman, and less about the strong ones, their advantages. Controversially, for men – only their strong points have been emphasised, and the weaknesses have not been mentioned as much (What are they?). I believe it is possible to argue that one of the greater weaknesses of men have always been women themselves. No man really likes being weak in any sense.

Another puzzling thought. Why do both man and women have in their minds the concept of rationality being *more important* than sentiment? Is this a question for *valuation* at all? But it exists in our society. We censure women for being generally emotional, beforehand valuating rationality more. Women have proved their intelligence capabilities do not distinguish from the men's. "Hardly anyone claims today that women lack the native ability to become neurosurgeons or executives" (Fels). Now, to keep their nature balanced and to show appreciation towards the same, it would be wrong if they would hide their sensitivity trying to play "by the rules of men". As Taylor Cox Jr cites, in the 1950s three of every four graduates in the States were men; in recent years most of graduates are women (around 54 per cent). Equally in 1971 there were only 4 per cent of women graduating from business schools. By the early 90s this percentage increased for more than seven times, up to 30 per cent. In requested technical fields such as engineering the share of women is even greater (Cox, p. 2).

Paul Tournier is pointing to Descartes, because it was only after him when the primacy of the rational principle was proclaimed in philosophy over sensitivity and the heart. He is saying that the great injustice towards women, her legal alienation, happened in the Renaissance, after the discovery of Roman law. The whole social improvement for women accomplished after the classical (Greek and Roman) period until the Middle Ages fell apart. The social liberation of women had not finished in the Middle Ages, but it had still reached much further than it was in the classical period. After the Renaissance, the rediscovered Roman law influenced the great political changes which were leading to modern states and their nationalism. And this has simultaneously initiated the neglect of women, by the example of the classical Rome. By the book of Benoîte Groult ("Ainsi soit – elle", Paris, Grasset 1975),

Tournier quotes Richelieu, who said at the time: "Nothing could harm the state as much as that sex", referring to women.

Tournier also speaks about two types of perception – logically-intellectual comprehension that predominates in the experience of men who are searching for different kinds of *how*, and intuitively-sensible comprehension in women's experience who are searching for *why*. Further on, he argues how an objective, scientific, logical thinking – is perfection, but its behaviour is inhuman. Our masculine civilization finds thought superior to behaviour. A woman cares more for the behaviour and what has been experienced. In his observation, men are embodiments of logical intelligence, women of the intuition of heart, because intelligence is the one that separates, divides and confronts (Descartes), but the intuition brings to fusion. He argues that men comprehend the basic unity of person as if 'their parts were glued together' after being dissected first, while a woman does it by a direct intuition.

> "We, the men, believe we understand everything, and spontaneously it does not occur to us to ask for help from a woman, in order to understand something we do not understand by our selves. This would be a real promotion of a woman: when a man would understand what he is missing and expect it from a woman." (Paul Tournier)

For the purpose of better understanding of the *women's way of knowing*, it is useful to mention a great contribution made in the project under the same name by Blythe McVicker Clinchy, Nancy Rule Goldberger and Jill Mattuck Tarule. The result of their study was formulated in a theory consisting of five types of knowing from which women approach the world: silence, received knowledge, subjective knowledge, procedural knowledge – consisting of connected knowing and separate knowing. The connected knower believes that truth is "personal, particular, and grounded in firsthand experience." They attempt to find the truth through listening, empathizing, and taking impersonal stances to information, whereas separate knower completely excludes feelings from making meaning and strictly rely on reason. The last way of knowing is constructed knowledge, where one integrates its own opinions and sense of self with reason and the outside world around them (Belenky, Clinchy, Goldberger, Tarule. *Women's Ways of Knowing,* (in Croatian)) The very essence of the female way of knowing was perhaps said by one of their interviewees explaining the truth as something we sense, as the voice inside of us we only need to know how to communicate, or to prove it in a reasonable manner. By the arguments of the reason solely, without listening the voice, we get nothing… The truth is not in the external arguments by themselves, they reflect it if they reflect the inner voice.

As a radically and specifically feminine voice, it comes out, therefore, out of typically feminine psyche. And to value feminine in respect to masculine psyche and vice versa, is a contradictory. There is no place for value comparison between male (typically ratio) and female voice (sentiment) voice, since they imply to different realities and in this manner together create a whole. On the same line, all social critics of newer history talk about 'coldness and alienation' as a product of a one-sided way of thinking.

Sometimes it seems funny to talk about social responsibility and caring relations of a large(er) unit when we even find hard to arrange the relations with the one closest to us, or see no meaning in it. Acceptance of differences and varieties we find our selves to be situated in is the only answer to the problems of creating a more nurturing and equitable world. But, starting from sexual differences, for some reason this seems to be the hardest thing to do. A chance of esteeming and better understanding of care (ethics) is being offered as the mean of uprooting that 'hidden' bias in human's minds. A character in a children's TV serial recently said: "It's very important to accept the differences and to learn how to be thoughtful of the interests of the other." So maybe the conclusion is – grownups should watch children's serials on TV, or read books for children more often – just to remind themselves of the simple lessons they were taught in kindergarten.

References

"Mobbing, How to defend from harassment" in: *Lider*, 3rd November, 2006, pp. 24–29, (in Croatian).

"The Holy Bible", http://www.biblegateway.com/passage/?search=Gal++3:28

Aronson, E., Wilson, T.D. and Akert, R.M. 2005 Social Psychology. Zagreb: MATE.

Brown A. 1996 "Apology of Woman, Feminism and Bible", STEPress, Zagreb, (in Croatian).

Clapp J.E. 1996 "Legal Dictionary", Random House, New York.

Crowther D. Jatana R. 2005 "Modern Epics and Corporate Well–Being", in: Crowther, Jatana (Eds.) "Representations of Social Responsibility" – Vol. II, The ICFAI University Press, Hyderabad.

Crowther, D. and L. Rayman-Bacchus (Eds) *Perspectives on Corporate Social Responsibility*, Ashgate, Aldershot).

Debeljak J. Krkač K. 2006 «Influence of culture on European business, ethics, and business ethics» in: Đ. Njavro, K. Krkač (eds.) «Business Ethics and Corporate Social Responsibility», International Conference Papers, MATE, ZSEM, 2006:110–125.

Debeljak, J., Krkač, K., 2006 "The role of culture in European Business, Ethics and Business Ethics" in: international conference proceedings "Business Ethics and Corporate Social Responsibility", Njavro, Đ. and Krkač, K. (eds.), ZSEM, Mate.

Fels A. "Do Women Lack Ambition?" in Harvard Business Review, October 2006, pp. 50–60.

Field Belenky M. McVicker Clinchy B. Rule Goldberger N. Mattuck Tarule J. 1998 "Women's ways of knowing", (in Croatian), Druga, Zagreb.

Held V. 2003 "Feminist Moral Inquiry: The Role of Experience".

Hoffman W.M. Frederick, R.E., Schwartz, M.S. 1998 (Eds) *Business Ethics: Readings and Cases in Corporate Morality*, Fourth edition McGraw-Hill Higher Education.

Kagin J. Krkač K. Mušura A. 2005 "Time, Credit and Debt, An Essay in Philosophy of Economics" in: F. Stadler, M. Stölzner (eds.) 2005 «Preproceedings of 28th

International Wittgenstein Symposium", Kirchberg am Wechsel, 2005:127–131

Krkač K. "Routine, Morality and Pragmatism", (in Croatian), Zagreb.

McCraw T.K. 2000 "Creating Modern Capitalism", Harvard University Press, Cambridge.

Noddings N. "The ethics of Care and Education" (http://www.infed.org/thinkers/noddings.htm)

Noddings N. "Two Concepts of Caring" (http://www.ed.uiuc.edu/eps/pes-yearbook/1999/noddings.asp)

O'Connor, M. and Cuevas, J. (1982) The relationship of children's prosocial behavior to social responsibility, prosocial reasoning, and personality. *Journal of Genetic Psychology, 140*(1), 33–45.

Posner R. A. 1983 *The Economics of Justice*, Harvard University Press, Cambridge.

Schneider, S.C., Oppengaard, K., Zollo Marizio and Huy, Q. 2005 Socially Responsible Behavior: Developing virtue in organizations. Retrieved from URL: http://faculty.insead.edu/zollo/personal/documents/Socially% 20responsible%20 behavior%203.pdf on December 26th 2006.

Tournier P. 1991 "Poslanje žene. Putovi i zadaci feminizma", Provincijalat franjevaca trećoredaca, Zagreb, (in Croatian).

Walker, L.J. and Henning, K.H. 2004 Differing conceptions of moral exemplarity: Just, brave and caring. *Journal of Personality and Social Psychology*, 86: 629–647.

Chapter 8

Critical Pedagogy as a Strategy for Management Development: Introducing Intersubjectivity as a Practical Application Tool

Ana Maria Dávila Gómez and Jair Nascimento Santos

The Problem: How Management Education can Contribute to the Social Responsibility of Organizations?

All kinds of organizations are responsible for society's development; therefore, all managers have the task to contribute towards the achievement of this responsibility. Consequently, management education as a contributor of director's formation, handles the power to develop in future directors some attitudes that help them to attempt and to achieve changes in organizations and societies.

Nevertheless, organizational reality practices have a lack in sharing and contributing achievements with the whole society (examples of these anomalies are treated by Alvesson and Willmott, 1996; Aktouf, 1989; Chanlat, 1998 amongst others). As the organization researchers we are, we found that many of these anomalies are caused by the messages transferred in management education, where students (future managers) learn theories and practices with a sole emphasis on monetary profit and with a consequent disregard of social dimensions. However, some academic researchers could argue with us that during the past fifty years, business education has already introduced the human concern in courses such as human resources and organizational behaviour. Despite the existence of these courses, we realize that they do not respond completely to our social concern as they seek to achieve the employee's commitment to assure the organization's economic growth, with disregard of other omnipresent dimensions such as diversity, culture and symbolism. In this case, the majority of methods utilized in management education do not enclose reflection or discussion about human and social consequences of management theory application.

Our research and practical experience has shown us that reality is the result of people's actions. Thus, even though many organizations are driven only by economic profit, we identified that changes in its reality are possible by the action of reflective managers. This need of reflection has guided us to find some propositions in the field of management education.

Therefore, we need a pedagogical approach that accepts the concepts of totality, where each element of the whole society is influenced by its other elements, given that all of them are interconnected. However, to accept this interdependence, we cannot finish our enthusiasm telling us "there's nothing to do, this aim is incommensurable." On the contrary, we have the opportunity to take a position and a positive attitude of hope in spaces where we can recognize that even though the isolated action of one person cannot change the total world; this isolated action is a step in the major success of a radical social change. In this sense, we talk of an emancipation from the standard organizational structures. In doing so, an isolated action relates with other people's actions and so forth. Thus, we take into account Foucault's (1980) concept of micro-emancipation to refer what a professor's action can produce in his students. As Alvesson and Willmott (1996) tell us:

> ... emancipation does not have to be conceptualized or realized only in terms of "grand" projects. Instead, it maybe partially and imperfectly fulfilled in everyday management and organization practice. (p.186)

In this chapter we propose an answer that facilitates both the professor's and the student's emancipation, in order to help future managers to become aware of their social responsibility. Our solution is the critical pedagogy approach, which we complement with two concepts: intersubjectivity and evaluative cognition. Even though critical pedagogy encourages reflection in students, most authors have treated the approach in a theoretical way and so little is told about practical examples and implementation methods. That is why the two complementary concepts aid the professors in their practical tasks. Thus, our paper develops four items. Firstly, in point 1, we have already presented the problem and the need to change the current reality. Secondly, in point 2, we present what critical pedagogy states. Thirdly, we dedicate most of the paper to present in point 3 our complementary propositions with practical applications, taking into account our experience as professors. Finally, we conclude about our proposition and our roles as contributors of the manager's development. Consequently, our contribution is from a practical sense.

Critical Pedagogy: Its Origins, Statements and Spaces to Fulfill

Research literature tells us that critical pedagogy approach takes into account our concerns about totality and social construction. It was Giroux (1981) who elaborated the bases of the critical pedagogy. According to him, coherence is the key to succeed in a process of awareness. Professors and institutions must be coherent between what they say, as need of reflection, and what they do in the classroom reality. In its general purpose, this approach can be implemented for any study discipline; it is not exclusive for management.

Giroux's takes inspiration from the critical theory which emerges from the Frankfurt school (with authors such us Habermas, Horkheimer and Marcuse). This school has been nourished from Marxism, post-structuralism (with Foucault) and postmodernism (with Derrida). From Marxism it takes the idea that education forms the people who will conduct the changes. Thus, education is a social change tool. Habermas (1972) develops a critique about the interest pursued by capitalist mechanisms and by the modern technology and economy; and consequently education answers to the social demands. By its own, as we have already said it in point 1, Foucault develops the concept of micro-emancipation as alternative. In addition, he illustrates power as a tool for change. By the same token, Derrida (1976) considers that the general social discourse can be de-constructed in order to identify the nature of pursued goals. In collective statements (e.g. a national declaration, a constitution or an organizational statement), the discourse's content exposes ideologies and power holders. Thus, in many cases, a collective discourse is accommodated to answer to the interest of the powerful ones, with disregard of general public opinion. In the de-construction method, questioning tools allow individuals to become aware of inequalities, injustices and consequences of actions.

Despite that the theoretical framework has existed for more than seventy years, it was only in the last decade that authors of organization studies had articulated it for management education. With our literature review, we conclude that the authors who articulate the most this approach are Reynolds (1997–1999) and Boje (1996), given that they construct a support frame to make reality the Giroux's statement of coherence. Here is their support frame:

Table 8.1   Hierarchical pedagogical approaches

Traditional Education	**Radical content**
Traditional content Traditional process	Radical content Traditional process
Radical process	**Critical Pedagogy**
Traditional content Radical process	Radical content Radical process

(Reynolds 1999, adapted form Giroux 1981)

What the authors seek is to have a classroom experience in the shaded box. In order to be coherent, what professors teach as course content must be aligned with what the pedagogical process is. Radical content implies for the professor to dispose of lectures, which treat culture, diversity and social interaction in organizations. Radical process implies a call to professors and institutions to identify if they allow the students a free or a conditioned speaking. Like that, the processes of planning and direction in the pedagogical cycle are fulfilled. However, little attention is given to the other processes, evaluation and controlling, exception being made of some professors whom apply self-questioning about the ideology that lies behind their course's contents and their disposition to modify their own methods after suggestions proposed by their students.

Furthermore, more recent works (Caproni and Prasad, 1997; Hardy and Palmer, 1999; Grey, Knights and Willmott, 1996; Rosile and Boje, 1996; Clegg and Ross-Smith, 2003) had the same aim as ours in terms of dispose of practical tips for the classroom. In general, these works have taken as their reference frames that of Benson's (1977) components of dialectical organization: social construction, totality, contradiction and praxis. The authors referred have transformed the contradiction component into power and ideology, in order to relate it with what authors of critical theory state. Some of the practices referred by the former authors, which can be applied by professors, are:

- In an advanced course, asking students to elucidate at what point their initial goals in taking administration studies have been fulfilled with what they have learned. Even if all goals are not completely fulfilled, professors must illustrate to the students that all previous living events are a necessary part of the continuous learning process.
- In courses of multiculturalism, leadership or communication skills, give to the students lectures about real cases of organizations that have had to resolve conflicts in those arenas. Before class, ask the students to read the lecture and to make a self-reflection about ways utilized by managers to solve conflicts and the restrictions imposed by stockholders and external regulatory organizations. Later, in the course, generate a group discussion in order to share the students' different points of view.
- In courses of social contents, ask students to deconstruct the discourses of the lectures they have been given. Ask them to elucidate the ideology that lies behind the lecture and the organizational theory that supports it.

In our understanding, Benson's core dialectic process is *praxis*, because it is in action where reality is changed. Nevertheless, analyzing all previous author's works, we realize that even if they fulfill the process of planning and direction, there are not yet deeply treated the issues of evaluation and controlling. Evaluation implies to compare what we obtained as reality after introducing changes with what were our planning goals. That's why even if the contribution of all the previous authors is very important, we have however a lack in the praxis components in terms of making critical pedagogy an alternative to act and to evaluate previous actions, and not only to make theoretical reflections. This gives us the opportunity to introduce in point 3 our propositions.

Our Complementary Propossal: Intersubjectivity as a Practical Tool

As we have said, to fulfill the need of more praxis in the critical pedagogy, we found it convenient to introduce another concept: intersubjectivity. We understand intersubjectivity as a group discussion in which people are taken in their dimension of subject, and therefore interactions of people are interactions of subjectivities. For social and human sciences the term of subject relates the condition of the person that is mostly forgotten in common life; this dimension enclose the psychic and the affective components, which go with the person wherever he or she goes (Freud, 1966).

According to Plato (399–348 B.C.), in one hand each individual has his own interpretation of reality, of the truth, but in the other hand, groups of individuals as a collectivity, construct another reality. That means that even though an actual social reality is accepted as a collective truth, it can always be changed and questioned by anyone. It is here where subjectivity takes place in the social construction.

Additionally, if we say that more than self-reflection (one student only) we need discussion to have group reflection, we find convenient to use Husserl's (1925) intersubjectivity concept. In general, what Husserl states as discussion of different subjectivities lies in the same interest of Socrates and Plato's dialectic. Husserl talks also about collective answers for problems.

On the one hand, the dialectic method is more orientated to a power relationship of professor-student (most of the times one student). The professor gives questions to the student in the aim that it will be the latter who will discover the answer, the nature, consequences and importance of the concepts to be learned. The student discovers answers by himself, which is the contrary of a traditional education where the answers are taught to the student as theoretical content before any questioning. In essence, the dialectic method in fact works intersubjectivity but more in the aim that the student realize for himself an answer that might be already known by the professor.

On the other hand, intersubjective method implies discussion in many-to-many relationships, in order not only to obtain the known answers by the professors, but also to solve problems with unknown or innovative answers. Even if the professor has some alternative solutions, it is more constructive for the student's development, the fact that in many-to-many relationships the answers, or alternatives, will emerge as a collective result. Thus, what does happen in intersubjectivity that could be so interesting? In interactions of subjectivities, the student expresses freely, given that the subject concept implies the wholeness of the person. Therefore, the student will interact with what he thinks and not with what he is imposed to; with what he believes and not what he is taught; with what are his interpretations and meanings. In doing so, when we speak of collective results, the common solution has taken into account everyone's concerns. Then, is that not what we pursue when we talk about organizational social responsibility? That is why intersubjectivity practices during courses will allow future managers to considerate the subjectivities of other people. We certainly know that most of the time, managers take into consideration only the stockholders' subjectivity, and very few times the subjectivity of employees or clients (only in behaviourist marketing studies, which tells us what to produce to increase sales). Thus, it is here where micro-emancipation can take place: where does management power lie, taking into account subjectivities of employees in different hierarchical levels, the families of the employees, and of course, the community served by the organization.

In the aim to have more intersubjective practices in management education, we have elaborated two aides. For the process of planning and evaluation, we propose questions and reflections based on Benson's theory; and for the process of direction and controlling, we present some practical examples.

In Planning and Evaluation

First, we understand evaluation as the improvement of the way we do things. Thus, oftentimes we use the term improvement rather than evaluation.

Planning and improvement include all the activities the professor must do before dictating his course. These activities have two moments: the first one is the syllabus course preparation, which is executed once in a period; and the second one is each class preparation, which includes revisions, lectures, students' questioning, appropriate methods and tasks. As we see, both of them demand at the same time planning and improvement. During improvement, the professor's critical reflection takes into account what he has learned from his previous courses and classes regarding student-professor power relationships and tasks unfolding. Thus, planning is a continuum of improvements. In this continuum process, critical pedagogy demands self-reflection from the professor, because him as a subject has learned from previous practices and therefore he can think about the meaning of his courses' contents, the influence of what he transmits to the students and the way students will apply what they have learned. Here are some examples of reflections using Benson's components.

Table 8.2   Benson's theory components in praxis reflections

Benson's theory component	Reflections for planning and improvement
Social construction	Are students conscious of the repercussion their actions as managers will have in society? What does life mean for them? Why do they study management? Do they recognize some institutional constraints in their own management school? In other words, do they know their immediate reality as students and the challenges of their future profession? Do we as professors, ask students questions of that nature? In addition, for us as professors, do we know, or do we ask ourselves, about all those former questions?
Power and ideology	In which parts of our course are taken into account the human dimensions of diversity, communication and culture in other way than the traditional idea of factors to be transformed into organization's assets? Were not the organizations created by people to fulfill people's needs? Do not we experience today an inverted order where many people must work to satisfy the organization's impersonal needs? Has not society worked for people in the beginning of times, but instead today most of the people work for only a part of society, which is mostly some firm conglomerates? Moreover, once students will graduate, what will be the ideologies they will take into account to work? As professors, how do we generate the latter reflections in the students? Which of our course lectures assist students in their reflections? Do we search in management literature other lectures with different ideological natures, in the aim to give broader options to the student? Are we conscious of the present ideology our school lies behind?

Benson's theory component	Reflections for planning and improvement
Totality	Do students ask themselves about the present ideology of their school? Are they encouraged to ask themselves about their preferences regarding the social motifs of firms and institutions where they are willing to work? How students conceive themselves as changing social agents once they will rule the organization they seek?
	As professors, how do we conceive ourselves as changing agents in our own school? How do implement changes in the way we teach ours courses, and also in the way we participates in academic comities or in formal and informal professors' reunions?
	How do we encourage changing actions in our students?
Praxis	Once students are on probation in organizations, are they also questioning the facts and the reality they meet? Do their papers talk about social concerns and repercussions of management actions?
	Are they asked – or allowed – by us as professors to make remarks about what probation period taught them in contrast with what they have learned in our courses?

© *Ana-Maria Dávila-Gómez, Jair Nascimento-Santos*

In Controlling and Direction

As professors, we are also managers of the students; therefore, in order to teach them how to become reflexive and conciliator managers, we have to conduct ourselves as such. We must seek the achievement of interaction between professors and students that denotes respect, freely expression, discussion and social construction. Here, intersubjectivity takes place. What are the professor's tasks in this intersubjectivity? They are direction and controlling in which we exercise power, more in a supportive way than in a vigilant or repressive one. To us, support includes answering students' questions about procedures as well as nourishing them with more relative lectures, and of course, assisting them in conciliation at the interior of their group discussions. In order to teach students intersubjectivity, professors can act as moderators inside students' discussions. These are some lines of conduct that a professor can utilize.

For Group-discussion and Collective Solution Construction

In order to obtain reflection about real life, in addition to theoretical *lectures*, professors utilize as one of their most precious pedagogical method that of the *case study*. With this method, students read about practical applications of theory, and by the activity of questioning-answering, students could interpret in a more personal way what a case teaches them. In a class activity of case study or theoretical lecture analysis, these are some tips for the praxis process.

- Previous to class, the professor can assign the students the task to interrogate themselves about the lecture's content in terms of: nature, theory application, social responsibility and spaces for changes. All students should do so because there will be a group discussion in class. Thus, each student will have his initial reflection.
- The day of class, depending on the amount of students, the professor can form more than one group of discussion. Sometimes the professor will form the groups, and other it could be the students' decision. In that way, students could evaluate the differences between being organized by another person who holds power, in contrast to being free to choose. In order to verbalize this difference, at the end of the course, the professor could ask what the students have learned regarding power implications.
- Once the groups are formed, the professor relates the lecture with a problem to be solved. Then, he asks additional questions that seek to be answered in-group, and given that it is a problem to be solved, discussion is needed and collective solution takes place. Like that, students will know that social changes are more complicated than isolated self-reflection, due to the fact that social interaction is needed. Hence, having increased the complexity of questions, the students of each group will have to discuss how to answer, and asking for the participation of each student, each one will utilize primarily what he has done by himself before. Therefore, even if social construction is more complicated, students will serve themselves of previous experiences and self-reflection tasks.
- During the discussion, the professor assists permanently the group, sometimes answering questions and some others demanding the group where they are in the solution elaboration. If the professor considers it necessary, he gives to the group more lectures references, authors or questions. As manager of the group discussions, the professor exercises direction. However, he must realize that inside group behaviours there are also power relationships. In student discussions it appears someone who naturally emerges as a leader, someone who does not express himself verbally so much but that can be very profound in writing tasks, someone who will not participate because of his own decision, someone conflictive or someone who tries to conciliate the group members each time conflict emerges. All these roles are the kind of people that students will encounter once they exercise as managers. The aim here is that in-group discussion experiences, having a task to resolve, students realize the roles of others, and doing so, they became aware that not everyone thinks or acts in an only possible way. Each one is different. Therefore, behaviour and role diversity are experimented inside the classroom. Nevertheless, as we know, even if that is the aim, it is also a professor's task to ask the students what they learned about roles, differences and diversity.

- At the moment, the students have experienced the diversity of roles and behaviours as a consequence of a natural occurrence. However, in the organization's real life, the role of manager (director of the group) is given to someone without necessarily being the natural and accepted leader amongst employees. That is why management education has developed so many courses regarding leadership in an attempt to provide to managers the characteristics of a real leader; however, we know as well that not all the managers develop those qualities. Thus, as we have shown the need to reflect about obligated or natural formation of groups, we as professors can also make students to think about natural leaders or imposed managers. In order to achieve student's awareness about this reality, in a posterior class task or discussion, the professor will assign the roles in order for the students to experience that in social interaction there are people whose role is not the desired or the appropriate one. For instance, we could assign the role of writing to the one student we know participates so much orally but does not do many writing papers; and to encourage management and direction, we can assign the role of group manager to whom is the conflictive one (in order to experience acceptance of disapproval from the other students); and other times assign the role of manager to whom is conciliator (in order to him and others experience cordial participation). These are only some of the possible roles and assignation possibilities. There are so many and each professor can develop more in his day-by-day experience.
- Given that a solution to the problem has been demanded, finally each group must write its own answer, including the reasons of taking one alternative solution and not others. In doing so, students will evaluate the causes and consequences of applying theory in a social context and not only in an economical performance context.
- Once the group activity is finished, each group is called to present its own solutions. If for instance the problem to solve was the same for all groups, the results obtained would show to the students that for a given problem there could be many possible answers. Each answer obeys to particular considerations that took place in the process of social reflection. Thus, each group will listen and understand other reasons, and therefore intersubjectivity facilitates here tolerance to diversity and relativity.

For Action Learning Tasks

In some advanced courses of management, *action learning* is a widely utilized method as an application of probation periods of practice inside organizations. Given that students have already experienced group discussion and group solution construction in class, they are now prepared to work in groups beyond the present professor's control. Thus, action-learning activities can take place.

- Here, the professor will ask a group of students to go visit an organization where they can observe in real life the application of course content. Students will be also asked to interview directors, managers and employees about what seems to be the cause of a particular problem to be solved, in order to identify the topics subjected to improvement with the application of course content. In taking in consideration other people's perceptions and points of view, students as future managers will exercise intersubjectivity in real organizations.

•   Then, for the final report, students will be asked to support their conclusions, answers and alternative solutions with social considerations. For instance, in a finance course students usually present as solution a capital expenditure program, budget forecast figures, long-term cash flows and operating working capitals for the organization object of their study. But now with our pedagogical approach, students will also be asked to justify their solutions regarding social repercussions to the employees and to the community in terms of salary inequities, net income redistribution, tax payments, governmental policies, ecological effects, ethical negotiations, etc.

•   Equally, for a course of logistics or production, the written report usually shows the most efficient chain process and information flux in terms of decreasing times, manual operations and production and distribution costs. But with our pedagogical approach, students will also be asked to evaluate how these solutions will affect employees in terms of their preparation to assume a new way to produce (new machines, new technology, new hierarchical structures), as well as social and cultural preferences to interact inside organization or with clients (e.g. face-to-face communication vs. e-mails, videoconferences, etc). For instance, employees who were used to writing the achievement of their tasks in a manual form, have now to do this directly in a computer, and now have to register more information (more fields of data bases) than before. Another example is a policy of cutting service costs, bringing as a result the replacement of a face-to-face customer care with a high technology structure of call-center where there is no more personal attention. Depending on the client's preference, the organization's solution to productivity could generate unconformity in clients that do not like to be attended by recorded messages, or by clients that do not have the time to wait unpredictable time in a phone before contacting an agent.

•   Other kind of social consideration can be included in courses of multiculturalism, diversity, communication skills, leadership, human resources and other related topics. Many of the actual organizational practices about multiculturalism are applied in multinational companies in order to achieve mutual understanding in international negotiations, given the presence of ethnic and cultural diversity in managers and stakeholders. However, there are some arenas not yet deeply treated. Thus, one example for students' task can be the evaluation of a company in which headquarters and stockholders are located in a developed country, but many of the subsidiaries that manufacture the products, are located in developing countries. Here, one question is how the company could implement programs to share in a more equitable way its income with all its members (including the distant employees whose salary is many times inferior to the minimum salary of the developed country). In this case, multiculturalism encloses more than different customs and behaviours. It demands respect for other worker's dignity. Additionally, we must realize that due to a more present globalization tendency, inside any national organization we will have more and more ethnic and cultural diversity given that employees, stakeholders and clients arrive from other countries due to the migratory global process. Thus, these themes of diversity and culture are not any longer exclusive of multinational companies. That is why it is very important to take into account these circumstances.

• Finally, groups of students are called to present their final papers to their classmates. Here, they will tell how they served themselves of the course contents and social considerations to elaborate solutions. Finally, if they want to, they will be invited to share the learning experience as human beings telling what they felt going to the organization object of their study, what were their expectations before the course and what are their conclusions.

The Professor Inside His Own Organization

The professor, as the manager he is, could be an example of respect and dignity in the way he conducts himself with his students and the staff personnel (secretaries, analysts, administration). We should remember that in coherence, students learn from example. They believe and learn more from a professor with a humanistic praxis than from another whose great intellectuality does not have an equivalent in human consideration.

Our proposals give students the opportunity to experience the manager's reality in a day-to-day basis. A manager is not only a financial or production expert, but also the person most consulted by his employees, the stakeholders and the community. Therefore, most of his time will be spent in interactions, which can give him the intersubjective experience, which we aim for.

Conclusion

Critical pedagogy success implies to be coherent between what we say and what we do. To achieve this reality, not only planning and improvement (evaluation) processes are crucial, as critical pedagogy states, but also direction and controlling issues must be taken into account. Elucidating this last need, we have proposed the complementary concept of intersubjective. This encloses many-to-many relationship in which not only student-professor relationships are encouraged, but also student-to-student discussion groups. Therefore, collective answering solutions are obtained. Thus, in the aim of micro-emancipation to change the reality, management education can contribute when it exercises social construction inside the classroom. In addition, intersubjective activity allows students to questioning consequences and purposes of the application of theories taught in courses. This last process implies the exercise of action learning, in which professors ask the students to go to visit real organizations, to read factual cases, and to evaluate the reasons of success or failure regarding the social contribution of these organizations. As we see, critical pedagogy does not stop in conceptualizing the need for reflections. It must go beyond into the process of social solution constructions and the evaluation of the organization's reality. Only in that case, students can realize the importance to propose alternatives to change the reality, and more important, the need and the reasons to do so.

To make it possible, students are not the only developing target of education; professors are as well. Our social reality is also present inside educational institutions. Therefore, if we want to have more critical pedagogical professors, institutional education has a responsibility to promote these kinds of pedagogical methods, and for doing so, there must be a continual process of development in professors. In that sense, the micro-emancipation concept can take place when one professor begins to change and influence its immediate environment. Later, when some professors share experiences with their colleagues, all of them begin to propose solutions, changes and innovative pedagogical methods. That is why changes can come from inside, and therefore, we, as professors are changing agents with micro-emancipation potential. It is then our decision to choose between the fact to continue with our society the way we know it or to contribute to have another one we would like to achieve. It is our power, it is our action.

References

Aktouf, O. (1994) *La administración: entre la tradición y la renovación.* (1989-trad. De la 3a. ed – de Gaëtan Morin Editor). Universidad del Valle, Cali, Colombia, p.483.

Alvesson, M. and Willmott, H. (1992) "On the Idea of Emancipation in Management and Organization Studies", *Academy of Management Review.* Vol.17, no.3, pp.432–464.

Alvesson, M. and Willmott, H. (1996) *Making Sense of Management: a critical introduction.* London, Sage.

Benson, J.K. (1977) "Organizations: a dialectical view", *Administrative Science Quartely.* Ithaca/New York, 22(1–22).

Boje, D.M. (1996) "Management Education as a Panoptic Cage". In: D.M. BOJE, R.P. Gephart and Thatchenkery, T. (eds.) *Postmodern Management and Organization Theory.* London, Sage.

Burrel, G. (1996) "Normal science, paradigms, metaphors, discourses and genealogies of analysis". In: S.R. Clegg, C. Hardy and W.R. Nord, *Handbook of Organization Studies.* London, Sage, chap. 3.8, pp.642–658.

Burrell, G. and Morgan, G. (1979) *Sociological Paradigms and Organizational Analysis.* New York, Heinemann.

Caproni, P. and Arias, M.E. (1997) "Managerial Skills Training from a Critical Perspective". *Journal of Management Education.* Sage, vol. 21, no.3, August, pp.292–308.

Cavanaugh, J.M. and Prasad, A. (1996) "Critical Theory and Management Education: some strategies for the critical classroom". In: R. French and C. Grey (eds.). *Rethinking Management Education.* London, Sage.

Chanlat, J.F. (1998) *Sciences sociales et management – Plaidoyer pour une anthropologie générale.* Les presses de l'Université Laval – Éditions ESKA. Québec, Canada.

Chia, R. (1996) "The problem of Reflexivity in Organizational Research: toward a postmodern science of organization". *Organization*. London, Sage, vol 2(1)31–59.

Clegg Et Ross-Smith. (2003) "Revisiting the boundaries: management education and learning in a positivist world". *Academy of management learning and education*. v.2, n.1, march.

Derrida, J. (1976) *Of Grammatology*. Baltimore, Johns Hopkins university Press.

Foucault, M. (1980) *Power / Knowledge*. Great Britain, The Harvester Press.

Freud, S. (1994) *Introducción al psicoanálisis*. Copyright Londres (1966). De Cast: Alianza Editorial S.A., Madrid, España, p.483.

Frost, P. (1997) "Building Bridges Between Critical Theory and Management Education". *Journal of Management Education*, Sage, vol. 21, n°.3, August, pp.361–367.

Giddens, A. (1984) *The Constitution of Society: outline of the theory of structuration*. Cambridge, Polity Press.

Giroux, H.A. (1981) *Border Crossings*. New York, Routledge.

Grey, C., Knights, D. and Willmott, H. (1996) Is a critical pedagogy of management Possible? In: French, R. and Grey, C. (eds.). *Rethinking Management Education*. London, Sage.

Habermas, J. (1972) *Knowledge and human interests*. London, Heinemann.

Hardy, C. and Palmer. I. (1999) Pedagogical Practice and Postmodernist Ideas. *Journal of Management Education*. Sage, vol.23, n°.4, August, pp.377–395.

Husserl, E. (1977) Phenomenological psychology – Lectures, summer semester 1925. Trad. from Scalon, J. (1962). Martinus Nijhoff, The Hague, Netherlands, p.186.

Ozmon, H. and Craver, S. (1999) *Philosophical Foundations of Education*. USA, Prentice Hall Inc.

Plato (399–348 B.C.) (1956) *Great dialogues of Plato*. (Rouse, W.H.D. 1863–1950 tr.) New York: New American Library, p.525.

Prasad, P. and Caprioni, P. (1997) Critical Theory in the Management Classroom: engaging power, ideology and praxis. *Journal of Management Education*. Sage, vol.21, n°.3, August, pp.284–291.

Raelin, J. (1997) Individual and Situational Precursors of Successful Action Learning. *Journal of Management Education*. Sage, vol.21, n°.3, August, pp.368–394.

Reynolds, M. (1999) Critical Reflection and Management Education: rehabilitating less hierarchical approaches. *Journal of Management Education*. Sage, vol.23, n°.5, October, pp.537–553.

Reynolds, M. (1997) *Learning Styles: A Critique. Management Learning*. London, Sage, vol. 28(2)115–133.

Reynolds, M. (1998) *Reflection and Critical Reflection. Management Learning*. London, Sage, vol. 29(2): 183–200.

Rosile, G.A. and Boje, D.M. (1996) Pedagogy for the Postmodern Management Classroom: greenback company. In: Boje, D.M., Gephart, R.P. and Thatchenkery, T. (eds.) *Postmodern Management and Organization Theory*. London, Sage.

Index